Praise for Finni

"Sahlberg has developed an international perspective on educational reform in general as well as the outsider's advantage in being able to make all that is familiar in Finland fresh to others."
—From the Foreword to Finnish Lessons 2.0 by Andy Hargreaves

"Finland's approach to education reform shows we must address student inequality before we can expect student excellence."
—The 2013 Grawemeyer Award Committee

"Like other professionals, as Pasi Sahlberg shows in his book Finnish Lessons, Finnish teachers are driven by a sense of intrinsic motivation, not by the hope of a bonus or the fear of being fired."
—Diane Ravitch in the New York Review of Books

"Finnish Lessons provides valuable evidence that investing in teachers and instruction—rather than in tests and inspections—can bring about admirable, even excellent, results."
—Connie Goddard in the Teachers College Record

"This book is an eye-opener for the ignorant. It makes clear why the development of school systems in Sweden (and in the U.S., UK . . .) is so miserable."
—Sven-Eric Liedman in Dagens Nyheter

"Simply put the one must read to begin to understand how Finland has built perhaps the world's most successful educational system over the past few decades."
—Kenneth Bernstein for Daily Kos

"Finnish Lessons kills 99.9% of GERMs."
—Niall MacKinnon in the Times Education Supplement

"The story of Finnish educational success as told by Sahlberg in the slim volume Finnish Lessons is remarkable. . . . Finnish Lessons is an important book and educators need to read it."
—Gaea Leinhardt in Educational Researcher

"Sahlberg's book contains important lessons for a broad range of academics, educators, politicians, and the public. I especially appreciated its demonstration that top academic performance can be achieved with low inequality, comprehensive school for all students, low dropout rates, low school-related anxiety, and a high degree of freedom for teachers. In fact, Finland teaches that all these aspects need to be considered when giving directions for effective and sustainable educational reform."
—Henrik Saalbach in Science

"I know many reformers and politicians will not want to read this book because it will negate all the 'reform' that has been embraced by our country, but we will all miss out on some very important opportunities if they don't. Neither the size of Finland nor the country's demographics should be used as an excuse by any state or by the United States not to pay attention to what works. This book will give hope, vision, and strategies to anyone who is sincere in bringing a great education to every child. Pick it up and read it."

—John Wilson in *Education Week*

Published by Teachers College Press,® 1234 Amsterdam Avenue, New York, NY 10027

Copyright © 2021 by Teachers College, Columbia University

Front cover image by shaunl / iStock by Getty Images.

Lyrics from "Rumblin" by Neil Young are reprinted with permission from Hal Leonard Corporation. Copyright © 2010 by Silver Fiddle Music. All rights reserved. Used by permission.

Library of Congress Cataloging-in-Publication Data

Names: Sahlberg, Pasi, author.
Title: Finnish lessons 3.0 : what can the world learn from educational change in
    Finland? / Pasi Sahlberg ; Foreword by Howard Gardner ; Afterword by Sir Ken
    Robinson.
Description: Third edition. | New York : Teachers College Press, Columbia
    University, [2021] | Includes bibliographical references and index.
Identifiers: LCCN 2020054597 (print) | LCCN 2020054598 (ebook) |
    ISBN 9780807764800 (paperback) | ISBN 9780807764817 (hardcover) |
    ISBN 9780807779293 (ebook)
Subjects: LCSH: Educational change—Finland. | Education—Finland.
Classification: LCC LA1013.7 .S34 2021 (print) | LCC LA1013.7 (ebook) |
    DDC 370.94897—dc23
LC record available at https://lccn.loc.gov/2020054597
LC ebook record available at https://lccn.loc.gov/2020054598

ISBN 978-0-8077-6480-0 (paper)
ISBN 978-0-8077-6481-7 (hardcover)
ISBN 978-0-8077-7929-3 (ebook)

Printed on acid-free paper
Manufactured in the United States of America

Finnish Lessons 3.0

What Can the World Learn from Educational Change in Finland?

THIRD EDITION

Pasi Sahlberg

Foreword by Howard Gardner
Afterword by Sir Ken Robinson

TEACHERS COLLEGE PRESS

TEACHERS COLLEGE | COLUMBIA UNIVERSITY
NEW YORK AND LONDON

For Reinhold Ferdinand Sahlberg (1811–1874)

I can feel the weather changing.
I can see it all around.
Can't you feel that new wind blowing?
Don't you recognize that sound that sound?
And the earth is slowly spinning.
Spinning slowly, slowly changing.

—*Neil Young: Rumblin' (2010)*

Contents

Foreword

I begin with a provocative statement. Whether held in your hands or displayed on your screen, the book that you are perusing is well on the way to becoming a classic—indeed, to coin a phrase, an "instant and evolving classic."

Let me unpack these terms.

One should not invoke the word "classic" lightly. A classic is a work that captures and sustains attention, that changes our understanding of an important topic or concept or facet or view of life, and, most important but most difficult to anticipate, a work that continues to remain alive and vital—as it were, "evergreen," despite the passage of time.

Although it's far too early to declare with certainty that *Finnish Lessons* is an educational classic, there is a good chance that it will achieve that exalted status—hence the descriptor "instant." Already there are encouraging signs—following its initial publication in 2011, there have already been two additional editions, each considerably revised. Then there are the enthusiastic readers across the globe (the book is a bestseller, with nearly 30 translations). Moreover, as happens with many bestsellers, the book is much cited and quoted even by individuals who have never laid their eyes on it. My guess is that you are reading this edition because you have heard it is a book that you *should* read—indeed, that you *need* to read—even if you have read an earlier edition.

And what of the descriptor "evolving"? Often when authors issue a subsequent edition of a work, they simply add some recent references, say a few words about the pleasure that they feel about the work's success, and touch on a few points that they might now express differently.

But *Finnish Lessons 3.0*, third edition, is far from a simple repackaging of the first and second editions. Rather, author Pasi Sahlberg digs deeper into the past of Finnish education; sketches the circumstances that gave rise in the latter half of the 20th century to its exceptional K–12 education system; details what has happened in Finland (and other corners of the educational world) in the past decade; and lays out a spectrum of possibilities—ranging from optimism to disappointment—with respect to the future course of education in the country of his birth.

Here are some of the reasons for my high opinion of *Finnish Lessons*. In every society, educators have searched for the best way to educate their children. This has been true since the time of Rousseau's *Emile;* indeed, since the time of Plato's *Republic* and the *Analects* of Confucius. There are always competing views, though they often cover only part of the spectrum—Plato versus Aristotle, Rousseau versus Mill, Confucius versus Mencius. And all too often, these idealized prescriptions come from individuals who may have thought deeply about the topic but who have not themselves tried to put their ideas into practice.

We live at a time when competition among nations is fierce, and when each nation seeks the "magic bullet" that will propel it to the top of the global rankings (PISA, TIMSS) and foster children who will go on to become "masters of the universe." And especially in the so-called developed countries—members of OECD, for example—there has been a virtual consensus: Have clear uniform standards; follow them assiduously; test students frequently; and award the students, teachers, and locations where the scores are high while penalizing or castigating (or even attempting to hide) those where the performances are mediocre or worse. There are nuances, of course, but this perspective has been the default position—whether one is in Singapore, South Korea, or the United States.

In *Finnish Lessons*, Pasi Sahlberg, the scion of a long line of Finnish educators and himself a classroom teacher, researcher, and policymaker both nationally and internationally, has challenged this consensus. Drawing on the Finland experience, he has provided an alternative model. In a phrase that still brings smiles to my face, he characterizes the global consensus as GERM—the Global Educational Reform Movement. And, as captured in the table (pp. 186–187 in the typed version), he critiques and contrasts this "one-size-fits-all" perspective with the lessons that have been learned in recent decades by educators in his native country. In this book, you will read how a country that—50 years ago—was barely on the radar screen of international comparisons rose to the very top. And far more importantly, Pasi Sahlberg explains in beautiful and memorable detail how Finland followed its own path—if I can riff on the words from the famous American ballad, how Finnish educators did it "their way."

Let me mention just some of the striking contrasts with the GERM approach:

In Finland, the following are true:

- Teaching is a highly valued profession—individuals vie to become teachers and are compensated like other professionals.
- Teachers remain in the classroom—they don't immediately vie for higher administrative positions and higher pay.
- Teachers don't fear research, they don't disdain it, and they don't claim that they can't understand it; instead they receive training in research, keep up with findings in the literature, think of themselves as researchers, and actually carry out "useful" research.
- Play is actively encouraged—it's not discouraged or even banned; school hours are limited as is homework.
- Ethics or morals are not ignored or ceded to religious authorities; one's personal standards of conduct matter and they are modeled with conviction.
- Student health and well-being are a proper concern of educators.
- Professional discourse goes beyond buzzwords—teachers don't just talk about "emotional intelligence" or "peer learning" or "individualized instruction"—they study it, put it into practice, reflect on the difference it makes, and, as good researchers, make adjustments when the prescription does not do what it is supposed to do.

Sahlberg believes ardently in these touchstones of an effective educational system. But in *Finnish Lessons 3.0*, he explains that they cannot be taken for granted or assumed. No more in education than in other sectors of society does time stand still. In just a decade following the original publication of *Finnish Lessons*, the performance of the Finnish educational system has at best remained stagnant and, according to several indices, has declined significantly. This disappointing situation may have come about because of fame or smugness, or, alternatively, because lessons learned from Finland have now been absorbed and applied skillfully by other competitive societies.

Sahlberg provides another explanation. Rather than learning from its own experiences in decades past, Finland has not revisited or recreated the distinctive blend—the cycle of experimentation and reflection—which in a few decades transported it from an educational backwater to a nation in a leadership position in the world of K–12 education. We might say it is no longer functioning as a "learning system."

Pasi Sahlberg sets a very high bar for future works of synthesis in education. We live at a time when large data sets can be readily assembled and analyzed. Scores of educational "think tanks" all over the world measure every conceivable variable—from test scores to class sizes to the variations in performances across classes, schools, cities, provinces, nations, and demographic groups. Accordingly, when a scholarly work is revised or a new text is issued, it is possible not just to *speculate* on how (and why) things might differ—but rather to *delineate* what's actually happened through charts, graphs, statistical tests, and other "hard data," and then to reflect on the factors that may have brought about reported changes.

As a seasoned researcher and analyst of data, Pasi Sahlberg handles these forms of information deftly. And reflective readers can join the author in trying to make sense of what happens from one year to another, from one country to another, from one variable to one another.

Finnish Lessons is a work by a polymath—teacher, researcher, data analyst, speaker, blogger, writer, loving family member, and cherished friend—the list of accolades could go on. But what most impresses me is that Pasi Sahlberg articulates and embodies deep values about equity, fairness, personal growth, community bonding, societal flourishing, and global harmony, as well as the importance of helping every young person find an area of passion and then enabling its nurturance. These values come through in page after page in this volume, and they are perhaps the chief reason that this book is destined to become a classic.

—Howard Gardner, Hobbs Research Professor of Cognition and Education, Harvard Graduate School of Education, September 2020

Preface

Just about 10 years ago today, I was writing a Preface to the first edition of *Finnish Lessons*. After working 5 years in Washington, DC, followed by another 3 in Torino, Italy, I had returned back to Finland with the manuscript to take a new job at the Ministry of Education and Culture in Helsinki. Since I left Finland in 2002, much had happened there. Finnish schools had become admired by many and envied by some. Finnish students had done very well in international student assessments compared to all other countries. The country's economy had become a poster child among politicians and business leaders after being ranked as one of the world's most competitive economies several years in a row. In global media, Finland was praised as happy and healthy but also a cultural lone wolf that finds its own way to do things rather than follow others. In August 2010, *Newsweek* magazine frontpage read, "The Best Country in the World Is . . . ," and the main story in that issue revealed the rest: "Finland."

I had a manuscript that I thought I'd never write. Education in Finland was simply too personal for me. I was born into a family of teachers, raised in a teachers' apartment in a small village schoolhouse, served as a teacher and teacher educator for many years, and spent a good part of my professional life in national education policy work that made Finnish education very familiar to me, so much so that it was often difficult to explain it to those unaware of my country's culture, traditions, history, and values that define much of what schools do.

Many of my colleagues in the United States urged me to write a book about Finnish education. Andy Hargreaves, who was a professor at Boston College, was researching international education reforms and insisted I tell the story about the Finnish Way. Linda Darling-Hammond's research on the teaching profession and teacher education included Finland, and she encouraged me as a former teacher and teacher educator to write a book that would explain the roles that great teachers play in building a successful education system. Stephen Heyneman, who had served 20 years at the World Bank and then became a professor of education policy at Vanderbilt University, convinced me that Finnish education deserved to be shared with scholars and policymakers in the United States and in the rest of the world. No more was needed to convince me to give this book a try in North American reader markets. Without these friends and some others, this book probably wouldn't be here.

Finnish Lessons was launched in Alberta, Canada, in November 2011. Honorable Dave Hancock, who was minister of education at that time, had invited me to talk about my new book to 500 Albertan school leaders. Under his leadership, Alberta was a world-leading education system, neck and neck with Finland in global charts. My book was soon widely acknowledged in Canadian media and became a bestseller there. After Fareed Zakaria featured *Finnish Lessons* on CNN, Tavis Smiley and Cornel West broadcast our conversation about Finnish schools on their new public radio show, and Diane Ravitch wrote a two-part review of my book in the *New York Review of Books, Finnish Lessons* was sailing in strong tailwinds. Against all odds, it went global, and two earlier editions of *Finnish Lessons* are now translated into almost 30 languages.

Much has happened in Finland since the appearance of the first edition in 2011. The financial crisis that hit the world a few years earlier caused massive cuts in public sector spending in the 2010s. Finland's performance in international education rankings—and some other global comparisons as well—had been declining. The mass migration of 2015 into and across Europe fueled by unrest and conflicts in the Middle East and northern Africa brought tens of thousands of immigrants and refuge-seekers to Finland and into Finnish schools. Then in 2020 came the global COVID-19 pandemic that closed school gates and locked children in to learn from home for several weeks. All these things have affected Finnish schools in ways that nobody could foresee in 2011 when the first edition was released. How the Finnish education system has coped with these changes is discussed in this new edition.

As I have done in other editions of *Finnish Lessons*, I begin this book with points of warning that readers need to keep in mind. First, my intention in this book is not to convince you that Finland has—or that it once had—the best education system in the world. International media and some experts have created the incorrect impression that there exists a global metric to determine what are the best—or the worst—education systems in the world. As I make it clear in this book, current international education rankings only include a small number of academic subjects in their indices—typically literacy, mathematics, and science. There are many other important aspects of education that need to be included when judging success of education systems or individual schools. I also emphasize that all social metrics are imperfect and that their ability to accurately measure success tends to be compromised. Most Finnish teachers and educators would agree that student test scores in literacy and numeracy tell something about how an education system performs but that those scores offer certainly too narrow a view to be used to determine overall success or failure of education systems.

Second, I am not claiming in this book that if only other countries would imitate the Finnish Model in reforming their education systems, then things in their schools would get better. If we have learned one thing about transferability of best educational ideas from one place to another, it is this: What seems to work in one place won't necessarily work somewhere else. Or, as I heard Dylan Wiliam say it: Everything works somewhere, nothing works everywhere. Too often, I must admit, I have met people who have visited Finland or studied its education system believing that if they only had Finland's curriculum, school buildings, and teachers, their own educational challenges would vanish and a miraculous transformation of teaching and learning would appear. This book is meant to emphasize that there is another way to improve education rather than those fashionable models offered by international organizations and consultants. I want to convince you that, yes, we can learn from one another, but we need to be mindful as well. Finland has inspired scores of educators in other countries to think more deeply about their own schools and cultures. There are lessons in this book that others can learn from us, just as Finland has been inspired by educators and school systems around the world and learned from them. This is where the real hope is for a better tomorrow.

Third, it is important to keep in mind that indeed much of the pedagogical innovation in Finnish classrooms and the inspiration for education policies has its origins in other countries. In the early 20th century, after Finland became an independent nation and its education system began to shape up, Germany and Switzerland served as models for Finnish schools. Then, the idea of an equitable, comprehensive school system came from neighboring Nordic countries, especially from Sweden. More recently, England, Scotland, Canada, Australia, and the United States have served as places where Finnish educators have found useful ideas to enrich teaching and learning in their schools and often in the education system as a whole. Curriculum theories, the idea of the human mind as a system of multiple intelligences, teaching methods to educate the whole child, authentic student assessments, and school leadership models are examples of the positive influence that American educational research and development has had in Finland since the 1980s.

Finally, I recognize and make it clear in this third edition that educational performance in Finland is not what it used to be at the time when the first edition was published in 2011. Students' test scores in international assessments have steadily dropped, equity of education has declined, and less young people read for pleasure, which has led to a growing number of poor readers, especially among adolescent boys. The most recent data that I have used in this edition shows what makes many educators and policymakers in Finland worried. This edition offers two kinds of lessons: On the one hand, it describes how Finland built its well-performing education system by the 2000s. On the other hand, it shows how the Finnish education system is reacting to eroding high performance in international rankings as well as challenges the schools are facing, including the recent disruption in schooling caused by the global COVID-19 pandemic.

This third edition of *Finnish Lessons* includes comprehensive updates on Finland's education scene as well as updates on international statistics measuring educational performance. I have used data from the international studies and surveys in which Finland has participated since 2000. Based on this updated evidence, this edition of the book also discusses how some key policies and practices are changing in Finland.

Finnish Lessons has had an unbelievable journey so far. I have presented the ideas in this book to the politicians at parliament houses around the world. I have been invited to comment on national education issues and tell stories about Finland's schools on national TV and radio, on dozens of podcasts, and in interviews in major newspapers. *Finnish Lessons* has given me scores of new friends and colleagues; I may also have lost some. In 2013, *Finnish Lessons* received the Grawemeyer Award, a prestigious prize given by the University of Louisville in Kentucky that recognizes important ideas in education that have the potential to change the world. In 2014, I got the annual Robert Owen Award from the Scottish government that honors inspiring educators for their work on equality and equity in education. Then, in 2016 the LEGO Foundation awarded its LEGO Prize to my work on genuine learning and creativity, which are the essential ingredients of *Finnish Lessons*.

I hope that *Finnish Lessons 3.0* inspires you and proves to you that there is a way to build good public school systems that can serve all of our children well. The Finnish recipe for good education is simple: Always ask yourself if the reform you plan to initiate is going to be good for children and teachers. If you hesitate with your answer, don't do it.

—In Sydney, Australia, October 2020

Acknowledgments

My journey with *Finnish Lessons* has lasted a decade now. Since the first edition, I have had conversations with teachers, parents, students, politicians, artists, entrepreneurs, and journalists about education in Finland and in many other countries in the world. I am grateful to all those who have read the earlier editions of this book, shared their impressions with me, and suggested improvements to this latest volume of Finland's education saga. It has been a privilege and pleasure as an author of this book to have access to so many conversations and debates about what education could be.

Since the first two editions of this book have been translated into almost 30 languages, it has been read around the world. I want to thank all those readers of the international editions who have been in touch with me, one way or the other, and have encouraged me to work on this third edition. But I am most thankful to those readers who have dared to disagree with me, thereby helping me to include some of those concerns in this new edition.

Special thanks to the following colleagues and friends who have had their say on this book: Erkki Aho, Howard Gardner, Martti Hellström, Peter Johnson, Hannele Niemi, and Veera Salonen, all of whom lent me their words to complement my story. Andy Hargreaves and Diane Ravitch have been critically important in writing earlier editions and helping the book to be read widely around the world. I also thank Jean-Claude Couture, Sam Abrams, and David Kirp for their kind help with this edition.

In December 2011, about a month after *Finnish Lessons* was published, I was invited to give a book talk at the Harvard Club in New York City. My editor had invited Howard Gardner, a distinguished professor at Harvard University, to be my discussant. I must admit that it was a nerve-wracking moment until I sat down with him for a dinner prior to the program. Howard has a magical skill to make people around him feel comfortable and relaxed. We had a lively conversation about education, Finland, America, and food. My talk later that evening to a roomful of guests was one of the most pleasant and memorable moments that I have had with *Finnish Lessons* anywhere. It is a huge honor to have the Foreword to this third edition written by Howard, who is one of my heroes and also a friend from my time in Cambridge a few years ago.

This book has been developed from two earlier editions of *Finnish Lessons*. I extend my appreciation to each and every one of those who helped me in writing those two editions in 2011 and 2015. As before, my editors Sarah Biondello and John Bylander and other colleagues at Teachers College Press did a fantastic job in turning my manuscript into this beautiful book you are now reading. Thank you all, again.

On August 21, 2020, Sir Ken Robinson, who was a friend and passionate proponent of creativity, passed away after a short battle with cancer. I can't emphasize enough his influence in sharpening the tone in this volume. I am grateful for his influence on my own thinking, for his words at the end of this book, and for being a prominent global voice in making the world a better place. Thank you, Ken.

I continue to be grateful to my family for their support and love while I was working on this book. My enthusiasm and passion never run out when Petra, Noah, Otto, and Eero are around. You make me a better man and hopefully also a better writer.

I dedicate this book to my grandfather's grandfather, Reinhold Ferdinand Sahlberg—a fearless explorer who traveled around the globe in the 1840s following his passion for research and discovery.

opportunities in an egalitarian manner, and makes efficient use of resources. Finnish education has recently attracted attention from many
international scholars. Linda Darling-Hammond (2010) writes exten-
sively about it in her book *The Flat World and Education*. Marc Tucker
(2011) included Finland as one example of a high-performing model for
the United States in his book *Surpassing Shanghai*. Andy Hargreaves
and Dennis Shirley (2012) chose Finland as an example of a nation that
has successfully transformed its education system in their book *The
Global Fourth Way*. Diane Ravitch (2013) refers to Finland in her book
Reign of Error as an example for Americans that shows why preserv-
ing public education helps bring about better education for all. Michael
Lawrence (2020) offered in his book a teacher's perspective on what
Australian education can learn from Finland. A chapter on Finnish education has become an integral part of any international handbook or
volume that reports contemporary thinking and practice in the field.
International development agencies, consulting firms, and media houses
refer to Finland as a good model and "a witness" of successful transformation of public education.[1] Monographs on Finnish schools and
teachers have been published in Australia, China, Korea, Japan, France,
Slovenia, Mexico, and Germany, to mention just a few countries. The
first edition of this book was translated into 20 languages—clearly, there
is a global interest in Finland's experience.

In leading the way toward educational reform in Finland in the early
1990s, Dr. Vilho Hirvi, then director general of Finland's National Board
of Education, said in a speech to his staff that "an educated nation cannot be created by force." He acknowledged that teachers and students
must be heard, and that the way forward called for active collaboration.
In Finland, teachers and students were insisting on more flexibility and
more freedom in deciding how to design instruction, what to study, and
when. "We are creating a new culture of education and there is no way
back," Hirvi said. Basic to this new culture has been the cultivation of
trust between education authorities and schools. Such trust, as we have
witnessed, creates reform that is not only sustainable but is also owned
by the teachers who implement it.

NORTHERN EXPOSURE

In the 1990s, education in Finland was nothing special in international
terms. All young Finns attended school regularly, the school network

was wide and dense, secondary education was accessible for all Finns, and higher education was a realistic option for an increasing number of upper-secondary school graduates. However, the performance of Finnish students on international assessments was close to international averages, except in reading, where Finnish students did better than most of their peers in other countries. The unexpected and jarring recession of the early 1990s brought Finland to the edge of a financial breakdown. Bold and immediate measures were necessary to fix national fiscal imbalances and revive the foreign trade that disappeared with the collapse of the Soviet Union in 1990. Nokia, the main global industrial brand of Finland, with its mobile communication products, became a critical engine in boosting Finland out of the country's biggest economic dip since World War II. Another Finnish brand not yet known to many people abroad at that time, *peruskoulu*, or the 9-year comprehensive basic school, was the other key player in this turnaround of the Finnish economy and society.

There are countries around the world where education leaders find their own educational systems in a situation very similar to what Finland faced in the 1990s. The global economic downturn has hit many schools, universities, and entire education systems hard. Take Ireland, Greece, England, or the United States, for example—student achievement is nowhere close to what it should be in these knowledge-based economies, where productivity and innovation are necessary conditions for competitiveness and a sustainable way of life. Students seem to find the teaching offered in schools and universities increasingly boring and irrelevant to their needs in a rapidly changing world. The story of Finland's educational journey in this book brings hope to all those who are worried about whether improving their educational systems is even possible. It also provides food for thought to those who are looking for ways to adjust education policies to fit the realities of economic recovery. The lessons from Finland should be refreshing because they depart from the ideas commonly presented in books or journals on educational development. Moreover, these lessons show that systemic improvement is indeed possible if only policies and strategies are designed in smart and sustainable ways and teachers and school leaders are involved in planning, implementing, and reviewing all aspects of intended changes.

Although these lessons hold great promise, they also call for patience. In this age of immediate results, education requires a different mindset. Reforming schools is a complex and slow process. To rush this process is to ruin it. The story told in this book makes this clear. Steps must be grounded in research and implemented in collaboration by academics, policymakers, principals, and teachers.

This book is about how such a process evolved in Finland since World War II. It is the first book written for international readers that tells the story of how Finland created a system praised as much for its equity as for its high quality of educational outcomes. Many of the world's great newspapers and broadcast services—the *New York Times*, the *Washington Post*, CNN, *Times of London*, *Le Monde*, *El País*, National Public Radio, NBC, *Deutsche Welle*, and BBC—have covered this Finnish educational miracle. Filmmaker Morgan Spurlock became intrigued by Finnish schools and included them in his education episode of *Inside Man* on CNN. Another documentarian, Michael Moore, featured the Finnish school model in a movie as one of the key lessons that the United States should import from other countries to make the country great again. Thousands of official delegations have visited Finnish authorities, schools, and communities to learn about what drives their excellence in education. This story, however, has until now not received the book-length treatment necessary for enumerating, linking, and explaining the many players, institutions, and impersonal forces involved.

My approach in this book is both personal and academic. It is personal because of my intimate relationship with education in Finland. I was born in northern Finland and raised in a village primary school, where both of my parents were teachers. Most of my childhood memories are in one way or another linked to school. I had the privilege of looking beyond the secrets of the classroom after everybody else was gone, and I found that world to be rich. It was my home—and it was an enchanted one. It is perhaps no surprise, then, that I went on to become a teacher myself. My first teaching position was at a junior high school in Helsinki. I taught mathematics and physics there for 7 years. Later, I spent enough time in educational administration and in university teacher education to understand the difference between education in school and out. As a policy analyst for the Organisation for Economic Cooperation and Development (OECD), an education specialist for the World Bank, and an education expert for the European Commission, I gained the global perspective necessary for a deeper appreciation of Finland's distinct place in education.

As a representative of Finland in these different capacities, I have also been forced to develop a keener understanding of what distinguishes Finnish methods by answering questions from colleagues, friends, and media around the world. During the past 20 years, I have given more than 600 keynote addresses and 350 interviews about the Finnish educational system around the world. I have had conversations with thousands of people, which has taught me to be sensitive to the complexity of education and how it might change. These conversations with people who are interested in education, as I am, have greatly advanced the writing of all three editions of this book. The following are some of the questions that I have been asked over and over again: "What is the secret of Finnish educational success?" "How do you make teaching such an attractive profession in Finland?" "How much does lack of ethnic diversity have to do with good educational performance there?" "How do you know that all schools are doing what they should when you don't test students or inspect schools?" "Why do Finnish parents and authorities trust teachers and schools to allow them to decide how teaching and learning are arranged for children?" More recently I have been asked: "Why Finland has been slipping down in recent international rankings?" Such questions, and also critical remarks related to the Finnish education story, have been essential in making this book what it is. Without them, I would never have been able to hone my assessment of Finnish differences.

This book also has an academic orientation because it stems from research that I have been part of over the past 3 decades as an author, scholar, policy analyst, or critic. This book is thus not a typical monograph, written as the result of a research project or a particular event. It is a synthesis of 2 decades of policy research, personal experience as a teacher and administrator, and dialogue with thousands of researchers and educators around the world. I have been privileged to spend enough time outside of Finland and to work with a number of foreign governments to better understand the true nature and peculiarity of Finnish education and life in Finnish schools.

By the time of updating this third edition of *Finnish Lessons*, I have spent some time working in the United States, Finland, and currently in Australia. This has provided me with more opportunities to talk about Finnish schools and what they might offer to educators and policymakers in other countries. Since the first edition of this book, much has happened in the world of international education. Many things have also changed in Finland since then as I wrote earlier. In this book, I will take a new look at the Finnish education system and return to the initial question: What can Finland offer to other countries who are trying to find a way to educate that would be fair, inclusive, and good for all children?

For many years I taught a course titled "Introduction to the Finnish Education System" at the University of Helsinki. Students came from all over the world, often to study for a full year in Finland because they wanted to better understand the structure and spirit of the Finnish school system. Teaching a course, "International Lessons from Successful Education Systems," at Harvard University's Graduate School of Education introduced me to American students who were interested in international education issues. Teaching Australian students at the University of New South Wales in Sydney has further enriched my experience in how educators elsewhere think about global education systems and what are their views about Finnish education. The opportunity to teach students in these academic institutions has been an excellent way to enhance my own understanding of the Finnish education system. I have improved and updated this third edition of *Finnish Lessons* through listening to my students and colleagues and then learning from them.

FINLAND AS AN INSPIRATION

Public education systems are in crisis in many parts of the world. The United States, England, Sweden, Australia, and Chile, to mention just a few nations, are among those countries where public education is increasingly challenged because of an endemic failure to provide adequate learning opportunities for all children. Tough solutions are not uncommon in these countries: Increasing competition between schools, stronger accountability with negative consequences for schools' performance, standardizing teaching to predetermined outcomes, turning direction to "back-to-basics" in curriculum, and closing down troubled schools are all part of the recipe to fix failing education systems. This book does not suggest that tougher competition, more data, abolishing teacher unions, opening more charter schools, or employing corporate-world management models in education systems will bring about a resolution to these crises—quite the opposite. The main message of this book is that there is another way to improve education systems, one that is different from the market-based reform ideology mentioned above. This other way includes improving the teaching force, limiting student testing to a necessary minimum, placing responsibility and trust before accountability, investing in equity in education, and handing over school- and district-level leadership to experienced education professionals. These are common education policy themes in some of the high-performing countries—Finland among them—in the 2018 PISA of the OECD (2019a, 2019b). The chapters of this book offer five revised reasons why Finland continues to be an interesting and relevant source of inspiration for other nations that are looking for ways to improve their own education systems.

One, Finland has a unique educational system because it has progressed from mediocrity to being a model contemporary educational system and a "strong performer" in about 2 decades since the late 1970s. Finland is special also because it has been able to create an educational system where most students learn well and where equitable education has translated into little variation in student performance between schools in different parts of country, as shown in all PISA studies since the year 2000. This internationally rare status has been achieved by using reasonable financial resources and less effort than other nations have expended on reform efforts.

Two, because of this proven steady progress, Finland demonstrates that there is another way to build a successful education system using solutions that differ from the market-driven education policies that have become common in many parts of the world. The Finnish Way of change, as described by Andy Hargreaves and Dennis Shirley (2009) in *The Fourth Way*, is one of trust, professionalism, and shared responsibility. Indeed, Finland is an example of a nation that lacks school inspection, reliance on externally collected data, standardized curriculum, high-stakes student testing, test-based accountability, and a race-to-the-top mentality with regard to educational change.

Three, as a consequence of its success, Finland can offer some alternative ways to think about solutions to existing chronic educational problems in the United States, England, and many other countries, such as high school dropout rates, early teacher attrition, and inadequate special education. The Finnish approach to reducing early school leavers, enhancing teacher professionalism, implementing intelligent accountability, and employing smarter student assessment in schools can offer inspiration to other school systems looking for a path to success.

Four, Finland is also an international high performer in commerce, technology, sustainable development, good governance, prosperity, gender equality, and child well-being, thus raising interesting questions concerning interdependencies between education and other sectors in society. It appears that other public policy sectors, such as health and employment, seem to play a role also in long-term educational development and change. In Finland, this holds true as well regarding income parity, social mobility, and trust within Finnish society, as the chapters that follow will show.

Finally, despite declining results in recent international education rankings, Finland continues to do well when it comes to overall learning outcomes and especially student engagement, well-being, and satisfaction with their schools. International observers should look beyond the PISA results and ask how authorities, politicians, and teachers are responding to the downturn in international school rankings. Increased emphasis on student well-being and engagement in school, keeping arts and music available to all in every school, and encouraging schools to design future-looking curricula where less focus is on traditional subjects and more learning takes place in real-world settings, are some of those answers to worsening test scores that hardly any other country has dared to try.

We should listen to the story of Finland because it gives hope to those who are losing their faith in public education and whether it can be improved (Sahlberg, 2020b). This book reveals that the transformation of educational systems is possible, but that it takes time, patience, and determination. The Finnish story is particularly interesting because some of the key policies and changes were introduced during the worst economic crisis that Finland has experienced since World War II. This suggests that a crisis can spark the survival spirit that leads to better solutions to acute problems than a "normal situation" would bring about. This book speaks against those who believe that the best way to solve chronic problems in many education systems is to take control away from school boards and give it to those who might run schools more effectively, by charters, businesses, or other means of privatization. Although there are limits to the ideas that can be transferred from Finland to other nations, certain basic lessons may have general value for other educational systems, such as the practices of building on teacher strengths, securing relaxed and fear-free learning for students, and gradually enhancing trust within educational systems.

As this book illustrates, there is no single reason why any educational system succeeds or struggles. Instead, there is a network of interrelated factors—educational, political, social, and cultural—that function differently in different situations. In October 2014, just about the time when the second edition of *Finnish Lessons* went to press, I was invited to give an address at the opening ceremony of the Frankfurt Book Fair that is the world's largest trade fair for books attended by more than a quarter of a million people each year. Being honored to speak alongside the president of Finland, Sauli Niinistö, and Sofi Oksanen, who is one of the most read modern Finnish writers and playwrights, I explained to the international audience that there is nothing magical in Finland's education story:

> Alvar Aalto, Finland's most renowned architect and designer, made the wise statement that we should work for simple, good,

undecorated things, but things that are in harmony with the human being and organically suited to the little man in the street. Similarly, one might say that Finnish teachers prefer traditional, reliable, calm teaching over the sort of heroic feats we've seen in the movies. If anyone thinks they're going to find a bunch of Robin Williamses from *Dead Poets' Society* in Finnish schools, they will be disappointed. Finns don't believe a few super-teachers can save their children and their schools. It takes a whole village to raise a child.

I did, however, cite three important elements of Finnish educational policies since the early 1970s that appear to transcend culture.

The first is an inspiring vision of what good public education should be: Finland has been particularly committed to building a good, publicly financed, and locally governed basic school for every child. This common educational goal, which placed equity in education as the key priority, became so deeply rooted in politics and public services in Finland that it survived opposing political governments and ministries unharmed and intact. Since the introduction of *peruskoulu* in the early 1970s, there have been 22 governments representing different political colors and 25 ministers of education in charge of educational reforms in Finland. This commitment to having a great public school for every child has been so strong that some call it the Finnish Dream. This name provides a hint for other nations when it comes to educational transformation: It is better to have a dream of your own than to rent one from others.

The second aspect of educational change that deserves attention is the way Finland has treated advice offered by friends and neighboring countries. Much of the inspiration in building independent Finland since December 1917 has come from its allies, especially Sweden. The welfare state model, health care system, and basic education are good examples of borrowed ideas from our Western neighbor. Later, Finnish education policies were also influenced by guidance from supranational institutions, especially the OECD (which Finland joined in 1969) and the European Union (which Finland joined in 1995). In this book, I launch an argument that, despite international influence and borrowing educational ideas from others, Finland has in the end created its own way to build the educational system that exists today. I call this the *Finnish Way* because it is different from what much of the rest of the world has done in educational improvement during the past 30 years. The Finnish Way of change preserves the best of Finland's own traditions and present good practices, and combines these with innovations received from others. Cultivating trust, enhancing autonomy, and tolerating diversity are just a few of the examples of the reform ideas found in Finnish schools today. Many pedagogical ideas and educational innovations are initially imported from other countries, often from North America or the United Kingdom. These include curriculum models from England, California, and Ontario; cooperative learning methods from the United States and Israel; idea of multiple intelligences from the United States; the pedagogies of science and mathematics from England, the United States, and Australia; and peer-assisted leadership and peer coaching from Canada, the Netherlands, and the United States, to mention just a few. At the same time, the Finnish Dream of education is "made in Finland" and therefore is owned by Finns rather than rented from others.

The third aspect of change is a systematic development of respectful and inspiring working conditions for teachers and principals in Finnish schools. This book raises an important question that is repeated when whole-system educational reforms are discussed: How do we get the best and the most committed young people to choose teaching as their career? Experience from Finland, as illustrated in Chapter 3, suggests that it is not enough to establish world-class teacher education programs or to pay teachers well. Finland has built world-class teacher education programs. And Finland pays its teachers relatively well. But the true Finnish difference is that teachers in Finland are expected to exercise their full professional knowledge and judgment both independently and collectively in their schools. They, not authorities or politicians, control curriculum, student assessment, school improvement, and community involvement. This is called teacher and leaders' professionalism. Much as teachers around the world enter the profession with a mission to build community and transmit culture, Finnish teachers, in contrast to their peers in so many countries, have the latitude and the power to follow through.

LEARNING FROM OTHERS

Can Finland be a model for educational change in other countries? Many people are fascinated by the fact that Finland has been able to transform its educational system from something elitist, unknown, and inefficient into a paragon of equity and efficiency. Finland is also one of the few nations among the 37 OECD countries that has had consistent good educational performance over time as measured by international indicators and student achievement tests. Furthermore, many foreign visitors have been particularly surprised to find out that teaching has become the number-one profession among young Finns—above medicine and law—and that primary teacher education in Finnish universities is one of the most competitive choices of study. All these aspects of the Finnish educational system are explored further in this book.

There are, however, those who doubt that Finland has much relevance to other educational systems because of its special characteristics. The most commonly presented argument is that because Finland is so exceptional, it hardly provides anything meaningful to the United States, England, Australia, France, or other much larger nations, or that it is "too different to serve as models for whole-system reform for North America as a whole," as Michael Fullan (2010, p. xiv) writes. Two points are often emphasized when the relevance of Finland as a model for educational change is considered.

First, Finland is culturally and ethnically still rather homogeneous and thus too unlike the United States, for example. Fair enough, but the same holds true for Japan, Shanghai, Korea, Estonia, or Poland. The proportion of foreign-born citizens in Finland was 4.4% in 2010 and 7.7% in 2020 (Statistics Finland, n.d.a). It is noteworthy that Finland is a trilingual country, where Finnish, Swedish, and Sami are all official languages. The largest language and ethnic minorities are Russian, Estonian, and Somali. The diversification of Finnish society since the mid-1990s has been the fastest in Europe, at a rate of 800% by 2010. When I began my teaching career in Helsinki in the mid-1980s, it was rare to have anybody in my classroom who looked or sounded different from the others. The number of foreign-born citizens in Finland has nearly tripled during the first decade of the 21st century. Finland is not that homogeneous anymore, but, of course, it still doesn't compare to the United States or Australia as a multicultural nation as far as ethnic diversity is concerned.

Second, Finland is considered too small to be a good model for system-wide reform for North America. This is a trickier argument to defend. When the size factor in educational reforms is considered, it is necessary to note that in many federal nations, states, provinces, or regions are to a large extent autonomous in terms of educational management and the running of their schools. This is the case in the United States, Canada, Australia, Brazil, and Germany, for example. The population of Finland today is 5.6 million. This is about the population of Minnesota in the United States or Victoria in Australia and just slightly more than the size of the population of Alberta in Canada or Nord-Pas-de-Calais in France. Indeed, about 30 states of the United States have a population that is close to or smaller than Finland's. These include the states of Maryland, Colorado, Oregon, and Connecticut. The populations of the states of Washington, Indiana, and Massachusetts are also smallish and are close to Finland in size. In Australia, only New South Wales has a slightly larger population than Finland's; all other Australian states are smaller. In France, Île-de-France is the only region that surpasses Finland in population size. In Canada, only Ontario is significantly larger in population (and land area) than Finland; all other provinces are similar in size. If these jurisdictions have the freedom to set their own educational policies and conduct reforms as they think best, then the experiences of an educational system the size of Finland's should be particularly interesting and relevant to them. France is the only country mentioned above that employs centralized educational management, and therefore the French education policymakers could argue for the irrelevance of smaller education systems as models for their reforms.

Finally, there are some who doubt that international comparisons are relevant or reliable in what they claim to show. One point of view is that academic achievement tests, such as the OECD's PISA, Trends in International Mathematics and Science Study (TIMSS), and Progress in International Reading Literacy Study (PIRLS), focus on areas that are too narrow to capture the whole spectrum of school education, and thus they ignore social skills, moral development, creativity, or digital literacy as important outcomes of public education for all (see Chapter 2 for references to this argument). There is also a growing concern that these comparisons are influencing educational policies and endorsing the culture of "governing by numbers" (Fischman et al., 2019; Grek, 2009; Meyer & Benavot, 2013; Sellar et al., 2017; Zhao, 2014). Another skeptical group simply argues that the chosen measurement methodologies in current international tests favor Finland because they match better with the culture of teaching in Finland; this group includes both Finnish and foreign scientists and experts.[2] Harvard's Howard Gardner warned his audience during a visit to Finland in 2010 to treat these current student assessment studies with caution,[3] contending that results in studies like these always depend on the subject-area knowledge tested and the respective methodologies of the studies used. In addition, these studies do not measure interpersonal, spatial, or creative skills, and these skill sets are increasingly important in our contemporary world. There seems to be a growing group of people who question the credibility of PISA and who challenge the new educational world order created in a large degree by this one measurement.

Although Finland has persistently outperformed other nations, its achievements have been downplayed in numerous accounts of recommended policy. In an influential report by McKinsey and Company (Mourshed et al., 2010), for example, Finland was not even listed as a "sustained improver" in the listing of potential model countries for education reformers. The consequence is that policymakers in many contexts will not consider Finnish strategies as they develop their repertoire of school improvement practices. National education strategies and policy guidelines, such as the 2010 *Schools White Paper* in England (Department for Education, 2010), *Lessons From PISA for the United States* (OECD, 2011), and the World Bank Education Strategy 2020 (World Bank, 2011), often refer to common features of high-performing education systems as desired criteria for improvement. Focuses on teacher effectiveness, school autonomy, accountability, and data are all central elements of education systems in Korea, Singapore, Alberta, and Finland, but in very different ways. As this book will show again and again, Finland is unique in terms of how these very aspects of education policy are employed. The Finnish experience shows that consistent focus on equity and cooperation—not choice and competition—can lead to an education system where all children learn well. Paying teachers based on students' test scores or converting public schools into private ones through charters or other means are ideas that have no place in the Finnish repertoire for educational improvement.

The size of Finland's population and the relative homogeneity of its society obviously make many aspects of setting education policies and implementing reforms easier than would be the case in larger, more diverse jurisdictions. But these factors alone don't explain all the progress and achievements in Finnish education that are described in this book, and they should not stop us from learning from one another as we strive to improve education for all students. Finland is, however, very unique among nations in terms of its values, cultural determinants, and social cohesion, as André Noël Chaker eloquently describes in his book, *The Finnish Miracle* (2014). Fairness, honesty, and social justice are deeply rooted in the Finnish way of life. People have a strong sense of shared responsibility, not only for their own lives, but also for the lives of others. Fostering the well-being of children starts before they are born and continues until they reach adulthood. Day care is a right of all children before they start school at age 7, and public health service is easily accessible to everyone during childhood. Education in Finland is widely seen as a public good and is therefore protected as a basic human right to all in the constitution. Adages such as "Small is beautiful" and "Less is more" are typical descriptors of everyday culture in Finland.

In this book, I describe how Finns have built a functional, sustainable, and just country with an equitable public education system by doing things in their own way. The Finnish government's Country Brand Delegation that was chaired by ex-CEO of Nokia Jorma Ollila wrote in 2010 that "in Finland, people do not aspire to do everything the same way as the others, to dress or to live like others. Rather than the 'done thing,' Finns do what they think is the rational thing to do" (Ministry of Foreign Affairs, 2010, p. 59). The intense individuality of Finns, blended with a low degree of hierarchy and a traditional willingness to work with others, has opened pathways to endless creative potential. The inspiration and vision to create a society with an education system that is good and accessible to all was drawn from this pool of creative potential.

In the early 2020s, the Finnish school system continues to outperform most other OECD countries' school systems in reading, mathematical, and scientific literacy at the end of lower-secondary education (at the age 15), has a more equitable and efficient education system, and has children who show one of the highest levels of life satisfaction in school compared to other countries. Since about 2010, however, there has been a decline in Finland's OECD PISA scores, especially in mathematics. Some have asked what is happening in Finland? Has the world-class system begun to erode because of wrong reforms or lack of focus on improvement, or is Finland simply becoming more like other countries in terms of how its schools teach children and what children think about learning in school. I will explore answers to these questions and others asked about the fate of Finnish schools in the chapters that follow.

Data for this book come not from one source alone, nor does this book claim that educational excellence could be justified by any single international study. Evidence is drawn from the available international databases, such as PISA and TIMSS, from global education indicators, and from versatile official statistics in Finland.

THE PLAN OF THIS BOOK

The first edition of *Finnish Lessons* offered me access to rich and detailed conversations about educational change in general and about the Finnish education model in particular. This third edition includes updates to international performance data, more detailed descriptions of equity in Finnish education, and a revised outline of the structure of Finland's education system after reforms made during the 2010s. I will also answer the question that many have asked since the PISA 2018 results became public: What explains Finland's decline in the global PISA league tables since 2012?

This book draws from the following 10 notions, which are explained in detail in the pages of this volume:

1. Finland has an education system in which young people learn well and where performance differences among schools are small—and all with reasonable cost and human effort.
2. This has not always been so.
3. In Finland, teaching is a prestigious profession, teachers are respected and trusted professionals, and therefore many young Finns aspire to be teachers.
4. Therefore, the Finns probably have the most competitive and academically challenging teacher education system in the world. As a consequence, teachers in Finland have a great deal of professional autonomy and access to purposeful professional development throughout their careers.
5. Finnish education policies since the 1970s have aimed at having a good school for every child rather than ranking high on international education tables.
6. After 9 years of comprehensive basic education, Finnish students have two equally attractive and educationally purposeful options: academic pathway and vocational pathway that both provide access to free, publicly funded higher education.
7. Special education is based on inclusion of most students in normal mainstream schools, and it is meant for all children. Almost half of Finnish 16-year-olds, when they move to upper-secondary education, have had some sort of special education, personalized help, or individual guidance during their time in school.
8. In Finland, teachers teach less and students spend less time studying, both in and out of school, than their peers in other countries. Finnish schools lack the census-based high-stakes standardized testing, test preparation, and private tutoring common in the United States and much of the rest of the world.

9. All of the factors that are behind Finnish success seem to be the opposite of what is taking place in the United States and much of the rest of the world, where competition, test-based accountability, standardization, and privatization seem to dominate.

10. Finland's strategy is also different when things don't go as planned. When learning outcomes are declining, the authorities invest in student engagement, teacher collaboration, and interdisciplinary curriculum rather than tighten the grip on schools, refocus on back-to-basics, and introduce more testing in schools.

After this introduction, the book has five chapters. Chapter 1 explains both the political and historical realities in Finland after World War II and how they shaped the move toward the idea of common basic school for all by the end of the 1960s. In telling the story of educational change in Finland to scores of foreign visitors, I have learned that it is important to go back further in time than the birth of *peruskoulu* (I use this Finnish term because there isn't an English equivalent to it) in 1970. Chapter 1 illustrates the process of reforming the old school system, which divided pupils into two tracks and relied heavily on privately governed and cofinanced grammar schools, into a comprehensive, publicly managed and funded system. It also outlines the main features of upper-secondary education that emerged soon after implementing the *peruskoulu* reform in the late 1970s. The main characteristics of the iconic Finnish Matriculation Examination, a high-stakes test students take when they leave general upper-secondary education in Finland, are also described in this chapter.

Chapter 2 tackles a fundamental question: Was Finland also a high performer in education in the past? The answer provided in this chapter is as expected: no. This answer immediately invites a corollary question: What constitutes a good educational system, and which educational reforms have made such impressive progress possible in Finland? The core of this chapter is the insight that Finnish educational success in international comparisons can, at least to some extent, be understood through paradoxes. We can crystallize this notion with a simple principle in educational reform: Less is more. Chapter 2 provides evidence-based examples of how this paradoxical idea appears in the Finnish educational system today. It also suggests some explanations for changing trends in

Finnish student performance in international student assessments since 2010.

Chapter 3 is about teachers and the teaching profession in Finland. It examines the crucial role that teachers play in Finland and describes the main features of the teaching profession, teacher education, and teacher responsibilities in Finland. This chapter suggests that whereas high-quality, university-based teacher education and continuous professional development are necessary conditions for attracting the most talented and committed young people into teaching, they are not sufficient alone. Teachers have to be provided with a professional working environment so that they feel dignified and are able to fulfill their moral purposes in schools. This chapter also looks at teacher leadership and its manifestations among Finnish teachers, including the findings from the OECD's latest Teaching and Learning International Survey (TALIS 2018) regarding the teaching profession in Finland.

Since Finland's amazing recovery from a grave economic recession in the early 1990s—and more recently from the global financial crisis of 2008—many have spoken about the Finnish Model of building an inclusive information society and a competitive knowledge economy (Castells & Himanen, 2002; Dahlman et al., 2006; Halme et al., 2014). What is significant in Finland's process of economic recovery is that at the same time when the Finnish economy and especially the public sector was adjusting to tougher competition and better productivity, the performance of the education system was steadily improving. Chapter 4 illustrates some interdependencies between Finnish educational policy and other public sector policies that are at the heart of the economic comeback. This chapter also describes how the COVID-19 pandemic affected the Finnish education system and how teachers responded to the shutdown of much of the society, including schools and universities in the spring of 2020. Furthermore, it suggests that progress in the educational sector has happened in tandem with changes in government that have improved economic competitiveness, transparency, and welfare policy.

Finally, Chapter 5 asks a question that is, surprisingly, not often asked of Finns by their visitors: What is the future of Finnish schooling? Being in the global limelight takes its toll. Although Finns have hosted thousands of foreign education pilgrims since late 2001, they have had only a little time and energy to think about what their own education system should look like in the future. The first signs of the impact of this were reported in the PISA 2009 study and were reconfirmed in the PISA 2012 analysis when Finland's top spot was taken by Asian school systems. Finnish performance continued to slip in subsequent PISA cycles in 2015 and 2018, both in student achievement in reading, mathematics, and science and in equity of these outcomes. Chapter 5 culminates by insisting that an important lesson for Finland from its own past is that it needs to be clear about what to do next. I conclude that being at the center of the education reform debate has prevented Finns from thinking about what kind of education will be needed in the future, especially one influenced by the global health crisis caused by the COVID-19 pandemic since 2020. The chapter closes with a discussion about the need to change, in spite of the fact that the current system is praised for its excellence and seems to be working well.

There is an important note that the reader of this book should keep in mind. In my research I have used data primarily from the databases of OECD and Statistics Finland, which are publicly available for interested readers. I have constructed graphs showing correlations, or absence of them, between two variables—for example, the relationship between cost of education and level of educational performance in different countries. Old wisdom in statistics and in social sciences states that correlation does not imply causation; this must be remembered also while reading this book. What this means is that even if there is a correlation between two variables, it does not automatically mean that one causes the other. Correlation is *necessary* for linear causation and often suggests that indeed one variable causes the other. Figures 2.8, 2.10, 4.1, and 5.1 present such linear correlations.

Another reminder is noteworthy before getting any further. It is a risky business to pick any individual aspects of the Finnish school system and believe that they are the ones that explain Finland's educational success. Explaining why complex social systems behave in a particular way is difficult. It continues to be hard to say exactly what is the winning formula in education, just like we don't know exactly why the winners start to lose their power. In this book I have done the best I can to be truthful to these complexities and not to promise any easy answers.

CHAPTER 1

The Finnish Dream
A Good School for All

> God mend us! The fact is that we don't even know the first letter of
> the alphabet, and that knowing how to read is the first duty of every
> Christian citizen. The power of law, of church law, may force us to it.
> And you know what kind of contraption the State has watching, eager
> to snap us up in its jaws if we don't obediently learn to read. The stocks
> are waiting for us, my brothers, the black stocks; their cruel jaws gaping
> wide like those of a black bear. The provost has threatened us with those
> hellish pincers, and he is bound to carry out his threat unless he sees us
> eagerly studying every day.
>
> —Aleksis Kivi, *Seven Brothers*

The story of Finland is a story of survival. It is eloquently captured by
Aleksis Kivi in the first Finnish novel, *Seven Brothers*, which was published
in 1870. It is a story of orphan brothers who realize that becoming literate
is the key to happiness and a good life. Since those days, reading has been
an integral part of Finnish culture. Education has served as the main strategy for building a literate society and a nation that is today known by the
world for its cultural and technological achievements. Therefore, *Seven
Brothers* belongs to the list of core texts in most Finnish schools today.

Being a relatively small nation situated between much larger powers of the East and the West has taught Finns to accept existing realities
and take chances with available opportunities. Diplomacy, cooperation,
problem solving, and seeking consensus have thus become hallmarks of
contemporary Finnish culture. These traits all play an important part in
building an educational system that has enjoyed global attention due to
its equitable distribution of good teaching and learning throughout the
nation.

This chapter describes how Finland has progressed from being
a poor, agrarian, and only modestly educated nation to a modern,

knowledge-based society with a high-performing education system and a world-class innovation environment. Expanding access to education from early childhood education all the way to the highest academic degrees and adult learning has been a long-term ideal in Finnish society. This chapter first provides a historic and political context for realization of this Finnish Dream. It then describes the evolution of the unified comprehensive basic school, or *peruskoulu* as it is called in Finnish, and some principles of upper-secondary education that are an important part of Finnish educational success.[1] Present structures and policies of the Finnish education system are briefly outlined at the end of the chapter.

POSTWAR FINLAND

War ranks among the most serious of imaginable crises for any democratic nation. Except for a short period of ceasefire, Finland was at war from December 1939 to the spring of 1945. The cost of war for that young, independent democracy with a population of fewer than 4 million was enormous: 90,000 dead and 60,000 permanently injured. In addition, 25,000 were widowed and 50,000 children were orphaned. A peace treaty with the Soviet Union was signed in Moscow on September 19, 1944, but military campaigns to remove German troops from Finland continued until April 1945. The conditions that the Finns accepted were severe. Finland had to hand over 12% of its territory to the Soviets and had to relocate 450,000 people—11% of Finland's total population. The Finnish concessions to the Soviets were estimated to reach 7% of its gross domestic product (GDP). A peninsula near Helsinki had to be rented to the Soviet army as a military base, political prisoners had to be released, and wartime leaders were judged in war tribunals. Several political associations were prohibited, and the Communist Party was established as a legal Finnish political entity. These concessions led to such fundamental political, cultural, and economic changes in Finland that some have identified the postwar era as the emergence of a "Second Republic."[2]

Most important, Finland had fought for its freedom and survived. External threats experienced during and after World War II united Finns, who still felt the wounds of the previous 1918 civil war. The post–World War II era was one of political instability and economic transformation, but it also gave rise to new social ideas and social policies—in particular the idea of equal educational opportunities. It is difficult to understand why education has become one of the trademarks of Finland without examining these post–World War II political and social developments. Even among Finns, there are those who argue that the search for key success factors in the Finnish educational system has to extend much earlier than 1970, a year often recognized as a historical milestone in Finnish education for reasons explained later in this chapter.

History is often easier to understand when it is segmented into periods or phases of development, and the recent history of Finland is no exception to this strategy. Although there are many ways to recount Finland's history, depending on the purposes and perspectives of its authors, in this case it is helpful to illustrate congruencies between the development of Finland's education system and four stages of economic development following World War II (Sahlberg, 2010a):

- Enhancing equal opportunities for education by way of transition from a northern agricultural nation to an industrialized society (1945–1970)
- Creating a public comprehensive school system by way of a Nordic welfare society with a growing service sector and increasing levels of technology and technological innovation (1965–1990)
- Improving the quality of basic education, strengthening upper-secondary education, and expanding higher education in keeping with Finland's new identity as a high-tech, knowledge-based economy (1985–2010)
- Building a more streamlined lifelong learning system by integrating early childhood education and care into the education system and shifting curricula foci from content to competencies at all levels of education (2010–present)

The 1950s were already a time of rapid changes to Finland's economic structure, but the 1960s have been characterized as phenomenal by international standards (Aho et al., 2006; Dahlman et al., 2006). The decade of the 1960s saw Finnish society, in more general terms, relinquish many of its old values, and traditional Finnish institutions began to transform. Public services—especially basic education—were among the most visible sites of change. When the time for decisive change arrived, its speed and thoroughness took many Finns by surprise.

The end of World War II prompted such radical changes to Finnish political, social, and economic structures that immediate changes to education and other social institutions were required. Indeed, education soon became the main vehicle of social and economic transformation in the postwar era. In 1950, educational opportunities in Finland were unequal in the sense that only those living in towns or larger municipalities had access to grammar or middle schools. Most young people left school after 6 or 7 years of formal basic education. Where private grammar schools were available, pupils could apply to enroll in them after 4, 5, or 6 years of state-run basic school, but such opportunities were limited. In 1950, for example, just 27% of 11-year-old Finns enrolled in grammar schools consisting of 5-year middle schools and 3-year high schools. An alternative educational path after the compulsory 7 years of basic education was 2 or 3 years of study in one of the so-called civic schools offered by most Finnish municipalities. This basic education could be followed by vocational training and technical education, but only in larger municipalities and towns that housed these institutions.

In 1950, there were 338 grammar schools offering further educational opportunities after the 6-year basic school in Finland (Kiuasmaa, 1982). The Finnish state operated 103 of these schools, and municipalities ran 18. The remaining 217 grammar schools, about two thirds of the total, were governed by private citizens or associations. The major burden of the rapid expansion of education following basic schooling was absorbed by these private schools. A significant social innovation in 1950 was the issuance of legislation that guaranteed state subsidies to private schools, and simultaneously extended the government's control over these schools. This change made it possible to respond to the public's growing interest in education by opening new private schools, as their financial risks were diminished through state funding.

In the early years after Finland's independence, teaching in primary schools was formal, teacher-centered, and focused more on moral than cognitive development. Although pedagogical ideas aimed at social gains and more holistic interpersonal development were known in Finland as early as the 1930s, school education was not greatly influenced by them (Koskenniemi, 1944). Three dominant themes in Finnish national education policy between 1945 and 1970 would come to change this traditional model:

- The structure of the education system would provide access to better and more education for all.
- The form and content of curricula would focus on development of individual, holistic personalities of children.

- Teacher education would be modernized to respond to needs arising from these developments. The future dream of Finland was built on knowledge and skills; thus, education was seen as a foundation for establishing the future (Aho et al., Pitkänen, & Sahlberg, 2006).

Finland's economic structure in 1950, comparable to Sweden's economy in 1910, was in transition. Key industries were shifting from farming and small business to industrial and technological production. The new political environment in the postwar era had also activated working-class families, who insisted that their children should have opportunities to benefit from extended public education. Consequently, a model for comprehensive schools offering universal access and a unified curriculum, first proposed in the 1920s, was revived and entered education policy discussions soon after the end of World War II. It was clear that to become a recognized member of the community of Western democracies and market economies, Finland needed a better-educated population. This was a vision for the entire nation.

UNIVERSAL BASIC EDUCATION

The first 2 decades after World War II were politically turbulent in Finland. The Communist Party returned to the main stage of daily politics in the first postwar elections in 1944, and identified education as one of its primary strategies for building a Finnish socialist society. In the 1948 elections, three political parties received nearly equal seats in the Finnish national Parliament: the Social Democratic Party (50 seats), the Agrarian Centre Party (49 seats), and the Communist Party (49 seats). The rebuilding of Finland began; political consensus was a precondition for reforms, including renewing the Finnish educational system. The Conservative Party increased its popularity in the 1950s and became a fourth political force to be reckoned with in Finnish parliamentary negotiations. The political education committees played particularly important roles as the groundwork for comprehensive basic schooling for all Finnish students was laid, and the vision was finally realized in 1970.

Three politically oriented education committees are particularly worth mentioning. First, in June 1945, the government established the Primary School Curriculum Committee. The secretary of that committee was Matti Koskenniemi (1908–2001), who had, a few years earlier, written a seminal book on primary school didactics (Koskenniemi, 1944). Through his contributions, perspectives on curriculum in Finland shifted from focusing on syllabi (the German term *lehrplan*) to describing educational objectives, process of education, and evaluation. These reforms were the first to modernize the Finnish curriculum by international standards, and they still resonate in contemporary curriculum thinking.

There are several reasons why this committee holds a central place in the history of Finnish education. First, the members devoted special attention to formulating new objectives for education, thereby deviating from German tradition in Finnish education. The committee put forth the idea that school should aim at educating young people to realize themselves as holistic individuals, possessing intrinsic motivation for further education. The content of education that would lead to this general aim was grouped into five thematic, cross-curricular areas, which later became a model for the Comprehensive School Curriculum Committee in 1970.

Second, curriculum reform was grounded in empirical studies conducted in 300 field schools involving 1,000 teachers. In this way, research became part of education policymaking. Third, and as a corollary of the previous two reasons, the quality of the committee's work was regarded as exceptionally high. The Final Memorandum of the committee, published in 1952, has merit in its systematic formulation of educational objectives, broad child-centered perspective, modernized presentation and richness of educational content, and emphasis on the primacy of social cohesion as one important goal in education. Significant milestones in the postwar history of Finland were realized in 1952: hosting the Summer Olympics in Helsinki, the coronation of Miss Finland Armi Kuusela as the first-ever Miss Universe, and completion of heavy reparations to the Soviet Union. It is appropriate, also, to include in Finland's 1952 milestones the new, internationally comparable curriculum for Finland's primary school system, which paved the way to educational success some half a century later.

A second committee of significance, the Education System Committee, launched its work in 1946 to establish regulations for compulsory education and a common framework of principles for determining how different parts of the education system should be interlinked. The committee included representatives of all of the leading political parties of that time and was chaired by the National Board of Education's director general, Yrjö Ruutu, ally of the Finnish Communist Party. Less than

2 years after commencing its work, this committee proposed that the foundation of the Finnish educational system should be an 8-year compulsory basic school that would be common to all children regardless of their socioeconomic situation. The committee advised that this school system ought to avoid tracking more able students to "academic" subjects and to "vocational" studies those preferring to learn manual skills, as was done in the then-current parallel education system.

However, the committee retained the standard that only those students who had learned foreign languages during basic school would be allowed to enter upper-secondary school or *gymnasium*—which represented the only pathway to higher education. Although the idea of comprehensive school was clearly formulated, it was not acted upon due to bitter criticism from universities and the Grammar School Teachers' Union. However, the committee's proposal stimulated further debate within Finnish society about social justice and equal educational opportunities—tenets that, 2 decades later, would be realized and entrenched as foundations of Finnish education policy.

Development of different sectors of education continued in the 1950s. The baby boom after World War II led to rapid expansion in the number of schools. New laws stipulated that compulsory education was to consist of 6 years of primary school and 2 years of civic school for those who didn't advance further to grammar schools. The new curriculum launched in 1952 began to change work and life in schools. Vocational education became part of the education sector. Finland's dream of common schooling for all was alive, but, in practice, parallel schooling structures remained. Consequently, a third committee of key significance, the School Program Committee, was established in 1956 to unify the Finnish education system and bring coherence to changes in various subsectors of education. The establishment of this committee under the leadership of Reino Henrik Oittinen, director general of the National Board of Education and a Social Democrat, was one step further step toward the big dream of Finnish education.

The work of this committee was built on an unprecedented analysis of international education policies. Particularly significant was the committee's observation that Nordic countries shared much in common regarding their education policies at that time. Increasing equality of educational opportunities—a priority at the time in England and the United States—became a central theme in the committee's strategic thinking. The period from 1956 to 1959, during which this politically broad-based committee conducted almost 200 meetings, was particularly turbulent: Global economic recession, tough political conflicts both domestically and with the Soviet Union, and the launch of *Sputnik* soon impacted educational reforms around the world. Nevertheless, the committee persevered, and its work became a cornerstone in the history of educational reforms in Finland.

The School Program Committee published its recommendations in the summer of 1959. The committee suggested that future compulsory education in Finland should be based on a 9-year municipal comprehensive school with the following structure:

- The first four grades would be common to all pupils.
- Grades 5 and 6 would constitute a middle school where pupils could choose to focus on either practical subjects or foreign languages.
- Grades 7 through 9 would have three streams: vocational and practical orientation, an "average" track with one foreign language, and an advanced stream with two foreign languages.

The committee was unable to unify political will around this structure of comprehensive school; indeed, strong disagreement arose even within the committee about main policy principles. The proposed system would, however, gradually merge private grammar and public civic schools into a new municipal structure, and diminish the role of private schools. Overall, the work of this committee initiated deep and significant debate about core values in education in Finnish society. The key question was: Is it possible, in principle, that all children can be educated and can achieve similar learning goals? Answers to this question created divided opinions, even within families. Primary school teachers believed all students could learn equally well, universities typically doubted the proposition, and politicians remained divided. At that time, given its need to advance both politically and economically on the world stage, Finland had no choice but to accept the proposition that anyone—if given adequate opportunities and support—could learn foreign languages and advance to higher levels of education than had previously been believed. It was more difficult for many politicians to accept that the educational architecture of the day, which maintained and actually more deeply entrenched inequality in Finnish society, would be unable in the long run to ensure that Finland would achieve its goal of becoming a knowledge society. Figure 1.1 illustrates the characteristics of the parallel educational system until the early 1970s, which divided pupils at

Figure 1.1. Structure of the Education System in Finland Before 1970

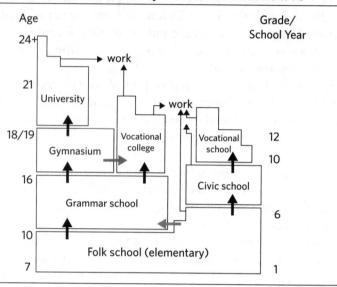

the age of 11 or 12 into one of two separated streams. There was practically no possibility to move between these streams once students had decided which pathway to follow.

The original 1959 proposal of the School Program Committee was further elaborated by the National Board of General Education in the early 1960s, and then finally taken to Parliament on November 22, 1963. The ensuing debate was harsh. Some predicted a gloomy future for Finland if the new ideas related to common unified public school for all were approved: declining level of knowledge; waste of existing national talent; and Finland, as a nation, being left behind in the international economic race. In the final vote, the proposal for the new educational system in Finland passed, with 123 voting in favor and 68 against. The celebration of the birth of the new school in Finland was disturbed by an announcement by the speaker of the Parliament: U.S. president John F. Kennedy had been assassinated in Dallas, Texas, just minutes earlier.

It would be inappropriate to claim that the birth of the new Finnish comprehensive school, or *peruskoulu* system, which is frequently identified as a structural foundation for Finland's educational fame today, was created by politicians and authorities alone. Many other people, including both school practitioners and academics, contributed to the process of defining Finland's new school system. Particularly significant was the role played by some of Finland's civil society organizations. It is beyond the scope of this chapter to conduct deeper analysis of the influence that many of these groups exerted on Finnish educational reform. However, a good example of civil society involvement in education policy development is the role played by the Finnish Primary School Teachers' Association (FPSTA). As early as 1946, FPSTA had expressed its support for the idea of a unified basic school system. In the mid-1950s, the association published its own education development program accompanied by a detailed, well-argued proposal for a unified, comprehensive school system. What was unusual about this proposed program was that, unlike the appeals of union-based teachers' associations, it was progressive and future-oriented. It was widely supported by the FPSTA members, representing nearly 90% of all Finnish primary school teachers. The FPSTA's proposal took 5 years to complete and stimulated a national discussion that was clearly focused on the need to enhance equality and social justice in Finnish society through a more equitable education system. Perhaps most important, the publication of the FPSTA's program proposal was a clear sign that schools and teachers were ready for radical change.

In 1956, the nation's grammar schools enrolled approximately 34,000 pupils. Five years later, enrollment had swelled to 215,000, and it continued to soar, rising to 270,000 in 1965 and to 324,000 in 1970 (Aho et al., 2006). Finland's old system could barely hold together as parents demanded an improved and more comprehensive basic education for their children in the hope of securing better lives for them. Such social pressure introduced a new theme in the education policy debate: the individual's potential for growth. Researchers then argued that an individual's abilities and intelligence always rose to the level required by society, and that education systems merely reflected these limits or needs.

THE NEW SCHOOL IS BORN

New legislation (1966) and a national curriculum (1970) were prepared in the second half of the 1960s. The social policy climate at the time had consolidated the values of equality and social justice across the social classes of Finnish society. The expenditures incurred by the ideal of a welfare state were seen, as argued by prominent Finnish political scientist Pekka Kuusi, as an investment in increasing productivity rather than a necessary social cost of maintaining an industrial society (Kuusi, 1961). The new comprehensive school system was poised for implementation in 1972. According to the plan, a wave of reform was to begin in the northern regions of Finland, and would reach the southern urban areas by 1978.

A fundamental belief related to the old structure was that *everyone cannot learn everything*; in other words, talent in society is not evenly distributed in terms of one's ability to be educated. In Finland, there were echoes of the Coleman Report published in the United States, favoring the view that a young person's basic disposition and characteristics were determined in the home, and could not be substantially influenced by schooling (Coleman et al., 1966). It was important that the new *peruskoulu* shed these beliefs and thus help build a more socially just society with higher education levels for all.

The central idea of *peruskoulu*, as shown in Figure 1.2, was to merge existing grammar schools, civic schools, and primary schools into a comprehensive 9-year municipal school. This meant that the placement of students after 4 years of primary education into grammar and civic streams would come to an end. All students, regardless of their domicile, socioeconomic background, or interests would enroll in the same 9-year basic schools governed by local education authorities. This implementation was revolutionary, although as noted previously, the idea behind it was not new. Critics of the new system maintained that it was not possible to have the same educational expectations for children coming from very different social and intellectual circumstances. Opponents argued that the entire future of Finland as a developed industrial nation was at risk because overall education attainment would have to be adjusted downward to accommodate less talented students. Despite these different views on what the new school in Finland should be, the nation was able to build necessary common consensus (see Box 1.1) for the decision and move on to its implementation.

As planned, the wave of implementation began in the northern parts of Finland in 1972. The National Curriculum for the Comprehensive School steered the content, organization, and pace of teaching throughout the country. Although the structure of the comprehensive school was similar for all students, the National Curriculum provided schools with tools to differentiate instruction for different ability groups and personalities. Foreign languages and mathematics teaching, for example, were arranged in a way that offered students options for three levels of study in grades 7 through 9: basic, middle, and advanced. The syllabus

Figure 1.2. Structure of the Education System in Finland Since 1970

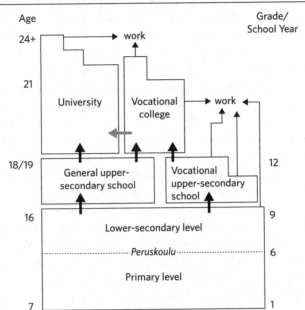

of the basic study program corresponded to what had previously been offered in civic schools, and the advanced study program was equivalent to that offered by the old grammar schools. The reasoning behind these differentiated syllabi was that if learning foreign languages was made a requirement for all, then there had to be different courses of study for different kinds of students.

The last of the southern municipalities shifted to the new comprehensive school system in 1979. Ability grouping was eventually abolished in all school subjects in 1985. Since then, all students have studied according to the same curricula and syllabi.

Comprehensive school reform triggered the development of three particular aspects of the Finnish education system, which would later prove to be instrumental in creating a well-performing education system. First, bringing together a wide variety of students with often very different life circumstances and aspirations to learn in the same schools and classes required a fundamentally new approach to teaching and learning. The equal opportunity principle insisted that all students be offered a fair chance to be successful and enjoy learning. From early on, it was understood that the education of pupils with special needs would

BOX 1.1: What Is the Finnish Consensus?

The Finnish Parliament reached a decision-in-principle for comprehensive school reform in November 1963. The decision was not unanimous; the basis of the majority consisted of the Agrarian Party and the leftists. This decision, perhaps the most important single consensus in the history of Finnish education, would not have been possible without the support of the Agrarian Party and wider national consensus for the common good.

The Agrarian Party had for a long time resisted the idea of a comprehensive school system. The youth wing of that party understood that restructuring of the Finnish economy and related urbanization required the development of the old-fashioned education system existing at that time. It was particularly important to secure access to good education in rural parts of Finland that were suffering from rapid migration to urban centers and to Sweden. The interesting question is: Why did the Agrarian Party support education reform that was based on the idea of common comprehensive school for all? A new generation of politicians who were close to the Primary School Teachers' Association became convinced that all children could have similar learning goals and that they could be taught in the same schools. The president of Finland and former Agrarian Party member Urho Kekkonen was one of the supporters of this reform.

The dream of a common public school for all Finnish children had existed since the birth of the Finnish Folk School in the 1860s. The process that led to Parliament's decision in 1963 was strictly a political one. It guaranteed that the political elite of Finland would be strongly committed to the comprehensive school reform. Political support for the reform was important because it made it possible to proceed swiftly without being halted by the new government. The foundation for a sustainable education policy was created. This same principle of the Finnish consensus has carried throughout the decades until today.

The implementation of comprehensive school reform required several other political compromises. Professor Pauli Kettunen has said that the Nordic welfare state was constructed using three political ideals: the legacy of liberated peasants, the spirit of capitalism, and the utopia of socialism. Equality, efficiency, and solidarity—the essential principles of these three political ideals—merged into a consensus where they all enriched one another. I think this is the root of the solid ground on which Finnish education policy has been established.

—Erkki Aho, Director General (1973–1991)
National Board of General Education

only be successful if learning difficulties and other individual deficits were identified early and promptly treated. Special education quickly became an integral part of school curricula, and all municipalities and schools soon housed experts trained to support special-needs pupils. Special education is discussed in more detail in the following chapter.

Second, career guidance and counseling became a compulsory part of the comprehensive school curricula in all schools. It was assumed at the time that if all pupils remained in the same school until the end of their compulsory education, they would need systematic counseling on their options after completing basic school. Career guidance was intended to minimize the possibility that students would make inappropriate choices regarding their future. In principle, students had three options: to continue education in upper-secondary general school, to go on to vocational school, or to find employment. Both types of upper-secondary education offered several internal options. Career guidance and counseling soon became a cornerstone of both lower- and upper-secondary education, and has been an important factor in explaining the low rates of grade repetition and dropout in Finland (Välijärvi & Sahlberg, 2008). Career guidance has also served as a bridge between formal education and the world of work. As part of the overall career guidance curriculum, each student in *peruskoulu* spends 2 weeks in a selected workplace.

Third, the new *peruskoulu* required that teachers who were working in very different schools—namely, the academic grammar schools and work-oriented civic schools—had to begin to work in the same school with students with diverse abilities. As Jouni Välijärvi explains, comprehensive school reform was not just an organizational change but a new philosophy of education for Finnish schools (Hautamäki et al., 2008; Välijärvi et al., 2007). This philosophy included the beliefs that all pupils can learn if they are given proper opportunities and support, that understanding and learning through human diversity is an important educational goal, and that schools should function as small-scale democracies, just as John Dewey had insisted decades before. The new *peruskoulu*, therefore, required teachers to employ alternative instructional methods, design learning environments that enable differentiated learning for different pupils, and perceive teaching as a high-status profession. These expectations led to wide-scale teacher education reform in 1979: a new law on teacher education, emphasizing professional development and focusing on research-based teacher education, that is discussed in detail in Chapter 3.

Another concrete consequence of the emergence of *peruskoulu* was a rapid expansion of upper-secondary education. Parents expected their children to study further, and young Finns themselves also hoped to reach higher in their self-development. Let us now take a look at how upper-secondary education provided pathways to improving human capital in Finland.

EXPANDING UPPER-SECONDARY EDUCATION

The general upper-secondary school had a traditional school-like organization until 1985 when the new Act on General Upper-Secondary Education abolished the old system and introduced a modular curriculum structure. Two annual semesters were replaced by five or six periods, per school year, based on how schools planned their teaching. This meant that teaching and studying were reorganized into 6- or 7-week periods during which students would complete the courses they had chosen. This change enabled schools to rearrange teaching schedules, and, in turn, affected local curriculum planning because schools had more flexibility to allocate lessons into these periods differently (Välijärvi, 2004). The next phase of development was to replace age cohort–based grouping of students with a nonclass organizational system in the mid-1990s. This new general upper-secondary school organization is not based on fixed classes or grades (previously called the 10th, 11th, and 12th grades). Students thus have greater choice available to them in planning their studies in terms of both the content and the sequencing of their courses. The new curriculum framework places a stronger emphasis on understanding students' cognitive development and also invites schools to make the best use of their own and their community's strengths. Although students now have more freedom to plan and choose their studies, all students are still obliged to study the basics of the 18 compulsory subjects. Students have to successfully complete at least 75 courses of 38 lessons each. About two thirds of these are compulsory, and the rest are freely chosen by students for their general upper-secondary education diploma. Normally, students exceed this minimum limit and study more, typically taking between 80 and 90 courses. The new National Core Curriculum for General Upper Secondary Education will be in effect from August 2021, and that will introduce a credit point system as a new way to quantify students' studies and build curriculum on six general transversal competences: Interdisciplinary and creative competences, civic competences, ethical and ecological competences, global and cultural competences, well-being competences, and interpersonal competences.

Student assessments and school evaluations are additional important factors affecting the nature of teaching and learning in general upper-secondary school. Teachers assess the achievement of each student at the end of each period or unit of study (of 6 or 7 weeks), which means students are assessed five or six times per school year. The National Matriculation Examination that students take after successfully completing all required courses is a high-stakes external examination (for students), and therefore it has a notable effect on curriculum and instruction. A frequently expressed criticism by teachers and school principals in Finland is that the matriculation examination results in "teaching to the test" and thus narrows curriculum and increases stress among students and teachers. As a former mathematics and science teacher, I concur.

Vocational upper-secondary education also underwent significant adaptations to better suit new economic and political situations. Structures, curricula, and methodology of vocational education were renewed to meet the expectations of a knowledge-based economy and provide required labor knowledge and skills. One of Finland's key policy targets has been to increase the attractiveness of vocational education at the upper-secondary level. Currently, about 41% of students who transit from *peruskoulu* to upper-secondary education start their studies in vocational schools (see Figure 1.3).

The *structure* of vocational education was simplified, and all initial vocational qualifications today consist of 120 credits, equivalent to 3 years of full-time study. One quarter of the study time is allocated to general or optional courses. The number of vocational qualifications was reduced from more than 600 to 52, and related programs of study to 113. In principle, vocational school students are eligible to take the matriculation examination, although very few do. Moreover, providers of upper-secondary education are required to promote transferability, ensuring that students have access to general upper-secondary schools from vocational schools and vice versa if they wish to include courses from other schools in their learning plans.

Curriculum and study programs in vocational schools were revised to match the changes made in upper-secondary education, especially the modular-based structure, as well as the needs of labor markets in a knowledge society. The new curriculum was designed to balance the need for more general knowledge and skills and specific professional competences required in each vocational qualification. Performance assessments of achieved professional knowledge and skills are developed via collaboration among three key stakeholders: schools, employers, and employees' representatives.

Methods of instruction and training have been gradually changing in vocational secondary schools. At least one sixth of the training has to be arranged as on-the-job learning, and this is an integral part of the curriculum. Alternative workshops, apprenticeship training, and virtual learning have become commonplace in upper-secondary education. A results-based component of the funding system for vocational schools allocates a factor of 6% at the top of the school's core funding for staff development. Vocational schools are increasingly investing these funds to upgrade their teachers' pedagogical knowledge and skills.

Two key factors appear to influence the efficacy of students' choices at the critical point of transition to upper-secondary education. First, when they enter upper-secondary education, Finnish students have no experience with high-stakes standardized testing in school, unlike their peers in many other countries where testing has become an integral element of school life. In a comparative study of teachers' experiences under different accountability regimes, we concluded that "the pressure of a structured instructional model of teaching and external assessment of pupils' achievement is having dramatic consequences according to some teachers" (Berry & Sahlberg, 2006, p. 22). Consequences of the high-stakes testing environment include avoidance of risk taking, increased boredom, and fear. The study also suggested that in Finland, most lower-secondary school teachers teach in order to help their students learn, not pass tests. The PISA studies provide further evidence for this argument: Finnish students experience less anxiety in learning mathematics compared with their peers in other countries (Kupari & Välijärvi, 2005; OECD, 2013c).

A second contributing factor to the successful transition to upper-secondary schooling is that students are well prepared to make decisions about their further education, because counseling and career guidance are widely available in basic school. During their 3-year lower-secondary school, all students are entitled to 2 hours a week of educational guidance and counseling. This reduces the risk that students will make ill-informed decisions regarding their further studies. It also helps students put more effort into those areas of their studies that are most important for their anticipated route in upper-secondary school.

Finnish students today enter the transition point between lower- and upper-secondary education with a more effective set of knowledge, skills, and attitudes than in the past. Implemented reforms to upper-secondary education in Finland have had a fundamental impact on school organization, especially with respect to teaching and learning. Traditional school organization based on presentation-recitation models of instruction, age grouping, fixed teaching schedules, and the dominance of classroom-based seatwork has been gradually transformed to provide more flexible, open, and interaction-rich learning environments, where an active role for students comes first. Ongoing school improvement has therefore been facilitated by the implementation of structural changes in upper-secondary school and by the enrichment of schools and classrooms with alternative instructional arrangements and teaching methods.

IMPROVING EDUCATIONAL ATTAINMENT

Comprehensive school reform has generated obvious consequences. As the number of graduates from these schools has increased, so too has the demand for upper-secondary education. Annually, almost all students who graduate from *peruskoulu* immediately continue their studies in one of the two types of upper-secondary education settings or enroll in an additional 10th grade of *peruskoulu*. Some students who do not continue their formal education immediately after *peruskoulu* enroll in nonformal educational programs, and will return later to adult educational programs. For example, about half of those who enroll in vocational upper-secondary schools are graduates of *peruskoulu* of that same year. Figure 1.3 illustrates the choices made by students leaving *peruskoulu* between 2000 and 2018, who were given the option of participating immediately after completing *peruskoulu* in general or vocational upper-secondary education, taking an additional 10th grade,[3] or exiting formal education. Vocational education has become a true alternative for many students because of its more generally oriented curricula and also because there are more opportunities to continue studies in higher education after receiving a professional qualification from vocational school.

As shown in Figure 1.3, in 2018 about 97% of those who completed basic education immediately continued their studies at the upper-secondary level or undertook an additional 10th grade of *peruskoulu*. In 2018, the number of students enrolled in general and vocational upper-secondary education stood at 53% and 41%, respectively. In absolute numbers, the 2009–2010 school year marked the first time when more

Figure 1.3. Transition from *Peruskoulu* to Upper-Secondary Education as a Percentage of Age Cohorts Between 2000 and 2018

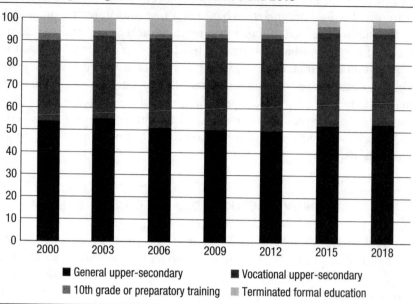

Source: Statistics Finland (n.d.a).

young people enrolled in vocational upper-secondary schools than in general upper-secondary schools when all students were counted (gross enrollment rate includes those who enroll in vocational schools after the age of 16). In 2018, about 3% of the students leaving basic school, opted not to continue studying in upper-secondary education or 10th grade of *peruskoulu*. Some of these students enrolled in other upper-secondary education programs, such as arts, crafts, or manual trades.

The number of students leaving basic school who don't continue their formal education immediately after graduation has become a social and political problem in Finland. Although the total number of young Finns who don't even apply to upper-secondary education is about 1,500 annually, those who leave the education system are, in the long run, becoming an economic burden for the society. It is estimated that each young person who doesn't complete upper-secondary school will, on average, cost US$1.5 million to the society in lost tax revenues, increased health and social costs, and often chronic unemployment. Recent governments have endorsed policies that have guaranteed a study place or apprenticeship to all students leaving *peruskoulu* and others under

25 years of age. The current coalition government has decided to extend compulsory education from age 16 to age 18, hoping that this would ease youth unemployment and the cost caused by insufficient education to the society. This decision has received wide opposition not only from political rivals, but also from the municipalities and many schools who would pay the bill for this reform and by those experts not convinced of the benefits of forced schooling for those not inspired to go to school. Total annual cost of extension of compulsory education until the completion of upper-secondary education (or when a student is 18 years old) is estimated to be US$150 to US$200 million. A strong argument against this spending that would mostly go to those who don't really need the financial support to buy textbooks and other study materials is that it should be invested in strengthening early childhood education and fixing the existing holes in providing timely support and guidance to students in lower secondary schools.

It is noteworthy that currently, until the new system goes into effect in the 2020s, upper-secondary education remains noncompulsory after a person has completed a 9-year basic education. Rather than making upper-secondary education compulsory, Finnish education policies have relied on developing equal opportunities for everyone to participate in upper-secondary education as a matter of individual choice, while at the same time creating incentives for young people to stay in the education system after completing their basic education. Since the introduction of the comprehensive school in the 1970s, the aims of education policy have been to provide a place of study for all young people in upper secondary education institutions (Aho et al., 2006). Most general and vocational upper-secondary schools today are under municipal (and in some cases regional) administration, and municipalities therefore determine policies regarding provision and accession for upper-secondary education. However, this does not mean that local authorities have complete freedom; curricula, teachers' professional requirements, and expectations regarding overall pedagogical environments are fairly unified throughout the country and create a common culture of schooling in Finland.

An important indicator of the success of upper-secondary education is the completion rate. As part of the education efficiency policies in Finland, state authorities collect systematic data and analyze completion rates in upper-secondary education. If an ideal completion time for vocational or general upper-secondary studies is set at 3.5 years, then about three out of four students successfully completed their studies in the desired time. Table 1.1 shows how many students terminated their upper-secondary and higher education in Finland in the academic year 2017–2018. Overall, graduation rates in Finland are internationally high. Practically everyone completes basic education in a normal route by attending basic school. A very small number of students annually receives a basic school diploma from an institute other than school; this is due to living abroad or being homeschooled. The first-time graduation rate in upper-secondary education in Finland in 2017 was 89%, compared with 85% in Canada and the United States. The OECD average upper-secondary education graduation rate is 86% (OECD, 2019d).

Because personalized learning plans in upper-secondary school are not tied to age groups or classes, some students will take more time to complete their studies than others. Some will leave the education system without a qualification or diploma. Early school-leaving rates thus provide a further measure of the quality and efficiency of secondary education. According to national statistics in Table 1.1, in recent years about 3% per annum of general upper-secondary school students terminate their studies without moving on to some other form of upper-secondary education or training. Approximately the same number of students moves from general to vocational secondary education and completes studies there. In vocational secondary education, the situation is a bit worse. For example, in the school year 2017–2018, 8.7% of vocational school students terminated their initial studies; of these some continued their education in some other school or institution.

Dropouts from formal education and training in Finland are slowly declining, and in upper-secondary education, dropout rates are substantially lower than those of most other countries. As far as all upper-secondary education is concerned, about 5% of students terminated

Table 1.1. Termination of Upper-Secondary and Higher Education in Finland in Academic Year 2017-2018 as a Percentage of the Total Number of Students

Type of Education	Academic Year 2017–2018
General upper-secondary	3.2
Vocational upper-secondary	8.7
Polytechnic	7.1
University	5.9

Source: Statistics Finland, n.d.a.

their studies during the academic year 2017–2018 without immediately continuing their studies in some other degree program. The need to prevent educational failure and dropouts is greatest in upper-secondary and higher vocational education. Keeping students in education has become a particular incentive for schools through a results-based central government funding scheme, which was introduced in upper-secondary vocational education in the early 2000s and was extended to all upper-secondary education in 2015. When the results-based financing index for education and training providers is calculated, reduced dropout rates and improved completion rates have a positive effect on the overall issued budget. Although the financing index concerns only a small part of overall education budgets, it has been a sufficient incentive to rapidly focus the attention of schools and teachers on measures to improve the early recognition and prevention of problems that might lead to dropout and on improved direct supports for students' learning and overall well-being in school. Moreover, because the basic funding of schools is tied to student numbers, success in preventing dropout has a positive impact on the school budget. Vocational schools in particular have developed innovative solutions for those students whose learning styles work best with a more practically oriented curriculum. For example, practice-oriented workshops where students can design and build concrete forms have become a popular way to increase the attractiveness and relevance of secondary education for many students who are at risk of leaving school.

Matriculation Examination

Students who have passed the required courses in upper-secondary general school are eligible to take the National Matriculation Examination. The examination is administered by the Matriculation Examination Board and is organized at the same time in all schools nationwide. There is no national examination for students graduating from upper-secondary vocational schools. Instead, vocational schools assess the form and content of certification examinations. Students who successfully complete either track can apply to institutions of higher education, namely polytechnics or universities. However, vocational school graduates make up a lesser share of total enrollment in higher education.

The Matriculation Examination first debuted in 1852 as an entrance test for the University of Helsinki. Students had to show sufficient evidence of general academic knowledge and be proficient in Latin. Today, the purpose of the examination is to discover whether students have as-similated the knowledge and skills required by the national core curricu-lum, as well as whether they have reached a level of maturity that is in line with the goals of upper-secondary general school. Students take tests in at least four subjects. Passing the matriculation examination, which is given only in upper-secondary general schools, entitles candidates to continue their studies at higher education institutions.

The Matriculation Examination is administrated by an external board appointed by the Ministry of Education and Culture. The board has about 40 members, who include university professors, high school teachers, and education policymakers. Exams are prepared and marked by separate subject committees that have altogether some 330 associate members, most of them current or previous schoolteachers. The secre-tariat of the board that who is responsible for technical matters related to employing, safeguarding, and managing the examination has a staff of 22 people. The typical examination fee per student for five exams is about US$200. The entire administration of the examination, which costs about US$10 million annually, is financed from these student-paid fees.

What is the structure of this exam, and what does it measure? Students must pass at least four individual tests in order to be awarded the Matriculation Examination certificate. First, an exam assessing stu-dents' competency in their mother tongue (Finnish, Swedish, or Sami) is compulsory for everybody. Second, each student chooses three ad-ditional tests from the following pool: a second domestic language (e.g., Swedish), foreign language (most often English), mathematics, and one test from the humanities and sciences category. Third, students may also add optional exams in the following subjects: various foreign languages, history, civics, biology, geography, physics, chemistry, health education, psychology, philosophy, ethics, and religious studies. Students have a maximum of 6 hours to complete each exam.

Exams are offered twice a year, in September and March–April. Students must complete all required tests of the examination within three consecutive exam periods—in other words, within 1 year from the time they sit for their first exam. All tests, except listening and read-ing comprehension in second domestic and foreign languages, typically require extensive writing in open-ended tasks. The examination pro-cess became fully digital in 2019 when students did their mathematics exam using computers, enabling the use of a wider range of materi-als in test items, such as video, audio, and dynamic graphs. Students bring their own computer to the exam. According to the Matriculation Examination Board (2020), "Candidates are not limited to a browser-based test system that only records their answers. The laptop they are using has a variety of applications that are also used in teaching. For example, a test item may contain spreadsheet data which must be analyzed using some of the statistical tools, and then be used as part of the answer." More about the structure of the Matriculation Examination, its tests, and administration can be found in English at https://www.ylioppilastutkinto.fi.

The Matriculation Examination Board assesses the tests of all candidates. Teachers whose students are taking the exam in school perform a preliminary assessment before the tests are sent to the board. Then the board's subject committee members (called as censors) give their final marks independently, not regarding what teachers have marked on each exam. This combined process then leads to a final score according to criteria that have been decided on by subject sections. After this scoring is done for all students, the board decides on which scores equal which grade. The relation may differ in every examination period.

Subject tests are graded using a 7-point scale that is adjusted to normal distribution. This means that the number of top grades and failed grades in each exam is approximately 5%. Students can have one failed exam if they perform well in the other exams. The exams and their grades are included in the Matriculation Examination Certificate that is awarded to students who successfully pass the mandatory exams and sufficiently complete the required high school studies.

The Finnish Matriculation Examination is a measure of students' general academic maturity, including their readiness to continue their studies in higher education. Students' successful performance on the Matriculation Examination becomes an asset to their university application. The nature of these individual exams is to try to test students' ability to cope with unexpected tasks. Whereas the California High School Exit Examination (CAHSEE),[4] for example, is guided by a list of potentially biased, sensitive, or controversial topics to be avoided, the Finnish examination does the opposite. Students are regularly asked to show their ability to deal with issues related to evolution, losing a job, dieting, political issues, violence, war, ethics in sports, junk food, sex, drugs, and popular music. Such issues span across subject areas and often require multidisciplinary knowledge and skills.

Here are some examples from the spring 2014 Matriculation Examination when exams were done by pen on paper by all students.

Sample essay topics (in mother tongue):
"Some politicians, athletes and other celebrities have publicly regretted and apologized for what they have said or done. Discuss the meaning of the apology and accepting it as a social and personal act."

"Has your body become your hobby?"

"Media is competing for audiences—what are the consequences?"

"Choose three world religions and compare the role and use of a holy image within them."

In 2020, all tests in the Matriculation Examination were digital, which changed the structure of these tests. The mother-tongue test, which is arranged in the Finnish, Swedish, and Sami languages, has two equally weighted parts, the textual skills test and the essay test. Both tests include resource materials that are for students during the test.

Sample health education questions:
"What is the basis of dietary recommendations in Finland and what is their aim?"

"Compare chlamydia and condyloma."

Sample psychology question:
"Design a study to find out how personality affects individuals' behavior on Facebook or other social media. Discuss the ethical considerations for that type of study."

Sample history question:
"Karl Marx and Friedrich Engels predicted that a socialist revolution would first happen in countries like Great Britain. What made Marx and Engels claim that and why did a socialist revolution happen in Russia?"

The Matriculation Examination in 2018 had a history test question on "the role of the United States in global politics" that students were asked to answer was based on two resources: a speech by Governor George W. Bush, "A Distinctly American Internationalism," in the Ronald

Reagan Presidential Library, Simi Valley, California, November 19, 1999; and an op-ed in the *New York Times* by Russian president Vladimir Putin, "A Plea for Caution from Russia," September 11, 2013. Students were asked: (1) What does it mean when the United States is called the World's Policeman?; (2) Compare the role of the United States in global politics based on the two provided resources; and (3) Think about the 21st-century events in light of Mr. Bush's and Mr. Putin's views of the role of the world's superpowers.

Sample philosophy question:
"In what sense are happiness, good life, and well-being ethical concepts?"

Sample ethics question:
"High school students often require that they are served a particular diet as their school lunch. Reasons may be medical, religious, ethical or moral. Describe students' requirements and their reasons; and assess the righteousness of having any particular diet in school."

Instead of a national examination, vocational students take a school-level assessment of learning outcomes and skills. The principle behind the assessment is to develop a positive self-image and personal growth in students with different kinds of competencies. Students are gauged according to their own self-assessments, as well as through interviews with their teachers. In addition, their on-the-job training instructors participate in workplace assessments. Performance is graded from 1 (satisfactory) to 3 (excellent). In the absence of a national vocational education examination, the National Agency for Education issues recommendations to ensure equality in school-based performance assessments.

A current topic of debate in vocational education is how to ensure the quality of certification from school to school. Parliament passed an act on this issue in 2005, and certification will now include both the teachers' assessment and a demonstration of skills to prove that a student has achieved the vocational proficiency set out in the curriculum. These skills demonstrations will take place, wherever possible, at work sites, mostly in conjunction with periods of on-the-job learning. Representatives of employers and employees will also take part in assessment. Depending on the program, students can expect to undergo from 4 to 10 demonstrations of proficiency during the course of their studies.

FOUR PHASES OF EDUCATIONAL CHANGE

Because the terrain of educational change has not been explored much in Finland, it is safe to suggest theories of change and conceptual models to organize the thinking about what has happened and why. After the comprehensive school reform in the 1970s, educational change in Finland can be described in terms of four phases (Sahlberg, 2009):

- Rethinking the theoretical and methodological foundations of teaching and learning (1980s)
- Improvement through networking, teacher leadership, and self-regulated change (1990s)
- Enhancing efficiency of structures and education administration (2000s)
- Internationalization and digitalization of education (2010s)

This process is illustrated in Figure 1.4. Each phase conveys a certain policy logic and theory of change. By the early 1980s, the structural reforms that led to creating *peruskoulu* were completed. After that, attention was focused on *conception of knowledge* and *conception of learning* in the school practices that were embedded into the philosophy of *peruskoulu*. The second phase emerged from the liberalization of Finnish education governance, a period characterized by the self-directed networking of schools and collaboration among individuals. The third phase was initiated by a need to raise productivity in the public sector, and was accelerated by publication of the initial PISA results in December 2001 and later by the 2008 economic downturn. This phase focuses on reforming the structures and administration of education and is careful to avoid disturbing the sensitive balance of a well-performing education system in the pursuit of enhanced efficiency. The fourth phase was focused on aligning education to the emerging needs of labor markets and the economy.

Phase 1: Rethinking the Theoretical and Methodological Foundations (1980s)

Several research and development projects launched within the new comprehensive school system in the late 1970s and the early 1980s led to criticism of then-current pedagogical practices, especially teacher-centered methods of teaching in Finnish schools. The new school system was launched with philosophical and educational assumptions that insisted

Figure 1.4. Phases of Educational Change in Finland Since the 1980s

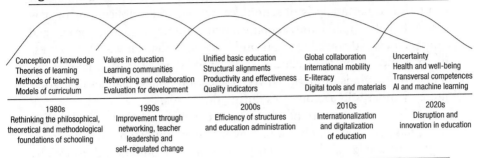

Conception of knowledge	Values in education	Unified basic education	Global collaboration	Uncertainty
Theories of learning	Learning communities	Structural alignments	International mobility	Health and well-being
Methods of teaching	Networking and collaboration	Productivity and effectiveness	E-literacy	Transversal competences
Models of curriculum	Evaluation for development	Quality indicators	Digital tools and materials	AI and machine learning

| 1980s | 1990s | 2000s | 2010s | 2020s |
| Rethinking the philosophical, theoretical and methodological foundations of schooling | Improvement through networking, teacher leadership and self-regulated change | Efficiency of structures and education administration | Internationalization and digitalization of education | Disruption and innovation in education |

that the role of public education must be to educate citizens to think critically and independently. One of the main themes of school development then was the realization of a more dynamic *conception of knowledge*. As a result, renewed approaches to teaching would lead to meaningful learning and understanding, teachers believed (Aho, 1996). A significant driver of this change was emerging information and communication technologies in schools at that time. Some feared, quite correctly, that the expansion of computers in classrooms would lead to problems, including isolated knowledge, unnecessary information, and technological determinism.

Technological development corresponded with the revolution in learning sciences. The dominance of cognitive psychology, along with the emergence of constructivist theories of learning and the advances in neurosciences on the horizon, attracted Finnish educational researchers to analyze existing conceptions of knowledge and learning in schools. Several influential and teacher-friendly readers were published and sent to schools. They included *Conception of Knowledge* (1989), *Conception of Learning* (1989), and *About Possibilities of School Change* (1990). Questions like "What is knowledge?," "How do pupils learn?," and "How do schools change?" were common themes for teachers' professional development and school improvement until the end of the 1990s (Lehtinen et al., 1989; Miettinen, 1990; Voutilainen et al., 1989).

From an international perspective, this first phase of educational change in Finland was exceptional. At the same time that Finnish teachers were exploring the theoretical foundations of knowledge and learning and redesigning their school curricula to be congruent with them, their peers in England, Germany, France, and the United States were struggling with increased school inspection, controversial externally imposed learning standards, and competition that disturbed some teachers to the point that they decided to leave their jobs. In England and the United States, for example, deeper analysis of school knowledge and implications of new research on learning mainly remained issues among academics or reached only the most advanced teachers and leaders. Perhaps it was due to these philosophical aspects of educational change that Finland remained immune to the winds of market-driven education policy changes that arose in many other OECD countries during the 1990s.

Although the nature of educational development in Finland during this phase was genuinely Finnish work, it is important to give credit to the knowledge and ideas that were brought from abroad, especially from the United States, Canada, and the United Kingdom, as well as other Nordic countries. Particularly significant was the role of teaching and student assessment methods—especially those published by the Association for Supervision and Curriculum Development (ASCD)— that were developed in the United States and then adopted into Finnish culture and educational practice. Two examples deserve to be mentioned here. First, Finland was one of the first countries to launch a large-scale implementation of cooperative learning in select Finnish universities and later in schools. Research and development work done at the University of Minnesota (David and Roger Johnson), Stanford University (Elizabeth Cohen), Johns Hopkins University (Robert Slavin), and Tel Aviv University (Shlomo Sharan and Yael Sharan) had an important role to play in the transformation of teaching and learning in schools according to the philosophical principles described in the Finnish readers mentioned above. Second, in the late 1980s, the National Board of General Education in Finland launched a national initiative to diversify teaching methods in science teaching. *The Models of Teaching* by Bruce Joyce and Marsha Weil (later with Beverly Showers) was the main source of inspiration and ideas for this work (Joyce & Weil, 1986). Bruce Joyce visited Finland in the late 1980s, and his work has left a permanent impression on the history of Finnish school improvement that still exists today in hundreds of Finnish schools through expanded repertoires of teaching methods. Work by David Berliner in educational psychology, Linda Darling-Hammond in teacher education, and Andy Hargreaves and Michael Fullan in educational change has have been closely studied and implemented in developing Finnish education since the 1970s. The secret of the successful influence of these educational ideas from the United States, the United Kingdom, and Canada is that there was fruitful ground in Finnish schools for such pragmatic models of change. Interestingly, the Finns themselves have developed only a little novel pedagogical practice that would have had more international significance.

There is surprisingly little reliable research on how this first phase of educational change actually affected teaching and learning in Finnish schools. Erno Lehtinen (2004), one of the key figures in Finland of that time and author of some of the readers mentioned earlier, was cautiously reserved about the impact:

> Discussion on conceptions of knowledge and learning has clearly affected how teachers talk about learning and teaching. Earlier discourse that was characterized by traditional values of socialization and teaching of facts and automated ideals of mastery has been replaced by understanding, critical thinking, problem solving, and learning how to learn. Expanding the conceptions of knowledge and learning was also reflected in implementation of the new curriculum in the mid-1990s at all levels of schooling, and also in the national curriculum reforms in this new decade. (p. 54)

This phase of educational change in Finland has been characterized as a time that challenged conventional beliefs, searched for innovation, and increased trust in schools and their abilities to find the best ways to raise the quality of student learning. Deeper understanding of knowledge and learning strengthened schools' moral foundations. A recent evaluation of education in Finnish comprehensive schools concluded that "teachers pay conscious attention to diversifying teaching and learning environments. Teachers think that the use of versatile teaching methods is important both to planning and classroom work" (Atjonen et al., 2008, p. 197). This suggests that schools have made progress in teaching and learning, at least modestly.

Phase 2: Improvement Through Networking, Teacher Leadership, and Self-Regulation (1990s)

The National Curriculum Reform of 1994 is often regarded as the major educational reform in Finland, along with the Comprehensive School Reform of the 1970s. The main vehicle of change was the active role of municipalities and schools in curriculum design and the implementation of related changes. Schools were encouraged to collaborate with other schools and to network with parents, businesses, and nongovernmental organizations. At the level of central administration, this new collaborative and self-directed movement culminated in the Aquarium Project, a national school improvement initiative enabling all Finnish schools, principals, and teachers to network with one another.[5] The aim of the Aquarium Project was to transform schools into active learning communities. According to Martti Hellström (2004), this project was "a unique self-directed school improvement network that was open to all active educators" (p. 179). As a form of practice, this was previously unheard of in Finnish educational administration, and only rarely found elsewhere.

The Aquarium Project offered schools a new context for improvement—something that combined traditional community work with modern social networking and teacher leadership. It has close links to the ideas of the Alberta Initiative for School Improvement (AISI), a unique long-term government-funded school and teacher development program in Alberta, Canada (Hargreaves et al., 2009). Research has shown that school improvement through networking and self-regulation has positively impacted the engagement level of schools in development in Finland and Alberta. Particularly important is the fact that the majority of schools involved in these initiatives reported that during a time of economic downturn and decreasing resources, teachers believed they had succeeded in improving their schools. Despite different educational governance systems, the Aquarium Project and AISI have stimulated local innovations and research activity among principals and teachers who pursued advanced educational studies in universities. They also have demonstrated that it is the school, not the system, that is the locus of control and capacity—a point reinforced by Hellström (2004) and Murgatroyd (2007). Alberta's government terminated funding for AISI in 2013 as part of the province's fiscal adjustment procedures.

At the beginning of 1997, there were more than 1,000 projects in 700 schools and 163 municipalities participating in the Aquarium Project. Our best estimate is that this included about 5,000 teachers and 500 principals who were directly involved in this school improvement initiative. The project was in accord with new ideas of decentralization, increased school autonomy, and stronger teacher leadership in the 1990s. As a strategy for school improvement, this project stressed shared responsibility in schools, personalization, and collaborative efforts to enhance the quality of learning. In this sense, the Aquarium Project incorporated features consistent with neoliberal education policies, and occasionally, these characteristics were seen as signals of increased competition among schools in the education sector. It is true that school choice creates a competitive environment, but the school improvement network transformed bold competition into mutual striving for better schools. The strong social aspect of the Aquarium Project valued sharing ideas and solving problems together, thus preventing schools from viewing one another as competitors. In this respect, the project relied on earlier values of equal educational opportunities and social justice, rather than competition and administrative accountability. Perhaps this political duality served as the Achilles' heel of the Aquarium Project. The project was terminated by a political decision in early 1999 at the dawn of the era of enhanced efficiency of administration and structural reforms.

Phase 3: Enhancing Efficiency of Structures and Administration (2000s)

The first OECD's PISA results, published on December 4, 2001, took everyone by surprise. In all three academic domains—reading literacy, mathematics, and science—Finland was the highest-performing nation of the OECD countries. This new international study revealed that earlier student performance gaps with Japan, Korea, and the European countries were closed. Finns seemed to learn all the knowledge and skills they demonstrated on these tests without private tutoring, after-school classes, or the large amounts of homework that are particularly prevalent among students in East Asia. Furthermore, the relative variation of educational performance between schools in the sample was exceptionally small in Finland.

Initial reactions after the first PISA results within the education community were confusing. Some Finnish educators wondered if there was something wrong with these new OECD tests because the test scores in academic school subjects were so high. Since the 1970s, education in Finland had had as strong a focus on music, arts, crafts, social studies, and life skills as there was on reading, mathematics, and science. The world media immediately wanted to know the secret behind good Finnish education. Within the first 18 months after the PISA results were published, several hundred official foreign delegations toured Finland to learn how Finnish schools operate and how their teachers teach. Questions from the foreign visitors regarding the "Finnish miracle" were often such that Finns themselves were not prepared to respond with reliable answers. The next two PISA cycles, in 2003 and 2006, advanced and consolidated Finland's reputation even further, thus elevating the world media's interest in Finnish education. PISA 2009 and 2012 showed some decline in Finnish students' academic performance, and similar trends continued in 2015 and 2018 PISA surveys as well. I will discuss these in more detail and possible reasons behind these trends in the next chapter. Overall, PISA data until 2018 show that Estonia, Finland, Canada, Japan, and Korea produce consistently high learning results regardless of their students' socioeconomic status (OECD, 2019b). England, Germany, Australia, Denmark, France, and the United States, among other countries, have both average achievement scores and a wider performance variance.

What PISA surveys, in general, have revealed is that education policies that are based on the principle of equal educational opportunities and equity in education and that have brought teachers to the core of educational change have positively impacted the quality of education systems. Further analysis of PISA data in Finland indicates that factors related to domicile and place of living also play visible roles in Finland in explaining the variations in assessed student learning and students' future career paths as well (Välijärvi, 2008). Apparently, the variations in student performance caused by students' socioeconomic factors are increasing. There is growing skepticism among teachers and researchers in Finland regarding limitations that international student assessments impose on their definition of student performance and educational success.

Combining PISA results with other global education indicators and national surveys of people's satisfaction with schools, it is safe to conclude that Finland's education system is in good condition by international standards. This is obviously a challenge to Finnish education policymakers and to the school improvement community—after all, it is difficult to renew a system that is already performing well. Perhaps this explains the rather conservative mode when it comes to reforming primary and secondary schools in Finland recently. Structural reforms have focused on regulatory changes related to the length of compulsory education, administration of postsecondary education, and the efficiency of the entire education system. In the Finnish school system, multiculturalism, special education, and abolishing the administrative line between primary and lower-secondary schools have been the main areas of development since the year 2000. Another significant change since the beginning of 2013 has been to move early childhood education away from social issues administration to make it an integral part of the Finnish education system. The National Core Curriculum for Basic Education and General Upper Secondary Education were revised in early 2000s, but no significant changes were introduced.

In 2014, Finnish state authorities revised the national core curriculum (NCC) for basic education. It came into effect during the 2016–2017 school year. The core curriculum provides a common direction and basis for renewing school education and instruction. Here are some basics of how that new national core curriculum works in practice.

First, education providers draw up local curricula and annual work plans on the basis of the NCC for Basic Education. Schools though actually take the lead in curriculum planning under the supervision of municipal authorities. Second, the NCC for Basic Education is a fairly loose regulatory document in terms of what schools should teach, how they arrange their work, and the desired outcomes. Schools have, therefore, a lot of flexibility and autonomy in curriculum design, and there may be significant variation in school curricula from one place to another. Finally, because of this decentralized nature of authority in the Finnish education system, schools in Finland can have different profiles and practical arrangements, making the curriculum model unique in the world. It is incorrect to make any general conclusions based on what one or two schools do.

This recent curriculum reform in Finland aims at those same overall goals that the OECD—which gives the PISA exams every 3 years to 15-year-olds in multiple countries—as well as governments and many students say are essential for them: to develop safe and collaborative school culture and to promote holistic approaches in teaching and learning. The NCC for Basic Education states that the specific aim at the school level is that children would:

- understand the relationship and interdependencies between different learning contents;
- be able to combine the knowledge and skills learned in different disciplines to form meaningful wholes; and
- be able to apply knowledge and use it in collaborative learning settings.

All schools in Finland are required to revise their curricula according to this new national framework. Some schools have taken only small steps from where they were before, while others went on with much bolder plans. These different ways of implementation are well tolerated by the authorities and accepted by parents and teachers. The logic of Finnish school is that rather than providing everyone exactly the same education in every school, the desire is to educate children who are different but still equal in terms of their opportunities and options.

A focus on enhanced efficiency and productivity has led to shrinking school budgets in many parts of the country, which means there is now a need to do more or the same as before with fewer resources. Many practitioners, among them school leaders and teacher leaders, have been waiting for new directions in school improvement to make up for these negative developments in resourcing. Some of the possible trends for Finnish primary and secondary education will be discussed in Chapter 5.

Phase 4: Internationalization and Digitalization of Education (2010s)

The global economic downturn created by the 2008 financial crash had severe consequences for the Finnish government budgets and particularly for its public sector spending. Although banks and other financial institutions in Finland were much stronger in 2008 than they were in the early 1990s, the Finnish economy suffered from declining international trade and the poor fiscal situation in Europe. The tone of education policies stressed efficiency, productivity, and doing more with less, reminding many of the days of the 1990s recession. This time, two new themes emerged to steer the efforts to enhance quality of education institutions at a time when resources had become scarce: Active engagement in internationalization of schools and universities and faster adoption of digital technologies to help boost efficiencies of administration and pedagogy.

The internalization of Finnish education has had two main approaches: on the one hand, to increase international cooperation and exchange between Finnish education institutions and those in other countries; on the other hand, to strengthen exports of Finnish educational products, expertise, and services to the world markets. The major facility to advance international cooperation and student mobility has been a group of different European Union programs, currently under the Erasmus+ umbrella program. Finland has been one of the most successful countries in Europe in making international cooperation and exchange a part of the work of schools and universities.

Education export has been much harder for the Finns. Efforts to root Finnish-Model schools in other countries have proved to be complicated. Despite some interesting new ideas that educators, experts, and researchers in Finland have been able to get out to the global education marketplace, the real breakthroughs that the government and some entrepreneurs had expected still have yet to be realized.

The new law that came into effect in August 2017 stipulates a minimum annual tuition fee in Finnish universities for students outside the European Union or European Economic Area that is 1,500 euros (US$1,700). In practice, graduate programs offered by Finnish universities to foreign students typically cost about US$13,500. In 2016, just before the new law did away with tuition-free higher education for many foreign students, there were 20,000 overseas students studying in higher education degree programs. In 2019, Finnish universities had 4,600 degree students who belong to the fee-paying category of international students. Most of these students received a scholarship that covered part of the full tuition fee.

Public policy directions in Finland are determined in each government's political program. In June 2011, the new conservative-led coalition government that was led by Prime Minister Jyrki Katainen built its program on strengthening international cooperation and education as the key drivers of productivity and sustainable economic growth. The aim was that Finland become the most educated nation in the world by 2020. Technology came to play an important part in improving education and efficiency of schools and universities. The next government, which was politically a center-right coalition, continued the direction of the previous government program, now setting the target for Finland to be among the most educated, skilled, and leading nations in modern learning. This government continued previously executed budget cuts, especially in vocational education and higher education sectors. Its spearhead strategic initiative was titled "New learning environments and digital educational materials to schools." In OECD's first TALIS survey in 2013, Finland was rated as a fairly conservative adopter of technology in teachers' pedagogical repertoires. Just one in five teachers at that time said that students are regularly allowed to use information and communication technologies in school projects or class work. By the next TALIS survey in 2018, this number exceeded 50% of lower-secondary teachers (OECD, 2019f).

The government that holds the power at the time of this writing is led by social democrat Sanna Marin and has a number of young female politicians responsible for some of the heaviest portfolios in that government. A government program titled "Inclusive and competent Finland—a socially, economically and ecologically sustainable society" takes a new route from what the previous three governments have done in education. The government states that "an equal society seeks to provide opportunities for every citizen to study to their full potential" and has four primary objectives (Finnish Government, 2020):

1. The level of education and competence among the population will rise at all levels of education, differences in learning outcomes will decrease, and educational equality will increase.
2. Children and young people will feel well.
3. Education and training will enhance gender equality and nondiscrimination in society.
4. Finland will be an internationally attractive place to study, conduct research, and invest.

This government made it clear that their view of the role of education in further developing Finnish society is very different from what the governments in the 2010s had described in their programs.

THE FINNISH EDUCATION SYSTEM IN 2020

One of the key messages of this book is that unlike many other contemporary systems of education, the Finnish system has not been infected by market-based education reform models, such as tougher competition between schools over enrollment, standardization of teaching and learning in schools, and using high-stakes standardized tests to measure schools' performance and hold them accountable. The main reason for this is that the education community in Finland has remained unconvinced that these globally fashionable directions for improving education would be good for Finnish schools. The ultimate success of a high-stakes testing policy is whether it positively affects student learning, not whether it increases student scores on a particular test (Amrein & Berliner, 2002). If student learning remains unaffected, or if testing leads to biased teaching as it increasingly does nowadays in many parts of the world, the validity of such high-stakes tests must be questioned. Finnish education authorities and especially teachers have not been convinced that frequent external census-based testing and stronger accountability for teachers would be beneficial to students and their learning.

Education policies are necessarily intertwined with other social policies, and with the overall political culture of a nation. The key success factor in Finland's development of a successful knowledge economy with good governance and a respected education system has been its ability to reach broad consensus on most major issues concerning future directions for Finland as a nation. The conclusion is that Finland seems to do particularly well in implementing and maintaining the policies and practices that constitute *sustainable leadership and change* (Hargreaves & Fink, 2006). Regardless of what political party is leading, education in Finland is seen as a public good and therefore has a strong nation-building function.

Education policies designed to raise student achievement in Finland have put a strong accent on teaching and learning by encouraging schools to craft optimal learning environments and establish instructional content that will help students reach the general goals of schooling. This is the opposite of policies in many other countries where externally designed directives are imposed upon schools, such as the Common Core State Standards in the United States, the National Standards in New Zealand, or the New Education Standards in Germany. It was assumed very early in Finland's reform process that teachers and teaching are the key elements that make a difference in what students learn in school, not standards, assessment, or alternative instructional programs. As the level of teacher professionalism gradually increased in Finnish schools during the 1990s, the prevalence of powerful teaching methods and pedagogical classroom and school designs increased. A new flexibility within the Finnish education system enabled schools to learn from one another and thus make their best practices universal by adopting innovative approaches to organize schooling. It also encouraged teachers and schools to continue to expand their repertoires of teaching methods, and to individualize teaching in order to meet the needs of all students. The structure and the internal dynamics of the education system in Finland are illustrated in Figure 1.5.

Since the beginning of 2013, early childhood education has been part of the Finnish education system. Until then, it fell under the umbrella of social and health administration. In Finland, early childhood education refers to the education and care children receive before they start primary school at the age of 7. Before they go to school, all children have the subjective right to day care, either family-based or in kindergarten. Under recent government budget savings this right was narrowed to half a day of early childhood education and care for those households who had one parent at home for one reason or another. The current government returned to the earlier practice, which gives all children a right to full-day early childhood education and care from August 1, 2020 onward. Let's take a closer look at what Finnish children do before they enter primary school.

Figure 1.5. The Education System in Finland in 2020

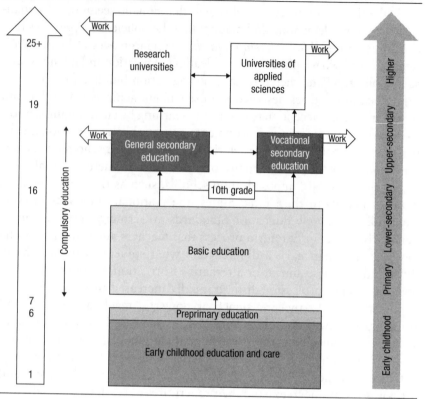

The Finnish social welfare system provides parents of newborns the right to parental leave to be at home with the baby. Mothers normally start maternity leave about 2 months prior to their due date and are entitled to continue that leave for about 5 months after the child's birth. Maternity leave is followed by parental leave, which should be shared by both parents and can last about 8 months. Parents who are employed will continue to receive their normal monthly salaries during these leaves through the State Insurance Institution of Finland (Kela). Fathers are continuously encouraged to more actively take part in parental leave, or paternity leave that is up to 9 weeks, and to spend time at home with family. In 2019, just 11% of total available parental leave in Finland (same as in Denmark) was taken by fathers, compared to 19% in Norway, 28% in Sweden, and 29% in Iceland (Statistics Finland, n.b.d).

The vast majority of children stay home during their first year—less than 1% of infants under 1 year are in day care (Table 1.2). The child's right to day care means that the municipality where the family lives is responsible for offering the child a place in kindergarten or family-based day care. There are three types of day care options for the child: municipal day care, privately provided day care, and private family-based day care. According to the National Institute for Health and Welfare in 2020,[6] about half of all 1- to 2-year-olds and four out of five 3- to 5-year-olds were in day care at the beginning of 2020 (Table 1.2). Preschool at the age of 6 is now compulsory for all children, and it will be extended to include all 5-year-olds as per the current government's policy. Preschool hours are normally only held in the morning, and most 6-year-olds stay in day care in the afternoons. Seventy-four percent of all 1- to 6-year-old children in Finland were in early childhood education and care in 2020, with 83% of these in public kindergartens or family-based day care and 6% in publicly subsidized private day care, and 11% received a service voucher from local authorities that parents can use to purchase early childhood education from private providers of their choice.

The new administrative system that made early childhood education part of the education system will help provide better-coordinated and higher-quality services to children and families. Probably most important, there is now a more seamless transition from early childhood to preschool and primary school for those children who require special

Table 1.2. Number of Children in Early Childhood Education and Care in Finland in 2020

Age	Number of Children	Percentage of Age Cohort
0	434	0.9
1	17,907	37.2
2	35,405	69.1
3	45,724	84.5
4	49,988	88.2
5	53,683	90.9
6	49,303	82.1
7	1,283	2.1

Source: National Institute for Health and Welfare (2020).

support. Currently, one third of the teaching staff working in kindergartens in Finland has a higher education degree. Most of them study in the departments of teacher education where all other teachers are educated in Finland. There is a shortage of qualified kindergarten teachers at the moment, and therefore the Ministry of Education and Culture, which regulates the number of new students in the universities, is temporarily increasing the intake of new kindergarten teacher education programs. What happens in kindergartens and preschools is steered by national frameworks for early childhood care and preschool education. The main principle of early childhood education and care (ECEC) in Finland is that it must be arranged according to the best interest of the child. The regulations that steer ECEC take this principle even further by stipulating that every child has a right to well-being, care, and protection and that children's opinions must be heard in decisionmaking regarding education and care. The National Core Curriculum for Early Childhood Education and Care of 2018 states the basic values for early childhood education and care (Finnish National Agency for Education, 2018):

- Intrinsic value of childhood
- Growth as a human being
- Rights of the child
- Equity, equality, and diversity
- Diversity of families
- Healthy and sustainable way of living

The National Core Curriculum for ECEC lays a foundation for a lifelong learning system in Finland. It links to curricula for preschool (6-year-olds) and 9 years of basic education, forming a logical continuum that not only provides smooth transitions from one level of education to another but also helps each and every child to learn and grow according to their individual needs, interests, and abilities. Kindergartens use the National Core Curriculum for ECEC to design their own locally adapted curriculum and work plan according to the characteristics and nature of the community. These local plans are made considering children's earlier experiences and learning, and children need to be involved in planning, implementation, and assessments according to their abilities. Internationally, it is not very common that ECEC is seen as the right of the child and that children are given an opportunity to have a say in how education for them is arranged.

How can these ideals be made to work in practice? The central mechanism is the Individual Education Plan that every child must have. It is prepared in kindergartens in collaboration with parents or guardians and children. This individual plan typically identifies child's areas of interests and strengths together with possible special educational needs. It also includes pedagogical guidelines for meeting the goals included in the plan and records regular assessments by the teacher, the parents, and the child. The aim of this inclusive process in Finland is to engage parents more closely to education of their children in kindergartens and also to make children more aware of goals and responsibilities regarding their own education.

Finland's educational philosophy today is based on sets of knowledge, skills, values, attitudes, and will that are called transversal competences. Early childhood education and school education that follows it aim at developing these competences so that individuals can use knowledge and skills that they learn in school in real-life situations. High-quality ECEC makes sure that all children will develop strong foundations of these competences for their future, not through traditional instruction but primarily learning through play (Sahlberg & Doyle, 2019). Transversal competences included in ECEC:

1. **Thinking and learning how to learn.** These competences can be achieved through projects, exploration, and play that starts with children's own interests, encourages them to become curious and ask questions. Children need enough time to find their own ways of working, in a safe and emotionally rich environment, and adults support them in reflecting their own learning.

2. **Interaction, self-expression, and cultural understanding.** These competences develop best when children work in small groups, or in organized events and celebrations. Unstructured play, music, art, and drama are common methods of learning these competences.

3. **Life skills and taking care of oneself.** These competences are best learned in close interaction and collaboration with children's homes. Daily routines should be scheduled so that children have time to learn these skills and receive feedback from adults about how they are progressing. Children often learn these skills through play.

4. **Multiliteracy and technological literacy.** These competences require that children can use media and different digital

technologies, and also create new ideas and products using digital devices. When children tell stories with technology and teach one another, their multiliteracy competences have chances to develop.

5. **Participation and influencing.** These competences can be learned when adults give children a genuine voice and take their interests and opinions seriously. Involving children in planning, decisionmaking, and reflection regularly are important steps in teaching children these important competences.

Play is an important part of ECEC in Finland. It is considered as the basic right of the child that every kindergarten must protect. The Finnish National Agency for Education[7] states that in ECEC, "The importance of play for the child and its pedagogical possibilities in the promotion of wellbeing and learning are understood. Play motivates children and brings joy while allowing them to learn new skills and create meanings about themselves and the surrounding world. Children's social relationships are supported and everyone's opportunities to take part in play and shared activities are ensured."

Similarly, preschool for 6-year-olds is guided by the National Core Curriculum for Preprimary Education, which stipulates the overall goals of preprimary education and specific educational objectives. Because preschool education is now compulsory, every child must enroll in kindergarten or primary school where preschool classes are normally arranged, or they must take part in other activities that meet the goals for preprimary education 1 year before the 1st grade. Preschool is provided under the Basic Education Act, and it is free of charge.

Again, the aim of preprimary school in Finland is not simply "school readiness" as it is in many other countries but rather to promote children's conditions of growth, development, and learning. Preprimary education should be planned from the child's perspective, and it should support positive advancement of children's understanding of themselves and their individual self-concepts. A leading educational principle in developing preprimary education in Finland is inclusiveness; that means that all children are welcomed to their neighborhood school and that these schools should be ready to support and help all children to succeed as they are (Finnish National Agency for Education, 2014).

The National Core Curriculum emphasizes the development of thinking in relation to language and communication, mathematics, ethics and religion, environmental issues, physical development, and arts and culture. All these domains must be handled in a way that supports children's holistic growth and must be discussed with children's parents. "School readiness" in Finland means that all schools must be ready to receive all children just as they are. This is one reason why Finland's early childhood education, including preschool, doesn't prioritize reading, writing, and mathematics as core skills to determine children's successful entry into primary school.

What the scheme shown in Figure 1.5 is not able to reveal are the principles of individualized education and the systematic care of all children that are typical in Finnish schools today. For example, schools are required to maintain strong support systems for teaching and learning—nutritious, free school meals for all pupils; health services; psychological counseling; and student guidance are normal practices in every school. These principles make the Finnish school system—as I see it—one of the most individualized and flexible school systems in the world.

THE FINNISH DREAM CHALLENGED

It would be a mistake to think that the education reforms of the 1970s that created Finland's *peruskoulu* were supported by all business leaders, politicians, and educators. The campaign against *peruskoulu* was particularly harsh from some parts of the business community. Finnish business leaders followed closely the way *peruskoulu* was implemented. Most of the privately governed grammar schools were amalgamated into the public school networks of the municipalities, and all school fees were abolished. The Finnish Business and Policy Forum (EVA), a policy and promarket think tank, gave funding to a foundation that was opposed to this ongoing school reform and wanted to see private schools as alternatives to these new schools. The Parliament's conservative right accused advocates of *peruskoulu* of being socialist, warning that the model would jeopardize the steady economic progress and prosperity of Finnish society. The other side of the aisle defended the reforms by saying they would secure a good education for every child in Finland and thereby raise the well-being and prosperity of Finnish society. There was also a debate in the 1970s about the ability of the new *peruskoulu* to keep up with the international race for a knowledgeable and skilled labor force. These critics feared that *peruskoulu* would not allow the most able and talented to progress as far as they should in school.

In the late 1980s, when opposition to ongoing education reform was particularly strong, some parents as well as politicians and business leaders voiced their criticism and dissatisfaction with *peruskoulu*, where all streaming and tracking had been abolished a few years earlier. According to these critics, the emphasis on social equality had led to a suppression of individuality. This concern was, in fact, voiced by the prime minister at the Finnish School Principals' Annual Meeting in November 1987:

> When believing that anyone can learn everything, the goals of the comprehensive school are set too high. When trying to educate the whole population to the unattainable comprehensive school level, the financial and mental resources of a small nation are being wasted on a hopeless task. These same educational resources would be badly needed to educate those who have proven to be talented in different areas to international high standards. Only that way can we maintain Finland's position in the hard international competition in science and the economy. (Aho et al., 2006)

Triggered by this perception of the political leadership, Finnish business leaders launched a survey in 1988 to find out the actual state of *peruskoulu* as the main medium of education in Finland. The grim conclusion was that *peruskoulu* was killing talent. In other words, it wasn't allowing able and gifted pupils to progress to their full potential because it insisted on social equality by employing a unified curriculum in all classrooms. This coincided with the deregulation of the economy. The education system had to support the transition of Finnish society into a more liberal and competitive market economy. There were those—including the then–prime minister of Finland—who argued that the economic transformation from postindustrial to knowledge economy requires that able and talented students should be offered opportunities to progress freely and not to "wait for the mediocre students," especially in mathematics and science.

The campaign to reform the Finnish education system according to the models of the emerging New Public Management Movement continued into the 1990s. The Education Reform Act of 1988 in England with the first national curriculum and common attainment targets for all, the outcome-based education policies of New Zealand, and the standards-based model of the United States were all seen by some Finns as suitable alternatives to the new Finnish Way in education. Increasing choice, competition, and specialization were cited as a way to improve education. National assessments and regular testing of student achievement were promoted as the necessary way to catch up to other education systems that seemed to be increasing the gap between them and Finland in education.

Criticism continued and sharpened until the end of the 1990s, although research findings did not support the contention that students were learning less because of *peruskoulu* (Linnakylä & Saari, 1993). Shifting the responsibility of curriculum planning, school improvement, and student assessment to municipalities and schools in the mid-1990s had strengthened support from teachers and principals to develop the Finnish school system without using models of marketplace management. The critical voices were suddenly muted in early December 2001 when news of the first PISA study was published in the global media: Finland had outperformed all other OECD countries in reading, mathematics, and science when measured at the end of *peruskoulu*. Indeed, the Finnish Way was validated, and as many have said, PISA had saved Finnish *peruskoulu* from the toxic influences of the Global Educational Reform Movement that is explained in detail in Chapter 4.

Andreas Schleicher (2006), who is director of the education department and the chief of PISA at the OECD, concluded in his analysis of Finnish education that building networks among schools to stimulate and spread innovation helps explain Finland's success in making "strong school performance a consistent and predictable outcome throughout the education system, with less than 5% variation in student performance between schools" (p. 9). The question is: Has Finland always had such a well-performing education system? If the answer is no, then it is worth asking another question: What factors have contributed to Finland's educational improvement?

CHAPTER 2

The Finnish Paradox
Less Is More

If everybody thinks the same way, nobody thinks very much.

—My grandmother's advice to me for succeeding in life

Today Finland is regarded as one of the world's most politically stable, socially equal, and economically successful countries. It is also among the most literate and best-educated societies. As a nation of modest people, Finland never actually intended to be the best in the world in education. Finns like to compete, but collaboration and teamwork are more typically characteristic of this nation. In the mid-1990s, when Finnish education was known internationally as average, the Finnish minister of education visited her colleague in neighboring Sweden to hear, among other things, that by the end of that decade when the first PISA survey would be carried out by the OECD the Swedish education system that had just a few years earlier introduced school vouchers and opened its equitable public school system to private for-profit operators would be the best in the world. The Finnish minister replied that the Finns' goal is much more modest than that. "For us," she said, "it's enough to be better than Sweden." This episode is an example of the close sibling-like relationships and coexistence between Finland and Sweden often expressed in the spirit of humor but most of the time in mutual respect and togetherness. In fact, companionship is more common than rivalry between these neighboring Nordic nations, which share many values and principles in their education systems and societies.

This chapter answers questions such as: Has the Finnish education system always been a top performer? What do we mean by a successful education system? How much does homogeneous society or culture explain Finland's good educational performance? This chapter also describes how Finland has been able to improve participation in education, creating equal educational opportunities for all, and how it has spread good-quality teaching to most schools and classrooms with modest overall cost. Rather than increasing time for teaching and learning, testing students more frequently, and insisting that students work harder on their homework, Finland has done the opposite, as this chapter illustrates. The key lesson from Finland is: There are alternative ways to build well-performing public education systems that differ from those commonly offered in world education policy forums.

FROM PERIPHERY TO LIMELIGHT

In the 1980s, the Finnish education system had only a few features that attracted any interest among international educators. Many aspects of education policy were adopted from Finland's wealthier western neighbor, Sweden. In international comparisons, Finnish education was exceptional on only one account: Finnish 10-year-olds were among the best readers in the world (Allerup & Medjing, 2003; Elley, 1992). Other than that, international education indicators left Finland in the shadows of traditional education superpowers such as Sweden, England, the United States, and Germany. What is noteworthy is that Finland has been able to upgrade human capital by transforming its education system from mediocre to one of the best international performers in a relatively short period of time. This success has been achieved through education policies that differ from those found in many other nations. Indeed, some of Finland's educational reform policies appear to be paradoxes because they depart so clearly from global educational reform thinking that often insists on hard-hand control, more standardized testing, tougher accountability, and harder work from all involved in schooling.

When the OECD countries in the mid-1990s first discussed the need to create new metrics and measurements to compare educational performance in the most developed countries, Finnish authorities were concerned about whether this was a good idea (Sahlberg, 2018). They questioned whether a fair single measure for such a diverse set of countries and economies as the United States, Japan, Italy, and Finland, for example, would be possible in the first place. They were also afraid that this new student assessment program would become an international league table, ranking entire education systems from the best to the worst by using one single criterion. These views were overruled and the inauguration of the Programme for International Student Assessment (PISA) was set for the year 2000. Because the massive amount of data from the 28 countries that were then OECD members and 4 partner countries took some time to process, the first results were scheduled to be released in December 2001.

PISA is a standardized assessment that measures the extent to which students at the end of lower-secondary education can apply their knowledge to real-life situations and how far they are equipped for full participation in society. OECD describes the essence of PISA (at pisa.oecd.org):

> Since the year 2000, every three years, fifteen-year-old students from randomly selected schools worldwide take tests in the key subjects: reading, mathematics and science, with a focus on one subject in each year of assessment. The students take a test that lasts 2 hours. The tests are a mixture of open-ended and multiple-choice questions that are organized in groups based on a passage setting out a real-life situation.

In 2018, altogether 79 countries (and regions) took part in the PISA test that focused on reading literacy. This number will increase to a total of 88 (of which 37 are OECD member countries) in the next cycle when the main assessed subject domain is mathematics in 2022. It is important to keep in mind that PISA is a sample-based assessment that uses statistical methodology to analyze collected data to make generalizations. PISA is methodologically similar to other international student assessments, such as TIMSS and PIRLS, but it measures different types of learning, as mentioned above.

Prior to the first cycle of the PISA in 2000, many countries thought that their education systems were world-class and that students in their schools were better learners than those elsewhere. Indicators about educational attainment, spending, and college graduation rates, as well as academic competitions such as the International Olympiads in mathematics, physics, and chemistry (and later in subjects such as computer science, biology, and philosophy), had given these nations reason to celebrate the respective performances of their school systems. In academic scholarly competitions, high school–aged students compete to demonstrate advanced-level knowledge in their fields. Naturally, those education systems that have established effective selection systems to identify talents and special abilities early on and then provide gifted students with superior learning opportunities have succeeded well in these games. Population-rich nations with large numbers of students, such as China, the United States, and the Russian Federation, have acquired reputations as high-performing education nations on the basis of academic Olympiads. Interestingly, several central and eastern European countries—among

Table 2.1. Finnish Upper-Secondary School Students in Mathematics Olympiads Compared With Their Peers in Selected Countries in 1959–2019

Rank, Country	Medals			Number of Participations	Number of Participating Students
	Gold	*Silver*	*Bronze*		
1. China	157	35	6	34	200
2. United States	130	112	29	45	282
3. Russia	99	57	12	28	168
4. Hungary	82	167	99	59	390
5. Korea	79	70	27	32	192
6. Romania	77	144	105	60	398
7. Soviet Union	77	67	45	29	204
8. Vietnam	62	108	73	43	258
9. Bulgaria	54	119	109	60	402
10. Germany	51	100	79	42	258
11. United Kingdom	48	109	125	52	338
12. Iran	45	97	43	34	199
21. Australia	22	70	92	39	218
23. Singapore	21	55	69	32	192
35. Netherlands	8	32	79	49	316
36. Sweden	7	31	79	52	337
52. Norway	2	14	35	36	208
60. New Zealand	1	11	54	32	192
62. Finland	1	9	52	46	290
66. Denmark	1	6	33	29	168

Source: International Mathematical Olympiad (www.imo-official.org).

them Hungary, Romania, and Bulgaria—are ranked high in the overall league tables of these Olympiads. Table 2.1 illustrates the top-20 countries in mathematics Olympiads and the position of Finland and some of its neighbors among them between 1959 and 2019. As this ranking shows, Finland has not much to celebrate as far its achievements in international mathematics competitions during the last half century.

Success in these academic Olympiads was often used as a proxy for the quality of national educational systems. Even if Finnish students' performance in mathematics is adjusted for population size, the relative position of Finland has fluctuated between 25th and 35th in the overall global rank list. Until 2001—and in some circles, for quite some time after that—a common conception in Finland was that the level of mathematical and scientific knowledge and skills of Finnish students was internationally average, at best. As mentioned earlier, academic competitions like the Olympiads for high school students don't tell much about the quality of teaching or learning overall in participating countries.

In 2008, OECD launched the Teaching and Learning International Survey (TALIS), which explored various aspects of teaching and learning in 24 participating countries. The second cycle of TALIS was conducted in 2013 in 34 countries and the third one in 2018 in 48 countries. Finland and the United States did not participate in 2008, but both did so in 2013 and 2018. TALIS asks a representative sample of teachers and school principals in each country about their working conditions and learning environments. According to the OECD (2014b, p. 26), "[TALIS] aims to provide valid, timely and comparable information to help countries review and define policies for developing a high-quality teaching profession." This survey, OECD says, enables teachers and school leaders to provide input into educational policy and development in key areas. TALIS results are based on opinions, views, and perceptions from teachers and school principals. Data that are collected for these surveys are therefore subjective. They include teachers' and school principals' voices, which sometimes differ from the objectively collected data in research projects. Some findings of TALIS are discussed in the following chapters.

Andreas Schleicher, who is director of OECD's Directorate for Education and Skills and in charge of its PISA study, says that "in Finland, for example, the country with the strongest overall results in the first PISA assessment, parents could rely on consistently high performance standards in whatever school they chose to enrol their child" (Schleicher, 2018). As Finland attracts global attention due to its high-performing education system, it is worth asking whether there has really been any progress in the performance of its students since the 1970s. If such progress in any terms can be reliably identified, then, consequently, the question becomes: What factors might be behind successful education reform? When education systems are compared internationally, it is important to have a broader perspective than just student achievement. What is significant from this analysis is the steady progress Finland has made during the past 3 decades within four main domains:

1. Increased levels of educational attainment of the adult population
2. Widespread equity in terms of learning outcomes and performance of schools
3. Improved student learning as measured by international student assessments
4. Efficiency in using human and financial resources, almost solely from public sources

Let us next take a look at each of these domains in more detail.

EDUCATIONAL ATTAINMENT

Finland's people remained rather poorly educated until the 1960s. Secondary and higher education was often accessible only to those who could afford it and who happened to live close to a grammar school and university. When *peruskoulu* was launched in the early 1970s, for three quarters of adult Finns, basic school was the only form of education they had completed. Holding an academic degree was rare, as only 7% of Finns held some kind of university degree. Overall progress since 1970 in educational attainment by the Finnish adult population (15 years and older) is shown in Figure 2.1. The current situation is congruent with a typical profile of the educational attainment pyramid in advanced societies, where about 30% of the population have higher educational attainments and about 40% are upper-secondary education degree holders.

Figure 2.1 indicates that there has been steady growth in participation in all levels of education in Finland since 1970. The growth was especially rapid in the upper-secondary sector in the 1980s and, then, within the higher and adult education sectors in the 1990s and up to the present. Policies that have driven Finnish education reform since 1970 have prioritized creating equal opportunities for all children to a good education, improving the quality of teaching and learning, and increasing participation within all educational levels across Finnish society. As a result, each year more than 99% of the age cohort successfully completes basic education, over 97% continue their formal education in upper-secondary schools or in the additional 10th grade of *peruskoulu* (2%) immediately after graduation, and about 90% of those starting upper-secondary education eventually graduate, which is a license to higher education (Statistics Finland, n.d.a).

Figure 2.1. Level of Educational Attainment Among the Finnish Adult Population (Over 15-Year-Olds) Since 1960

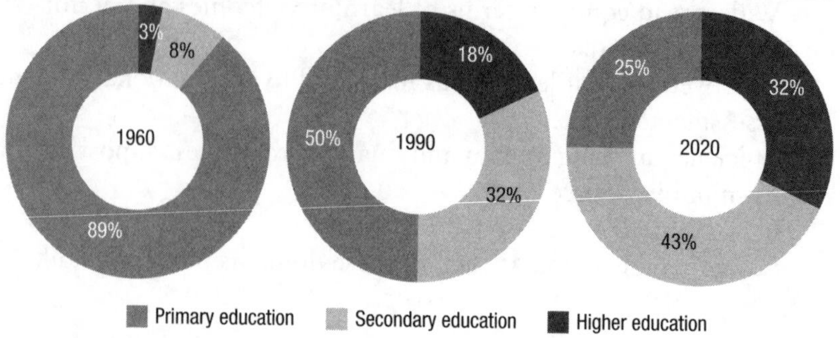

Source: Statistics Finland (n.d.a).

According to OECD, 54% of the Finnish adult population (age 25–64) participated in formal or nonformal adult education programs in 2016, compared to 47% in the OECD on average (OECD, 2019a). What is significant about this expansion of participation in education is that it has taken place without shifting the burden of costs to students or to their parents. According to recent global education indicators, in 2016 only about 3% of Finnish expenditure on educational institutions (primary to tertiary education) comes from private sources, compared with an average of 17% of total educational expenditure in OECD countries (OECD, 2019a). For example, in the United States 32%, in Australia 32%, and in Canada 25% of funding for educational institutions come from private sources.

OECD conducted the first cycle of the Programme for the International Assessment of Adult Competencies (PIAAC) study in 24 countries, including Finland, in 2012 (OECD, 2013c). The study assessed selected basic skills that adults need in different life situations, including work and everyday living. Reading literacy, numeracy, and practical problem solving in technology-rich environments form the main areas of the PIAAC study. This study provides further information about the quality of educational attainment among adult Finns and how they are likely to cope with different issues as citizens and in working life.

So, what does PIAAC 2012 tell about adult Finns' knowledge and skills related to everyday life? The average reading literacy skills in Finland are excellent. Only Japan has better overall adult competences. Two out of three adults in Finland are either good or excellent readers. In Canada, just over half and in the United States almost half of adults reach these same levels in reading literacy. The mathematical skills of

Finnish adults are at the same high international level; 57% of all adult Finns have either good or excellent skills in numeracy. Again, Japan was the only country that exceeded Finland in numeracy. In both Canada and the United States, adults' everyday mathematics skills fall below the OECD average, with the proportion of good or excellent numeracy skills being 45% and 34%, respectively. In Finland, 41% of adults have good or excellent problem-solving skills in technology-rich contexts. And again, in Canada and the United States, the numbers of adults with good or excellent problem-solving skills are 36% and 31%, respectively. Sweden is the only country that did better than Finland in this aspect of adult competencies. Finland's good performance in PIAAC 2012 was in a large degree thanks to the younger segment of adults between the ages of 20 and 39. Proficiency in basic reading, mathematical, and problem-solving skills is strongly connected to educational background in all countries that participated in this survey, including Finland.

Finland's school life expectancy, which predicts the duration of a citizen's formal education at the age of 5, is one of the highest in the world, at over 19 years in 2018, according to UNESCO's Sustainable Development Goals education database. This is mainly because education is publicly financed and hence available to all but also because education and training are held in high value in the Finnish culture. The two types of higher education institutions offer a place of study for about three of five young people of the age cohort (see Figure 1.5). Because studying in Finnish universities and polytechnics is tuition-fee free for all Finnish students, as well as those from European Union and the European Economic Area, higher education is an equal opportunity for all those who have successfully completed upper-secondary education. The government has introduced new conditions for financial aid for students that encourage students to graduate on expected time. The total monthly financial aid for higher education students is about US$1,000, of which 65% is government-guaranteed bank loans, and the rest is government grant. A student who graduates on time may deduct annual interest paid for her student loan from her income tax.

EQUITY OF OUTCOMES

People sometimes incorrectly assume that equity means the same as equality in education. In other words, that all students should be treated the same way in school—taught the same curriculum, given the same amount of instruction—or that they should achieve the same learning outcomes in school. This was also a common belief in Finland for a long time following the equality-based school reform that was first launched in the early 1970s. Rather, equity in education means that students' educational achievement in school is not primarily determined by their home background, that is, wealth, occupation, positions, or power of their parents or guardians. The basic starting point of equitable education is that all students must have access to high-quality curriculum, teaching, and learning regardless of where they live or what school they attend. In this sense, more equitable schools or school systems ensure that differences in educational outcomes are not the result of differences in students' family background.

Equity in education has become a hot topic in international education policy circles. One reason for this growing amount of research, and other evidence from around the world showing that smart public policies create educational conditions that can boost social mobility and success for many more children than if these policies were not introduced. The other reason is that today there are different ways to measure equity of education systems by linking students' measured achievement and their home background data to calculate estimates of the association of these two variables. Equity of education systems is often measured in international student assessments by calculating the strength of the relationship between students' achievement in school and various aspects of their home background. OECD uses an index that includes economic, social, and cultural status (ESCS) by calculating a value for equity based on parents' education, occupations, wealth, and some aspects of socioeconomic background. In more equitable education systems, students' learning in school is less dependent on their family background. Countries vary greatly in terms of how much of student achievement is associated with family background, just like they are different with regard to student achievement in reading, mathematics, and science in school. Measuring equity in education now also includes quantitative values for academic resiliency, distribution of resources across the education system, and performance variations between immigrant and native students and between girls and boys (OECD, 2019b).

Equality of educational opportunity and equity of outcomes are important features in Nordic welfare states. They mean more than just ensuring that everybody has access to school. In Finland, equity means having a socially fair and inclusive education system that provides everyone with the opportunity to fulfill their intentions and dreams through education. As a result of the comprehensive school reform of the 1970s, education opportunities for good-quality learning have spread rather evenly across Finland. In the early 1970s, at the start of the implementation of the comprehensive school reform, there was a significant achievement gap among young adults due to very different educational orientations associated with the old parallel system (see Figure 1.1). This achievement gap strongly corresponded with the socioeconomic divide within Finnish society at the time. Although students' learning outcomes began to even out by the mid-1980s, the streaming of pupils according to ability grouping in mathematics and foreign languages kept the achievement gap relatively wide.

After abolishing streaming in comprehensive school in the mid-1980s and raising learning expectations for all students, the achievement gap between low and high achievers began to decrease. This meant that all pupils, regardless of their socioeconomic conditions or interests, studied mathematics and foreign languages in the same nonstreamed classes. Earlier, these subjects had three levels of curricula to which pupils were assigned based on their prior academic performance in these subjects and also often on their parents' or peers' influence.

Until the first PISA study in 2000, it was not clear if equality-based education policies and heavy investments in enhancing equity were actually any good for raising the quality of learning outcomes at the system level. Many thought that having equity as the key driver in national education policy would prevent the system from cultivating individual talent and thereby improve quality. One of the unexpected aspects of the first three PISA cycles was that most of the education systems with high overall student learning were also the most equitable. Since then PISA has revealed, among other things, that Finland has the smallest performance variations among schools in reading, mathematics, and science scales of all OECD nations (OECD, 2018, 2019b).

Calculating how much of the total variation in student performance is associated with variation within schools and how much with between-school variation indicates another aspect of equity in education systems. Between-school variation in performance indicates how different schools are statistically in any given country. In the Netherlands and Israel, for example, variation of student learning between schools is larger than within schools, which suggest that there is a big gap between schools in terms of their performance overall. Figure 2.2 shows performance variance within and between schools in the OECD countries as assessed by the reading literacy scale in 2018 (OECD, 2019b). Across OECD

Figure 2.2. Variance Within and Between Schools in Student Reading Literacy Performance on the 2018 PISA Study

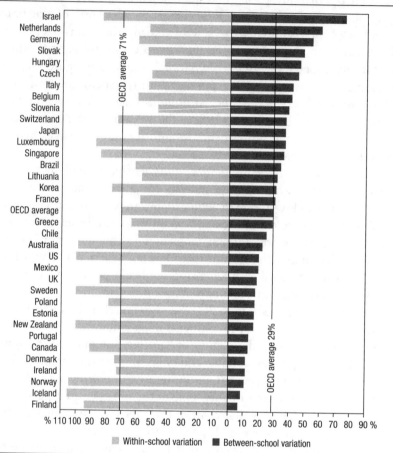

Source: OECD (2019b).

countries in 2018, 29% of the overall performance differences are observed between schools and 71% within schools.

According to Figure 2.2, Finland has just 6.7% between-school variance on the 2018 PISA reading literacy scale, whereas the average between-school variances in Canada, the United States, and the United Kingdom are 12.8%, 18.4%, and 19.7%, respectively. Performance variation between different schools in Finland in 2018 was at a level similar to what was shown in the previous PISA cycles. The fact that almost all variation of student learning occurs within schools, as shown in Figure 2.2, means that the remaining differences are probably due to variation in students' natural talent. Accordingly, variation between schools mostly relates to social inequality. Because this is a small source of variation in Finland, it indicates that Finnish schools successfully deal with these social inequalities caused by home background and peer influence. Furthermore, this suggests, as Norton Grubb observed in his review of equity in education in Finland, that Finnish educational reform has succeeded in building an equitable education system in a relatively short time, a main objective of Finland's education reform agenda set in the early 1970s (Grubb, 2007; OECD, 2005). Relatively small between-school variation in performance means that in Finland parents rarely are worried about the quality of their neighborhood school. Although choosing a school other than the neighborhood school is an increasing phenomenon in larger urban areas in Finland, parents most often look for an ordinary, safe school for their children. OECD's own analysis (Schleicher, 2018) confirms that successful education systems often have deliberately aimed at an ideal that the best school for any child is the neighborhood public school.

Strong emphasis on equity in education gives different meaning to *school performance* and how it is measured. Standardized testing has become the most common way to measure school performance in many parts of the world. Test-based accountability relies on data from these tests. Teachers and administrators are held accountable for their students' learning based on these data—but not in Finland. The absence of standardized tests in Finland leaves schools responsible for assessing student achievement themselves. A high-performing school in Finland is one where *all* students perform beyond expectations. In other words, the greater the equity, the better the school according to the Finnish criteria.

An educational system that is equitable and where students learn well is also able to redress the effects of broader social and economic inequalities. Since the 1970s, Finnish education policies have fostered high overall levels of student achievement while limiting the influence of student backgrounds on learning outcomes and thereby attaining a high level of equity. Some have wondered why Finns think this is so important. Inequity in educational systems in Finland is seen as particularly problematic because it demonstrates a failure to utilize students' human potential fully. As a small nation, Finland cannot leave any child behind. Evidence also shows that strengthening equity in education can be cost beneficial. The OECD, after examining the PISA data over time, concluded that the highest-performing education systems across OECD nations are those that combine quality with equity (OECD, 2012, 2018). Other research (Cunha & Heckman, 2010; Hausstätter & Takala, 2010) demonstrates that investing as early as possible in high-quality education for all students and directing additional resources toward the most disadvantaged students as early as possible, is a cost-effective strategy that will produce the greatest impact on improving overall academic performance.

How has Finland turned these findings into practices that enhance equity in schools? The universal right that all Finnish children have to high-quality early childhood education is one thing. The other, equally important, is the inclusion of children with special educational needs in mainstream schooling, which is an important guiding principle of Finnish education. All schools must have special education teachers and classroom assistants who can help children with special educational needs. There are notable differences between how special education is defined and delivered in Finland and in many other countries, including the United States. Most important, special education in Finland is for all students, based on the assumption that at some points in our lives all of us need support and help to move forward.

First, in Finland, special education is defined primarily as addressing difficulties related to learning, such as reading, writing, mathematics, speech, and increasingly today also languages of instruction. In the United States and many other nations, students are identified as possessing special education needs if they meet criteria that often refer to a variety of disabling conditions, such as sensory and speech-language impairments, intellectual disabilities, and behavioral difficulties.

Second, in Finland special education needs are identified and addressed as early as possible; *prevention* is a common strategy within special education. This means that there is a larger number of special education children in Finland compared with the United States or other nations, especially during the early years of schooling. In Finnish comprehensive schools, corresponding to K–9 education in the United States, almost one third of all pupils were in part- or full-time special education in 2012 (Statistics Finland, n.d.a). That number has dropped to 20% in 2019 as a consequence of the special education reforms in 2010 and 2011 that are described in detail by Raisa Ahtiainen (2017) in her doctoral dissertation.

Finally, the new special education system in Finland is defined under the title *Learning and Schooling Support,* and all special education students are increasingly integrated into regular classrooms. There are three categories of support provided to those pupils with special needs:

(1) general support, (2) intensified support, and (3) special support. The first includes actions by the regular classroom teacher in terms of differentiation, as well as efforts by the school to cope with student diversity. The second category consists of remedial support by the teacher, coteaching with the special education teacher, and individual or small-group learning with a part-time special education teacher. The third category includes a wide range of special education services, from full-time general education to a placement in a special institution. All students in this category are assigned an Individual Learning Plan (ILP) that takes into account the characteristics of each learner and thereby personalizes learning to meet each learner's abilities. As a consequence of this renewed special education policy, the number of students in intensified support has increased and in special support decreased. In school year 2019–2020 in *peruskoulu*, 11.6% received intensified support and 8.5% special support (Statistic Finland, n.d.a). This means that in that school year one of five students in *peruskoulu* received some kind of individualized support in school.

Education reforms around the world recently have included principles that promote inclusive education (i.e., integrating all students in mainstream schools and classes) and thereby reducing the identification rates for special education needs students. Special education reforms in Finland that were implemented by two separate laws mentioned earlier—the funding of special education in 2010 and the Basic Education Act of 2011—followed that same principle. These reforms aimed to shift schools' attention from assigning children to full-time special education to early identification of those children who have special educational needs and then support to them through a range of part-time special education arrangements. According to a recent study on these Finnish reforms, "the funding reform has incentivized municipalities to decrease identification rates for students in special education and to diminish special education provision" (Pulkkinen et al., 2020). Latest available statistics show that a number of students identified as having any kinds of special educational needs in *peruskoulu* has decreased by 10 percentage points since 2010. Many teachers today think that special education is insufficiently resourced, especially in smaller municipalities, and as a consequence, many children are left without proper support.

Regardless of these recent trends, many believe that Finland's special education system is one of those key factors that explain the world-class results in achievement and equity of Finland's school system in recent international studies. My personal experience, based on working with and visiting hundreds of Finnish schools, is that most schools pay very particular attention to those children who need more individual help to become successful, compared with other students. Many foreign teachers and administrators who have visited Finnish schools think the same way, but they are often stuck in the middle of *excellence versus equity* quandaries due to external performance demands and regulations in their own countries. Standardized testing that has a narrow academic definition of intelligence combined with using test results to compare individual students to statistical averages in schools jeopardize most efforts to enhance equity through teaching. None of these factors exists in Finnish schools.

At the dawn of *peruskoulu* reform, Finland adopted a strategy of early intervention to help those children with special educational needs of some kind. This means that possible learning and development deficits are diagnosed during early childhood development and care, before children enter school. In the early years of primary school, intensive special support—mostly in reading, writing, and arithmetic—is offered to all children who have major or minor special needs. As a result, the proportion of students in special education in Finland in the early grades of primary school is relatively higher than in most other countries. As Figure 2.3 shows, the proportion of students who receive special support in school in Finland declines by the end of primary school and then slightly increases as students move to subject-based instruction. The reason for the increased need for special support in upper grades of *peruskoulu* is that the unified curriculum sets certain expectations for all students, regardless of their abilities or prior learning. The common strategy internationally is to repair problems in primary and lower-secondary education as they occur rather than try to prevent them from happening (Itkonen & Jahnukainen, 2007). Countries that employ the strategy of repair have an increasing relative number of special-needs students throughout primary and lower-secondary education, as my estimate in Figure 2.3 shows.

The highly equitable education system in Finland is not a result of educational factors alone. Basic structures of the Finnish welfare state play a crucial role in providing all children and their families with equitable conditions for starting primary school at the age of 7. Extended parental leave, comprehensive and preventive health care for all infants and their mothers, and systematic monitoring of children's physical and mental development are accessible to everybody regardless of life circumstances or wealth. Every child's right to high-quality early childhood education and care, obligatory preschool for 6-year-olds, comprehensive health services, and preventive measures to identify possible learning and development

Figure 2.3. Estimated Proportion of Students in Special Education in Relation to Different Special Education Strategies in Basic Education

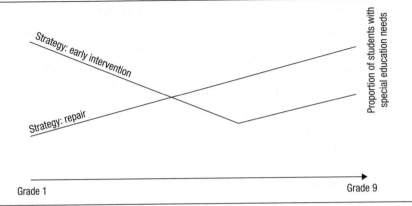

difficulties before children start schooling are accessible to everyone. Finnish schools also provide each child with a free and healthy lunch every day, regardless of their home socioeconomic situation. Table 2.2 summarizes Finland's systemic strategy for educational equity.

Foreign observers of Finnish education often state that it is easier to build a high-performing education system in a more equal society as compared to the United States, for example, where income inequality and people living in poverty are much more common. That is true and exactly the reason why Finland and other Nordic countries decided decades ago to have societies where equality defines the lives of all citizens and every child will have a fair go in their lives starting before they are born. Child poverty in all Nordic countries is at a very low level—below 5% of the child population—compared with over 20% in the United States (see Chapter 5). In order to prevent primary school pupils from being ranked according to their academic performance in schools (which often is a good measure of children's socioeconomic background), grade-based assessments are not used during the first 4 years of *peruskoulu*. This has been an important principle in developing emotionally positive elementary education in Finland: Structural elements that cause student failure in schools should be removed.

Bullying is one of the most harmful behavioral aspects of school. It is a significant worldwide concern also in Finland. Therefore, there are several interventions available for schools to prevent bullying and address its consequences. One of the most widely used is KiVa (that

Table 2.2. Key Educational Factors to Promote Equity in Education in Finnish Schools

Drivers of Equity	Finnish Model
Anyone can learn Common expectation that all children can learn what is generally expected by the school if appropriate support and individual help are made available.	Children are individuals, and they grow and learn in their own personal ways. All children are capable of learning what is expected if their individual needs are supported early on. Teacher education prepares all teachers to think about children and their human capacities in positive ways.
Right to early childhood education All children are guaranteed access to high-quality early childhood education and care preceding basic education.	Every child in Finland has a right to high-quality early childhood education and care. Access to early childhood education and care is heavily subsidized by the government. It aims to promote children's holistic growth, development, and learning in collaboration with parents. Learning through play is essential. Understanding the power of play and pedagogical possibilities it brings to the child in the betterment of well-being and learning is the foundation of early childhood education and care.
Fair funding and resourcing Funding to schools is based on the needs of the children in schools and socioeconomic characteristics of the community they serve.	Fair funding means that schools are able to build their budgets based on the needs of the children and communities they serve. The Finnish model of funding schools follows the idea of "positive discrimination" that means that public funds and allowances paid to schools are based on the socioeconomic status of pupils' parents, the number of immigrant families in the area, and other special education needs in school. Research (Silliman, 2017) shows that it is limiting social exclusion and lowers the likelihood of dropping out in education.
Student and teacher well-being Physical, mental, and social well-being are necessary conditions for high-quality teaching and learning in school.	Happiness, wellness, and health are considered important aspects of education, both as inputs through teaching and outcomes as student learning and development. School days are designed so that children and teachers have sufficient time on their own or with their peers to take a break from learning and work. School curricula also offer a healthy balance between academic seatwork and active engagement through physical activity in nonacademic learning. Play is an important part of the work of every school.

Drivers of Equity	Finnish Model
Health education and care in school Children learn to live a healthy and good life, and basic health care services are provided in school.	Every school provides all children with basic health care, dental care, mental health counseling, career guidance, and preventive care regardless of the makeup of student population or the community that the school serves. Annual health checks are part of students' lives at school. Again, every school serves free, healthy, warm lunch to all children.
Balanced curriculum Curriculum has equal emphasis on academic and nonacademic aspects of child development and learning.	National Core Curricula for different levels of schooling stipulate the aims, goals, and guidelines for designing how the school will operate. An important principle is that all children must have equal opportunities to experience a wide range of learning from traditional subjects to interdisciplinary topics and music, arts, physical activity, and play.
Broad-based special needs education Children's special educational needs are determined using classifications that include a wide range of developmental, behavioral, social, and medical criteria.	A basic assumption underlying special education is that all children have special educational needs—some of them don't need attention in school but many of them do. Special needs education is a flexible arrangement that relies on early intervention, cross-sector collaboration between teachers, health care personnel, and social workers, and that is provided by highly educated teachers in each and every school.
National youth policy Cross-sectoral policy that covers all decisions and mea-sures that concerns lives of young people in a range of areas, including employment, housing, education, health, leisure, culture, and influence.	Finland is famous for being the country that has its own law to respect the rights of young people. It promotes social inclusion, opportunities to participate in the decisionmaking over matters of concern, development of individuals' abilities, improvement of living conditions, and access to free-time hobbies and youth work. National youth policy is part of the strategy of the Ministry of Education and Culture.

means nice in Finnish).[1] It is an evidence-based antibullying program developed by researchers in the University of Turku, Finland, with financial support from the Finnish Ministry of Education. KiVa—the most studied antibullying program in the world—prevents bullying and helps to tackle the incidences of bullying constructively. Research on over one thousand schools in Finland revealed that the KiVa program reduced all forms of bullying significantly (Kärnä et al., 2011). It had positive effects on children's liking of their school, motivation, and learning. Moreover, this program reduced anxiety and depression and improved students' perception of their peers. The National School Health Survey 2019 shows that approximately 6% of students in grades 8 and 9 report that they experienced bullying at least once a week in school (Finnish Institute for Health and Welfare, 2019). The same data indicate that bullying in Finnish schools has been slightly declining during the 2010s.

STUDENT LEARNING

The ultimate criterion of the quality of a national education system is how well students learn what they are expected to learn. International comparisons of education systems put a strong emphasis on scores in standardized achievement tests, which are highlighted in Table 2.3. Although it is difficult to compare students' learning outcomes today with those in 1980, some evidence of progress in student achievement in Finland can be offered using International Association for the Evaluation of Educational Achievement (IEA) studies, and from research records since the 1970s (Kupari & Välijärvi, 2005; Martin et al., 2000; Robitaille & Garden, 1989). Because it is impossible to conclude for sure whether there has been progress in student learning in general, let us look at some school subjects individually instead.

Mathematics is often used as a proxy for general academic educational performance. The studies available include the Second International Mathematics Study (SIMS) in 1981 (8th grade, 20 nations); Trends in Mathematics and Science Repeat Study (TIMSS) in 1999, 2011, and 2015 (4th and 8th grades); and seven PISA surveys since 2000 (15-year-olds). These and other international student assessments in which Finland has participated are listed in Table 2.3. Because the nations participating in each international survey are not the same and the scope of IEA and OECD surveys are different, the international average as a benchmarking value does not always provide a fully comparable or coherent picture.

Table 2.3 shows Finland's performance in international student assessment studies since the early 1960s when the First International Mathematics Study was launched. These studies normally compare student achievement in reading comprehension, mathematics, and science at three points of education: at the end of elementary school (age 10), at the end of lower-secondary school (age 14), and toward the end of upper-secondary school (age 17). Finnish students' performance on the Second International Mathematics Study (published in 1981) was, in all areas of mathematics, at the international average. The national average performance of Finland was clearly behind that of Hungary, the Netherlands, and Japan in lower- and upper-secondary education. In 1999, the Third International Mathematics and Science Study ranked Finland 10th in mathematics and 14th in science among 38 participating countries. In TIMSS (Trends in International Mathematics and Science Study) 2011, Finnish 4th- and 8th-graders were ranked eighth of all participating countries and one of the best education nations outside of East Asia.

Progress has been similar in science since the Second International Science Study in the early 1980s. It is noteworthy that Finnish students have always performed well internationally in reading: Finnish 4th-grade students were the best readers in the Reading Literacy Study in the late 1980s, and Finnish 15-year-olds achieved top rankings in all four PISA cycles.

IEA published its 2011 results of 4th- and 8th-grade student achievement in reading (PIRLS) and mathematics and science (TIMSS) in December 2012. Finnish 4th-grade pupils took part in reading literacy tests for the first time since IEA's Reading Literacy Study in 1988. Finland had opted out of TIMSS after a 1999 repeater study because it joined PISA in 2000. In the late 1980s, Reading Literacy Study, Finnish 4th-grade pupils were the best readers of all 32 participating countries. TIMSS 1999, which measured mathematics and science, included a representative sample of Finnish 7th-grade students that deviates from normal procedure of IEA, which normally includes a representative sample of 4th- and 8th-grade students. The results of the 1999 TIMSS study showed that among 38 participating countries, Finnish students were doing well above the international average, and among participating OECD countries, Finnish students were close to the OECD average.

The release of TIMSS 2011 and PIRLS 2011 results in 2012 received much less international media attention than when PISA studies were published in 2013.[2] One major difference in these two types of

Table 2.3. Performance of Finnish Students in International Student Assessment Studies Since the Early 1960s

	Population	Countries	Rank of Finland
IEA			
First International Mathematics Study (FIMS), 1962–1967	13-year-olds and high school completion	12	Average performer
First International Science Study (FISS), 1967–1973	10- and 14-year-olds and high school completion	18	Average performer
Study of Reading Comprehension, 1967–1973	10- and 14-year-olds and high school completion	14	Average performer
Second International Mathematics Study (SIMS), 1977–1981	13-year-olds and high school completion	19 (13-year-olds); 15 (high school)	Average performer
Second International Science Study (SISS), 1980–1987	Primary, middle, and high school completion	23	10-year-olds: High performer; 14-year-olds: Average performer
Written Composition Study, 1980–1988	Primary, middle, and high school completion	14	Average performer
Reading Literacy Study, 1988–1994	9- and 14-year-olds	32	Top performer
Third (later Trends in) International Mathematics and Science Study (TIMSS)	4th and 8th grade	1995: 45	Didn't participate
		1999: 38	Above average
		2003: 50	Didn't participate
		2007: 59	Didn't participate
		2011: 63	Near the top
		2015: 47	Above average*
Progress in International Reading Literacy Study (PIRLS)	4th grade	2001: 35	Didn't participate
		2006: 45	Didn't participate
		2011: 48	Top performer
		2016: 50	Near the top

	Population	Countries	Rank of Finland
International Civic and Citizenship Education Study (CIVED and ICCS)	8th grade	1999: 31	Top performer
		2009: 38	Top performer
		2016: 24	Near the top
OECD			
Programme for International Student Assessment (PISA)	15-year-olds	2000: 43	Top performer
		2003: 41	Top performer
		2006: 57	Top performer
		2009: 65	Top performer
		2012: 65	Top in OECD
		2015: 72	Near the top OECD
		2018: 79	Near the top OECD

*Only 4th-grade students.

international student assessments is that all OECD member countries take part in PISA, whereas only some of them are included in PIRLS and TIMSS. In 2011, PIRLS covered 48 and TIMSS covered 63 countries or regions around the world. Overall, Finnish students were close to the top in all PIRLS and TIMSS scales in 2011. Finnish 4th-grade pupils were second in reading and third in science. In mathematics, Finnish 4th- and 8th-grade students were eighth overall. IEA's TIMSS and PISA 2011 studies suggest that Finnish students are close to the world's top performers in all measured school subjects. However, the main concern that these studies also reveal is a low level of motivation and engagement among students in Finnish schools. In TIMSS 2015, only 4th-grade students were included, and their performance was above the average of 47 countries and regions that took part in that cycle. Finnish students were near the top in the PIRLS 2016 study.

What might explain these upward and then declining trends in student achievement in Finnish schools on the international student assessments since the 1980s? There has been some earlier research on this question, but it has produced more speculation and qualitative analysis than reliable answers (Hautamäki et al., 2008; Linnakylä, 2004; Ministry of Education, 2019; Ofsted, 2010; Rautopuro & Juuti, 2018; Välijärvi et al., 2007). Three possible explanations for the steady improvement from the 1980s until about 2010 appear.

First, mathematics teaching is strongly embedded in curriculum design and teacher education in Finnish primary schools. For example, in the University of Helsinki each year about 15% of students in primary school teacher education programs specialize in teaching mathematics. As a consequence, most primary schools in Finland have professionals who understand the nature of teaching and learning—as well as assessing—mathematics.

Second, both teacher education and mathematics curriculum in Finland have a strong focus on problem solving, thereby linking mathematics to the real world. Mathematics tasks on PISA tests are based on problem solving and using mathematics in new situations rather than showing mastery of curriculum and syllabi.

Third, the education of mathematics teachers in Finland is based on subject didactics and close collaboration between the faculty of mathematics and the faculty of education. This guarantees that newly trained teachers with master's degrees have a systemic knowledge and understanding of how mathematics is learned and taught. Both faculties have a shared responsibility for teacher education that reinforces the professional competences of mathematics teachers (see Chapter 3).

PISA is increasingly being adopted as a global measure to benchmark nations' student achievement at the end of lower-secondary education. All 37 OECD member nations participate in these triannual assessments of reading, mathematics, and science literacies of 15-year-olds. There is also an increasing number of countries and jurisdictions (e.g., East Asian cities) taking part in this study. PISA focuses on young people's ability to use their knowledge and skills to meet real-life challenges. PISA uses the concept of literacy to refer to "students' capacity to apply knowledge and skills in key subjects, and to analyze, reason and communicate effectively as they identify, interpret and solve problems in a variety of situations" (OECD, 2013a, p. 24). It is noteworthy that PISA is based on testing a sample of 15-year-old students in each participating country, not all the students in that age cohort. PISA results are therefore an outcome of complicated statistical calculations that are explained in the technical documents available on their website (www.pisa.oecd.org).

Finland was the top overall performer among the OECD countries in 2000 and 2003 PISA studies, and the only one that was able to improve performance. In the 2006 PISA survey, Finland maintained its high performance in all assessed areas of student achievement. In science, the main focus of the PISA 2006 survey, Finnish students outperformed their peers in all 56 countries (OECD, 2007). In the 2009 PISA study, Finland was again the best-performing OECD country, with high overall educational performance and equitable learning outcomes with relatively low costs. Significant in this national learning profile is a relatively large number of best performers (level 6) and a small proportion of low achievers (below level 2). More than half of Finnish students reached level 4 or higher in comparison to the United States, where approximately one quarter of all students was able to do the same (OECD, 2010). The Canadian provinces of Alberta, British Columbia, Ontario, and Quebec also have more than 40% of students showing at least level 4 performance.

The fifth PISA cycle in 2012 confirmed the weak signal that the previous cycle had sent to the Finns: Student achievement in this international ranking had continued to decline. In PISA 2009, reading slid 11 points from the 2006 results, from 547 to 536; math, 7 points, from 548 to 541; and science, 9 points, from 563 to 554 (OECD, 2010). National student assessments and academic research in Finland had showed already, before PISA 2012 results became public, that students' knowledge and skills in reading and mathematics were not what they used to be. A study from the University of Helsinki that compared learning outcomes in *peruskoulu* in 2001 and 2012 found a significant drop in 15-year-old students' "learning to learn" skills (Hautamäki et al., 2013). PISA 2012 therefore revealed no big surprises in Finland. The score in reading dropped 12 points since the last administration of the exam 3 years earlier, from 536 to 524; in math, the score dropped 22 points from 541 to 519; and in science, it dropped 9 points, from 554 to 545 (OECD, 2013a).

When PISA 2015 results were published in December 2016, the trend that started in 2012 continued: Finnish students' performance in all three subject areas continued to get worse (Rautopuro & Juuti, 2018). Again, national evaluations of students' performance in school had already indicated that there was a growing number of low-performing students in schools. This was especially an issue among adolescent boys who were reading much less than before and were often disengaged in learning. Finland was still among the best-performing countries in the OECD with the following scores: science 531, reading literacy 526, and mathematics 511 (OECD, 2016). Finnish authorities were particularly worried about the increasing number of very low-performing students and the big performance gap between boys and girls. In 2015, Finnish girls outperformed boys in all three subject domains—this is a unique situation compared to other countries.

According to the latest PISA survey in 2018, Finland is one of the top three education systems overall, along with Canada and Estonia, among OECD countries, but its actual scores in reading, mathematics, and science literacies have come down from the previous figures in 2015 (Ministry of Education, 2019; OECD, 2019a). On average, if all three subjects are included, Finland's aggregated national score in 2018 was 519 compared to 527 in 2015. As in the previous test in 2015, the proportion of those students who don't reach the minimum level of proficiency is relatively large compared to earlier years in the 2000s. Girls continue to perform better than boys in all subject areas. Worryingly, once the world's most equitable education system where students from different backgrounds had a fair chance to succeed in school, Finland is now losing some of that strength. Any good news? Finland was the only country where a high level of reading literacy correlates with students' expression of life satisfaction.

When these inconvenient trends in Finland's educational performance are considered, it is worthy of note that 36 other OECD countries are not performing better in 2018 compared to the past, on average. Indeed, many countries have been in decline in student achievement in reading, mathematics, and science as measured by OECD's PISA test. The OECD (2019c) concluded that "there has also been no real overall improvement in the learning outcomes of students in OECD countries, even though expenditure on schooling rose by more than 15% over the past decade alone."

Another important indicator of educational success is equity of these education outcomes that is also measured in OECD's PISA survey. Equity of education outcomes refers to the strength of the relationship between students' family background, or Economic, Social and Cultural Status (ESCS) index, and student test scores in reading, mathematics, and science in school are considered a basic element of educational performance. Finland continues to be among the most equitable education nations, which means that students' home background has less influence on their academic learning in school than in most other countries. Furthermore, schools across the country are still very similar in terms of their educational results unlike in many other countries where most of the variation of students' learning is based in variances between schools, which makes them very different in terms of overall educational performance.

It has been equally difficult to explain exactly why PISA scores in Finland have been dropping as it has been to explain what was behind Finland's world-class performance to start with. You may ask if something has happened in schools that is negatively affecting the quality of teaching.

Or has Finland implemented wrong education policies since the 2010s that have derailed teaching and learning, causing worsening outcomes?

There is not much research or systematic analysis that would help answer these questions. A closer look at data—both from the OECD and from Finland's own statistics—reveals the following three possible factors that directly or indirectly affect student engagement and their learning in schools.

First, the Finnish economy was hit hard in the aftermath of the 2008 global financial crisis; this negatively affected funding of schools, which is largely a responsibility of local governments. Class sizes increased, opportunities to attend professional learning for teachers were reduced, and many schools were forced to cut significant parts of their learning support services like classroom assistants under a constraint of shrinking budgets. This has certainly been one important reason why performance gaps between schools and also within schools has widened since 2010. Perhaps the most critical conclusion from the last three PISA cycles is that students' family background has had a stronger impact on their measured achievement in school. Parents' education is a particularly strong factor explaining variation in Finnish students' performance in school. Figure 2.4 offers an illustration of how levels of parental education in years of schooling is associated with student achievement in Finland in 2009 and 2018. This figure shows that the relationship between student's socioeconomic factors and educational performance has become stronger, and that has affected more of the lower-performing students than others (Kirjavainen & Pulkkinen, 2017).

Second, the new policy of special education in Finnish schools shifted more students that previously were served in smaller classes or focus groups with expert support to mainstream classes that had growing class sizes as mentioned above. It became not uncommon for a teacher with a class of 25 children to have four or five students who just a few years earlier would have had a special assistant or would have spent at least part of the day in a smaller group receiving individualized attention. At the same time with this trend, Finnish schools welcomed rapidly growing numbers of newcomers who didn't speak Finnish (or Swedish) at home, and they often attended classes with insufficient ability to understand everything that was going on. It must be stressed that this situation varies greatly from municipality to municipality in Finland.

Finally, Finnish young people have been affected by the same phenomenon as most of their peers around the world: spending more and more time connected to their digital devices, consuming media, and

Figure 2.4. Aggregate National Average PISA Score and Levels of Parental Education Converted Into Years of Schooling in Finland in 2009 and 2018

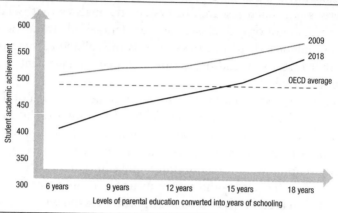

Source: OECD database.

entertaining themselves. Just like in other countries, it is typical that a big part of teenagers' daily time is spent in front of digital screens that include TV, video gaming, social media with their own device, and using the Internet for learning and fun. This increased time with media and digital technology is oftentimes taken away from reading, physical activity, and sleep. National health statistics in Finland show that at the same time, more young people are being diagnosed with serious mental health challenges and are being medicated to cope with their daily lives. An understandable assumption, therefore, is that there are many more students in schools who are not ready to learn or find it difficult to pay proper attention to teaching and concentrate on learning properly. Whatever the reasons for Finland's slight downturn in student learning, there are no signs that teachers are losing trust as professionals or that schools' ability to find the best solutions to these challenges would be questioned.

Those who think that Finland's education system is going downhill because of curriculum policies, classroom pedagogies, or a lack of accountability or testing should think again. There is no evidence that would link declining reading, mathematics, and science literacy scores to these or other in-school factors. More convincing explanations are those made by academics who have been cracking the data from OECD databases and domestic research. For example, a large team of researchers from the University of Jyväskylä and the University of Oulu came to a conclusion using PISA 2018 data that there are two main drivers affecting student learning at school (Ministry of Education, 2019). One, the number of low achievers in all three measured academic domains has increased since 2009. The small number of low-achieving students was one reason for high performance between 2000 and 2006. Two, from an equity point of view, the bad news is that the relationship between the pupil's socio-economic background to the level of performance is still as strong as in 2015, when this relationship was at the OECD average for the first time in the history of PISA assessments. Previously, this inequity had been clearly weaker in Finland than in the OECD countries on average. The conclusion is that "the strengthening of the relationship can be seen, above all, among the weakest students. The average performance of students from socioeconomically disadvantaged backgrounds (and boys in particular) is significantly lower, while the performance of students (and especially girls) from more affluent families has remained high" (Ministry of Education, 2019, p. 125). The achievement gap between immigrant background students and native students has not narrowed, and it remains the largest in the OECD countries. This doesn't explain poorer educational performance in Finland but is part of the larger eroding equity trend.

Some explanations go even further than this. There are those who argue that a big explaining factor behind declining test scores in many other OECD countries, not just Finland, is students' diminishing motivation to take low-stake tests seriously. OECD's PISA is a low-stakes test because the results have no consequences to students, unlike the Matriculation Examination or university entrance exams in Finland that are high-stake tests for students. One of the advocates of this explanation is professor emeritus Jarkko Hautamäki, who has led Finland's national PISA research team and is a founder of the Center for Educational Assessment at the University of Helsinki. He believes whereas it is clear that Finnish students' PISA scores have declined there is no evidence that this would reflect the worsening of their real knowledge and skills. "The real reason seems to be students' lack of motivation in test taking," he said in an interview to *Yliopisto*, an academic periodical of the University of Helsinki (Yliopisto, 2018). "I believe that if students really wanted, they would do as well as others before them in these tests," Hautamäki claimed. He may be right. OECD's own data show that 70% of Finnish students (compared to 68% in the OECD on average) who were selected to the 2018 PISA sample said they did not fully try in taking the test; in other words, they didn't make a full effort in doing their best (OECD, 2019a). This same factor may be one reason for slipping PISA results elsewhere as well.

Whatever the reasons behind the changes, Finns must adopt smart responses and avoid hasty, false recoveries; they must analyze past data again; and they must learn more from other countries, both their success stories and their failed reforms. A particular challenge seems to be the widening learning gap between girls and boys in school. In the 2018 PISA study, Finnish girls outperformed boys by 6 points in mathematics; only Norway and Iceland of the 37 OECD countries had a large difference in favor of girls. In science, Finnish girls beat boys by 24 points, larger than in any other OECD country. Girls are typically better readers than boys; in the OECD countries on average girls scored 30 points better than boys in the reading literacy test (OECD, 2019a). In Finland, girls were 52 points ahead of boys—a larger gap than in any other country.

Figure 2.5 shows proportions of Finnish girls and boys in different reading literacy proficiency levels in 2018. It appears that a potential factor behind Finland's declining learning outcomes points toward boys' performance in school, especially the growing crowd of underperforming boys in reading, mathematics and science.

Finland's response so far to declining performance in international student assessments has been surprising. In most other countries that have been in similar situations, the policy response is to increase instruction time and to add more learning time to students outside of school hours. As Figure 2.6 shows, on average 15-year-olds in the OECD countries spend 44 hours per week in learning tasks in and outside school. The

Figure 2.5. Percentage of Students at Each Proficiency Level by Gender on the PISA 2018 Reading Literacy Scale in Finland

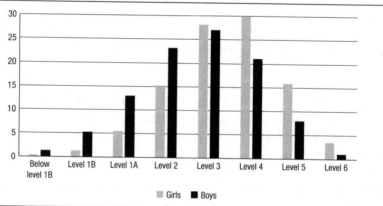

Source: OECD, 2019a.

Figure 2.6. Science Performance and Total Learning Time per Week in OECD Countries in 2015

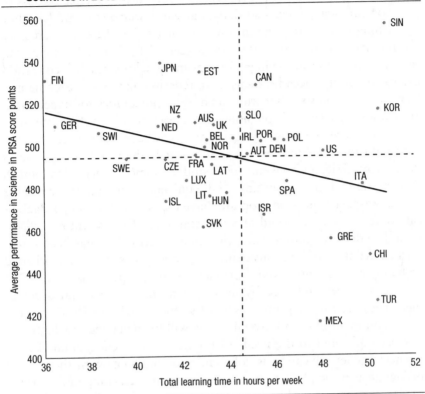

Source: OECD (2016); OECD database.

total weekly learning time of Finnish students is 8 hours less. Still, most educators in Finland think a better way than making students work longer hours is to find smarter ways to teach, discover, and learn. Therefore, the resources that would have gone to harder and longer teaching and learning have been used to make teaching more interesting and learning more engaging through focusing on interdisciplinary curriculum, giving students more of a voice in school regarding their studies, and developing more effective methods of teaching. Finnish policymakers and authorities have not made changes in education policies or national curricula just to do better in PISA. Nor have national strategies included any intentions to restore Finland's former top spot in international school rankings.

Another intriguing question emerges from Figure 2.5: What could explain Finnish students' relatively good performance in science with the least time spent in learning? The strength of Finland's schools, as far as its success in PISA is concerned, seems to be the effectiveness of pedagogical arrangements so that even when students spend less time in learning than their peers in other countries their learning outcomes are relatively higher. Some factors suggested by Finnish science educators include the following: First, primary school teacher education has for the past 2 decades focused on redesigning science teaching and learning in schools so that students have opportunities for experiential and hands-on science throughout their basic school. At the same time, more and more new primary school teachers have studied science education during their teacher education—more than 10% of graduates of the University of Helsinki have studied some science education in their master's degree programs. These university studies, as part of the normal teacher education program, have focused on building pedagogical content knowledge and an understanding of the scientific process in knowledge creation. Second, the science curriculum has been transformed from traditional academic knowledge-based to one oriented to hands-on experiments and problem solving in the classroom. This change has been followed by massive national professional development support for all primary school science teachers. Third, teacher education in all Finnish universities, as will be explained in Chapter 3, has been adjusted to the needs of the new school curriculum. Today, science teacher education is coherent and consistent with the current pedagogical principles of contemporary science teaching and learning that have been inspired by ideas and innovation from the United States and England.

There are few international student assessments that focus on subjects other than reading, mathematics, and science. The IEA International Civic and Citizenship Education Study (ICCS) is one such assessment, and it is the third IEA study designed to measure contexts and outcomes of civic and citizenship education (Schulz et al., 2018). The 2016 ICSS that built on IEA's Civic Education Study 1999 and ICCS 2009 studied the ways in which young people in lower-secondary schools (typically grade 8) are prepared to undertake their roles as citizens in 24 countries in Europe, Latin America, and the Asia-Pacific region. A central aspect of the study was the assessment of student knowledge about a wide range of civic- and citizenship-related issues. In this study, *civic knowledge* refers to the application of the civic and citizenship cognitive processes to civic and citizenship content. *Civic knowledge* is a broad term that includes knowing, understanding, and reasoning. It is a key outcome of civic and citizenship education programs and is essential to effective civic participation.

In the 2016 ICCS, Finnish 8th-grade students scored the third-highest average score in civic knowledge, right after Denmark and Sweden (Figure 2.7). As in the PISA and TIMSS results, Finland had the smallest between-school variation in student performance on the ICCS 2016 study. The ICCS 2016 shows a strong relationship between the human development index (HDI) (a summary measure of average achievement in key aspects of human development, such as a long and healthy life, being knowledgeable, and having a decent standard of living), and civic knowledge at the country level. This shows that national averages of civic knowledge are related to factors reflecting the general development and well-being of a country. This finding is similar to those from other international studies of educational outcomes, but it does not necessarily indicate a causal relationship between civic knowledge and the

Figure 2.7. Civic Knowledge of 8th-Grade Students in the 2016 International Civic and Citizenship Education Study (ICCS)

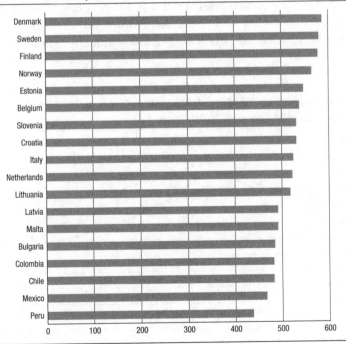

Source: Schulz et al. (2018).

overall development of a nation. Paradoxically, this study also found that Finnish youth don't feel engaged in politics and civic issues in their everyday lives. Despite their good civic cognitive and attitudinal knowledge, teenagers were among the least confident as to their own capabilities for action in society. This has been one focus area in educational development for Finland since 2010.

In conclusion, there have been two distinct trends in educational change in Finland. First, the quality and equity of Finnish public education as measured by international student assessment studies have been steadily improving since the early 1970s until about 2010. These comparative assessments provide a unique opportunity to look at the trend in how well students understand and can use what they have learned in reading literacy, mathematics, and science in school. Second, since 2012 Finnish students' position in international league tables has come down until the latest PISA cycle in 2018. Although the national averages of student performance since 2012 has declined, especially in mathematics, as Figure 2.8 shows, Finnish students' overall performance among the other OECD countries remains at a high level. What is alarming in the most recent PISA data, however, is related to finding that Finnish young people (especially boys) read less for pleasure today than they did 10 years ago. Half of 15-year-old Finnish boys reported that they don't read for pleasure. This is also clearly visible in national studies of

Figure 2.8. Performance of Finnish Students in Reading, Mathematics, and Science on PISA Surveys, 2000–2018

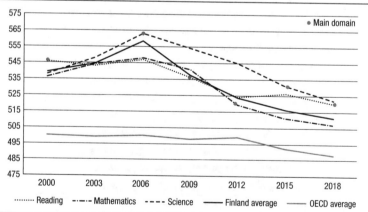

Source: OECD PISA database.

reading comprehension and habits in Finland. It appears that the observed downturn of Finland's educational performance may be associated with boys and their looser grip on school learning.

After the 2009 PISA study, the OECD (2011a, p. 117) stated that "Finland is one of the world's leaders in the academic performance of its secondary school students, a position it has held for the past decade. This top performance is also remarkably consistent across schools. Finnish schools seem to serve all students well, regardless of family background, socio-economic status or ability." For most parents this has meant that they can rely on consistently good-quality teaching and learning in whatever school they chose to send their child to. Internationally, the strength of Finland's school system is a relatively high level of student learning, which is equitably distributed across schools throughout the country.

COST OF EDUCATION

Until now we have seen how Finland has transformed its education system by increasing youth and adult participation in all levels of education, making a publicly funded education system accessible to a large proportion of its population, and achieving internationally high learning outcomes with very small performance differences between schools across the nation. All of this has been accomplished by financing education, including higher and adult education, almost exclusively from public sources. One more question regarding a successful education system remains to be addressed: How much does all this cost Finnish parents and other taxpayers?

In OECD nations for which data on comparable trends are available for all educational levels combined, public and private investment in Finnish education increased 34% from 1995 to 2004 in real terms, while the OECD average for the same period was 42%. Total public expenditure on primary to tertiary educational institutions as a percentage of GDP in Finland was 6.5% in 2011 (OECD, 2014a) and dropped to 5.5% in 2016 (OECD, 2019c) due to government's massive budget cuts in education in the 2010s. The OECD average in 2016 was 5.0% and in the United States (6.0% of GDP) and Canada (5.9% of GDP). Of the total Finnish expenditure on education institutions (including higher education), only 0.1% of GDP, or less than 3% of the total, comes from private sources.

The Relationship Between Cost and Student Performance

Figure 2.9 summarizes students' mean performance on the 2015 PISA science literacy scale in relation to cumulative educational spending from public and private sources per student (between 6 and 15 years of age) in 2015 in U.S. dollars and adjusted to purchasing power parities (OECD, 2016, 2019d). These data, first of all, indicate that there seems to be no correlation between spending and measured academic outcomes in education. Second, Finland and some other countries have accomplished good educational performance at a reasonable relative cost. For example, Luxembourg and Norway have high levels of spending in education, but their student outcome results are only moderate. This, of course, does not suggest any causal logic between education expenditures and learning outcomes, although regression indicates a positive association ($R^2 = 0.27$) between education spending and measured student achievement in OECD countries. Efficiency is more important to good educational performance than level of expenditure. In other words, money alone is not the solution to the problems in education systems, but it is necessary in building more inclusive and fair education systems.

Figure 2.9. Relationship Between PISA Performance and Total Cumulative Expenditure per Student Between Ages 6 and 15 in OECD Countries in 2015

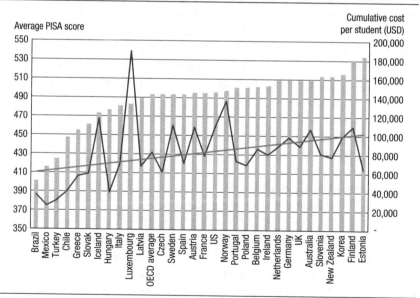

Source: OECD (2016, 2019d).

The Cost of Grade Repetition

One of the cost factors in education is grade repetition. This means that a student is asked to repeat a grade because he or she failed to successfully master the subject(s) covered the first time. Repetition is a commonly used method of treating individual deficits and problems. Not only is grade repetition an ineffective way to help students who are in need of help, but it is also expensive for education systems. How does Finland cope with this common global phenomenon?

Grade repetition in the old Finnish parallel school system was not rare in elementary schools, and it was an integral educational principle of grammar school. In some cases, a student repeated the 3rd grade of elementary school in order to improve knowledge and skills required in the grammar school admission test at the end of the 4th grade. At the time of the introduction of the new 9-year school, approximately 12% of students in each grammar school grade did not progress from their grade. Grade repetition at that time was not evenly distributed between schools or grades. For example, in general upper-secondary school, one in six students repeated a grade. We have estimated that up to half of those graduating from upper-secondary grammar school repeated one or more grades at some point in their schooling (Välijärvi & Sahlberg, 2008). Furthermore, significant numbers of students dropped out of school before completion—often after not being able to progress from one grade to the next. Inadequate progress in mathematics or Swedish (as a second language) were the most commonly cited reasons for grade repetition, although some students had to repeat a grade because of behavioral or attendance problems.

Peruskoulu (comprehensive basic school) was built on the social value of equity and was driven by the idea that all students are able to achieve common academic and social goals through choice-based educational streams in the upper grades of comprehensive school. In the old school system, grade repetition was a method of differentiation for teachers. Problems related to retention were well known at the inception of the new school system in the early 1970s. The impact of being sent back to the same grade with younger students was often demoralizing and rarely paved the way for the expected academic improvements among students repeating a grade (Brophy, 2006; Jimerson, 2001). After all, repeating an entire grade was an inefficient way to promote learning because it did not focus on those specific parts of the curriculum in which a student needed targeted help. Studying for a second time those subjects that a student had already successfully completed was rarely stimulating for either students or their teachers. Students were sent to the same class without any plan to specify the areas that needed improvement, let alone the methods of achieving most effectively the required levels of knowledge and skills.

In the early days of comprehensive school reform, grade repetition was seen as an inadequate and incorrect strategy for fixing individual learning or social deficiencies. In the elementary school, grade repeaters who had difficulties in one or two subjects were often labeled "failing" students who also had behavioral and personality problems. This educational stigma normally had a dramatic negative impact on students' self-esteem and thereby their motivation and efforts to learn. It also lowered teachers' expectations regarding these students' ability to learn. Grade repetition created a vicious circle that for many young people cast a negative shadow right into adulthood. Educational failure is linked to an individual's role in society and is characterized by unfavorable attitudes toward learning and further education. Leaving this role behind was possible only for young people who had strong identities and high social capital in the form of friends, teachers, and parents. Finnish experience shows that grade repetition, in most cases, led to increased social inequality and did not help students overcome academic and social problems.

Peruskoulu changed grade repetition policies and practices. Although the new system did not completely remove the problem of repeating grades, the number of students who repeated grades in the comprehensive school decreased significantly. Personalized learning and differentiation became basic principles in organizing schooling for students across society. The assumption that all students can achieve common educational goals if learning is organized according to each student's characteristics and needs became another foundation. Retention and ability grouping were clearly against these ideals. Different students have to learn to work and study together in the same class. Diversity in students' personalities, abilities, and orientations has to be taken into account in crafting learning environments and choosing pedagogical methods in schools. This turned out to be one of the most demanding professional challenges for teachers. Even today, schools are searching for an optimal educational and economic solution to deal with the increasing diversity.

Minimizing grade repetition has been possible primarily because special education has become an inclusive and integral part of every school in Finland. Every child has the right to have personalized support provided early on by trained professionals as a normal part of schooling. This special support is arranged in many different ways today. As described earlier, special education in Finland is increasingly organized within general mainstream schooling. Special education has a key role to play in improving equity and combating educational failure in Finnish schools. Figure 2.10 shows the percentage of students who had repeated a grade by the time they take the PISA test at age 15 in Finland and other OECD countries in 2015.

Figure 2.10. Percentage of Students Who Had Repeated a Grade by Age 15 in OECD Countries in 2015

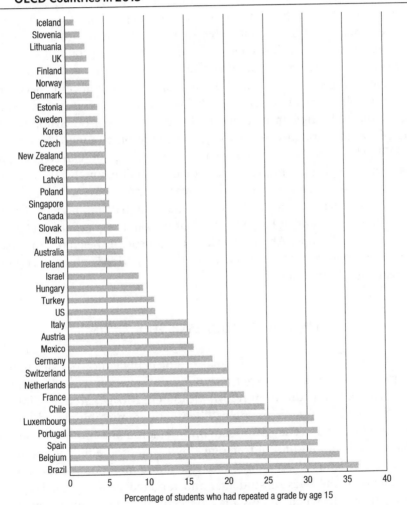

Percentage of students who had repeated a grade by age 15

Source: OECD (2016).

Upper-secondary schools—both general and vocational—operate using modular curriculum units rather than year-based grades. Thus, grade repetition in its conventional form has vanished from Finnish upper-secondary schools. Today, students build their own personalized learning schedules from a menu of courses offered in their school or by other education institutions. Studying in upper-secondary school is therefore flexible, and selected courses can be completed at a different pace depending on students' abilities and life situations. Rather than repeating an entire grade, a student only repeats those courses that were not passed satisfactorily. Most students complete upper-secondary school in the prescribed time of 3 years, although some progress faster while others need more time. This structure that is not tied to yearly classes has also abolished cohorts in which the same group of students moves from one lesson to another and from one grade to the next.

Finland has chosen a policy of automatic promotion combined with the principle of early intervention to help students with special needs. Such attention to dynamic inequalities in all schools, as Norton Grubb points out, is what distinguishes Finland from many other countries (Grubb, 2007). This process requires systematic counseling and career guidance as young people start to think about their educational pathways. Indeed, about 2% of students who leave the 9-year comprehensive school today at the age of 16 have repeated a grade at some point in their schooling. Grade repetition is at a similar level in other Nordic countries but is much higher elsewhere in Europe: About one third of students in Belgium, Portugal, and Spain and one fifth of students in the Netherlands and Switzerland repeat a grade at least once.

FINNISH PARADOXES OF EDUCATION

Finland has been a popular destination for many educators and politicians looking for a way to get out of lower-than-expected educational performance and education reform deadlock. Most visitors to Finland discover elegant school buildings filled with calm children and highly educated teachers. They also recognize the large amount of autonomy that schools enjoy: little interference by the central education administration in schools' everyday lives, systematic methods for addressing problems in the lives of students, and targeted professional help for those in need. Much of this may be helpful in benchmarking other countries' practice in relation to a leading education nation such as

Finland. However, much of the secret of Finland's educational success remains undiscovered:

- What has the educational change process been like?
- What is the role of other public sector policies in making the education system work so well?
- What role do culture and other invisible factors play?
- How much did Finnish educators take note of Global Educational Reform Movement (see Chapter 4) in creating their own approaches?
- How does a well-performing education system deal with bad news of slipping position in international education rankings?

In many ways, Finland is a nation of strange paradoxes. Home of the telecommunication industry and one of the highest mobile phone densities, Finland is also known for its introverted, less talkative people. Finns often prefer isolation to social interaction, but they love to dance the tango. They even select a national tango queen and king during the annual tango festival. Furthermore, with their tough, northern climate, Finns rank among the world's happiest people and live in one of the world's most prosperous nations. Finnish *sisu*, a cultural trademark that refers to strength of will, determination, and purposeful action in the face of adversity, coexists with calmness and tenderness, as Chaker (2014), Lewis (2005), and Panzar (2018) have noted. Similar to other Nordic nations, Finland has been successful in building a socially equitable welfare state through a globally competitive market economy (Sahlberg, 2016b). Indeed, paradoxes are more helpful than rational logic when it comes to understanding some of the key features of the Finnish people and their education system.

Avoidance of small talk is a well-known cultural characteristic of the Finns, as the following traditional story illustrates. Two men met unexpectedly after a long time. Because they had been good friends since boyhood, they decided to go and celebrate their pleasant, unexpected encounter with a drink or two. They soon found a bar, looked for a quiet table, and ordered their first drinks. No words were exchanged, and the drinks were soon finished. Their second drinks were ordered and enjoyed, yet there was still no talk. Their third drinks went down in silence, but when the fourth drinks were about to be sipped, one of the men raised his glass for a toast and cheerfully said, *"Kippis"* (which is equivalent to "cheers" in English). The companion gave him a puzzled look and replied, "Did we come here to drink or to talk?"

Minimalism is also favored in other walks of life in Finland. Arts, music, design, and architecture all draw their inspiration from small, clear, and simple ideas. Finnish people think that "small is beautiful." In business, politics, and diplomacy, Finns rely on straight talk and simple procedures. They want to solve problems, not talk about them. Inventions and innovations in Finland are often such that simple ideas make a big difference. It is perhaps not surprising, then, that these same principles and values are embedded in Finnish education. One of Finland's educational values is to put teaching and learning before anything else when education policies and reforms are under consideration. Most of all, Finns don't seem to believe that doing more of the same in education would necessarily make any significant difference for improvement. Instead, they think that working smarter, not harder, is a way to better outcomes.

Paradox 1: Teach Less, Learn More

The Finnish experience challenges the typical logic of educational improvement thinking that tries to fix lower-than-expected student performance by increasing the length of education, duration of teaching, and students' homework load. For example, when students are not learning enough mathematics, a common cure is a revised curriculum with more hours of classroom instruction and homework. In most education systems, this also requires more teaching time for teachers. Two international indicators provide a vivid picture of national differences in how much students are exposed to instruction and how much time teachers spend teaching.

First, as Figure 2.11 shows, there are big differences in the total number of intended instruction hours in public institutions in primary and lower-secondary education in OECD countries. There appears to be very little correlation between intended instruction hours in public education and resulting student performance, as assessed by PISA. Interestingly, high-performing nations rely less on formal teaching time as a driver of student learning (e.g., Finland and Estonia), whereas nations with much lower levels of academic achievement (e.g., United States, Israel, and Mexico) require significantly more formal instruction for their students. When these differences are converted into school years, Australian 15-year-olds, for example, have attended almost 5 more years of schooling than their Finnish peers. Moreover, in Finland, children start primary school at the age of 7, whereas many Australian children start school at the age of 5 (OECD, 2019a). These statistics don't tell anything about how much time students spend in private tutoring or other after-school classes on top of their formal school hours—common practice in most East Asian high-performing school systems. Overall time that students spend on learning in and out of schools is much less in Finland than other countries as was shown in Figure 2.6 earlier in this chapter.

Furthermore, according to the OECD statistics, Finnish 15-year-old students spend less time on homework than do any of their peers in other nations. This is yet another difference between Finland and many other countries where "minimum homework minutes" and other means

Figure 2.11. Total Number of Intended Instruction Hours for Students in Primary and Lower-Secondary Schools in OECD Countries in 2018

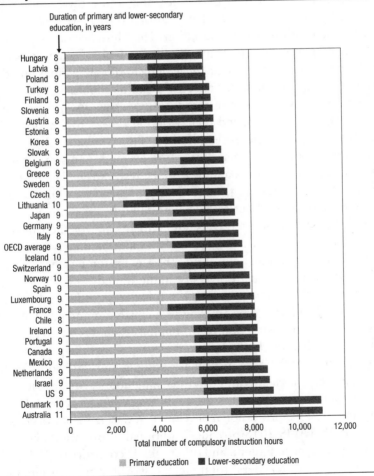

Source: OECD (2019a).

have been introduced to make sure that students are kept busy studying after school. Finnish schools seem to follow Sugata Mitra's idea of "minimally invasive education," which proposes that children can learn in unsupervised environments by themselves and by helping one another.

With school days running shorter in Finland than in many other countries, what do children do when their classes are over? In principle, pupils are free to go home in the afternoon unless there is something offered to them in the school. Primary schools are required to arrange after-school activities for the youngest pupils and are encouraged to offer educational or recreational clubs for older ones. Finnish youth and sport associations play an important role in offering youth opportunities to participate in activities that support their overall learning and growth. Two thirds of 10- to 14-year-olds and more than half of 15- to 19-year-olds belong to at least one youth or sport association. The Third Sector, as the network of these nongovernmental groups is called in Finland, contributes significantly to the social and personal development of young Finns and thereby also to the educational performance of Finnish schools.

Another way to illustrate the *quantity* versus *quality* paradox is to examine how teachers spend their working time across nations. Again, variance among countries is significant, as shown in Figure 2.12. In lower-secondary schools and primary school, on average, Finnish teachers annually teach about 614 hours and 677 hours, respectively (i.e., 830 and 900 lessons of 45 minutes each, respectively), according to OECD (2019d). This corresponds to about four lessons daily. A different source is used here for the United States because the OECD data for the United States have been documented as significantly exaggerated. Bases on detailed analysis by Sam Abrams who leads the Center for Benefit-Cost Studies of Education at Columbia University, in the United States the average annual total teaching time in primary and lower-secondary schools is 865 hours and 770 hours, respectively, which equals 5.5 and 4.9 daily lessons or other forms of instruction of 50 minutes each, respectively (Abrams, 2015).[3] Canadian teachers (the numbers vary across the provinces) teach approximately 800 hours in primary schools and 750 hours in lower-secondary schools each year. Lower teaching hours provide teachers with more opportunities to engage in school improvement, curriculum planning, and personal professional development during their working hours.

OECD's TALIS 2018 provides additional information about teachers' working time in Finland and other OECD countries (OECD, 2019f). Lower-secondary teachers' total weekly working time in Finland was 33.3 hours; that is significantly less than in Australia (44.8 hours),

Figure 2.12. Number of Statutory Net Teaching Hours in Public Primary, Lower-Secondary, and Upper-Secondary Schools Over the School Year in Some OECD Countries in 2018

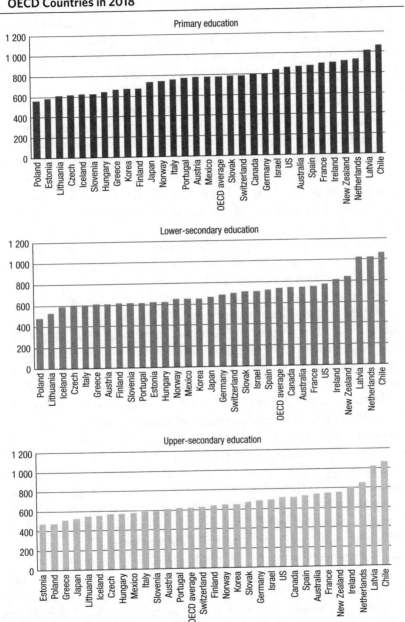

Source: OECD (2019a); U.S. numbers are from Abrams (2015).

the United States (46.2 hours), England (46.9 hours), Singapore (45.7 hours), Alberta (47.0 hours), or in the surveyed 48 countries on average (38.3 hours). On average, about 80% of lower-secondary teachers' working time is spent teaching and learning with students. Finnish teachers reported that they teach on average 21 hours a week, whereas their peers in Alberta teach 27 hours, in the United States 28 hours, and in Singapore 18 hours. In the OECD countries, lower-secondary teachers teach an average of 20 hours a week.

How is a typical school day different in Finnish and American upper-secondary schools (or high schools)? First of all, American teachers spend almost twice as long every week teaching or working with students as their Finnish peers. Teaching 6 hours (or four periods) daily is a tough job that leaves many teachers too tired to engage in anything professional when teaching is done. Teachers' work in the United States is therefore primarily defined as teaching in and out of classroom. In a typical Finnish upper-secondary school, on the other hand, teachers teach, on average, 4 hours a day. Despite the fact that teachers are paid by the number of lessons they teach, they also have time every day to plan, learn, and reflect on teaching with other teachers. Teachers in Finnish schools have many other responsibilities besides teaching: They assess their students' learning and overall progress, prepare and continuously develop their own school curriculum, participate in several school health and well-being initiatives concerning their students, and provide remedial support to those students who may need additional help. Many Finnish schools are, by virtue of a unique definition of teachers' work and by their nature, professional learning communities. Of course, there are exceptions to this general image of teachers' work. Most primary schools, nevertheless, are truly professional learning communities where teaching is a multidisciplinary profession that combines work with students in the classroom across a wide range of subjects and collaboration with colleagues in the staff room on common issues related to the school.

Finnish educators don't believe that more homework necessarily leads to better learning, especially if pupils are working on routine and intellectually unchallenging drills, which is unfortunately what school homework assignments often are. According to some national surveys and international studies, Finnish students in primary and lower-secondary school have the lightest load of homework of all. The *Wall Street Journal* reported that Finnish students rarely get more than half an hour of homework per day (Gameran, 2008). Data from recent PISA surveys show that 15-year-olds in Finland spend less than 3 hours a week on homework

(OECD, 2019a). It is true that many primary and lower-secondary school pupils are able to complete most of their homework before they leave school for the day. According to the OECD, Finnish 15-year-old students don't take private tutoring or additional lessons other than what is offered by their school (OECD, 2019b). Seen in this light, the high achievement of Finnish students on international tests is amazing. In Korea, Japan, Singapore, and Shanghai, China—jurisdictions that are on par with or above Finland in reading, mathematics, and science—most children spend hours and hours after their regular school days and on weekends and holidays in private classes and test preparation schools.

Interestingly, evidence indicates that Finnish students experience less anxiety and stress in school than many of their peers in other countries (OECD, 2004, 2007). PISA concludes that only 7% of Finnish students said they feel anxiety when working on mathematics tasks at home, compared with 52% and 53% in Japan and France, respectively (Kupari & Välijärvi, 2005). In 2015 less than one of five Finnish 15-year-olds said that that they "feel very tensed when they study" compared to 53% in the United Kingdom, 48% in Australia, and 43% in the United States (OECD, 2016). Similar observations from Finnish classrooms have been reported by scores of journalists around the world. A relaxed culture of learning and a lack of stress and anxiety certainly play a role in the achievement of good overall results in Finnish schools. Interestingly, when exploring the association between students' performance in school and how satisfied they were in their lives in 2018, Finland was alone in the category where both reading literacy and life satisfaction were at a high level (Ministry of Education, 2019). In most high-performing Asian countries students were not satisfied with their lives, and in other places where students' life satisfaction was high, their learning outcomes often were not (see Figure 2.16).

Paradox 2: Test Less, Learn More

The global educational reform thinking includes an assumption that competition, test-based accountability, and clear focus on numeracy and literacy are prerequisites for improving the quality of education systems. Corporate management ideas that have become common in many school systems have made competition, effectiveness, and productivity the key areas of interest in education policies and improvement strategies. As a result, teachers spend longer hours teaching and students more time in learning in school and doing homework after school than they did before. A common assumption among parents and education authorities is that more instruction in school leads to improving learning outcomes. An important question is: *Are those education systems where teachers teach more and students study harder showing better performance in international comparisons?*

Using the OECD education database to construct such a comparison, a suggestive answer emerges. Figure 2.13 demonstrates how students' overall net instruction time received in primary and lower-secondary school correlates with their reading literacy in 2018 (OECD, 2019a).

First, let's look at those countries where students' required instruction time in school is higher than the OECD country average and see how students performed in recent PISA studies. Correlation between these two variables is zero; in other words there is no association between net instruction time in school and measured academic outcomes at the end of lower secondary education. These data also show that Finnish students perform rather well in measured academic subjects with much less instruction time than most of their peers in other OECD countries.

Second, let's compare how children experience school days in Finland and some other countries (e.g., the United States or Australia). Figure 2.13 suggests that since Finnish students have just about 6,300 hours of required instruction in primary and lower during secondary education, their school days during 190-day school years must be shorter than elsewhere. Indeed, they are, much shorter. Finnish children spend about 3,900 hours in attending lessons in a 6-year primary school. For comparison, in OECD countries on average students have 4,600 hours mandatory instruction, and in in the United States and Australia these figures are 5,800 hours and 7,000 hours, respectively. In Finnish primary school students' daily learning time increases as they climb up from year to year so that in first two years the school week has about 20 lessons of 45 minutes and in years five and six about 25 lessons per week.

Figure 2.14 illustrates what a typical day in primary school in Finland looks like. Lessons are normally 45 minutes, which are always followed by a 15-minute recess break or longer lunch break. Children spend recess outdoors, even in cold and rainy days doing their own things, often playing games or engaging in physical activity. Every day Finnish children spend at least 1 hour outside with their friends. Most teachers value this free unstructured time during school days as an important

Figure 2.13. The Relationship Between Students' Compulsory Net Instruction Time in Primary and Lower-Secondary School and Their Performance in 2018 PISA Test

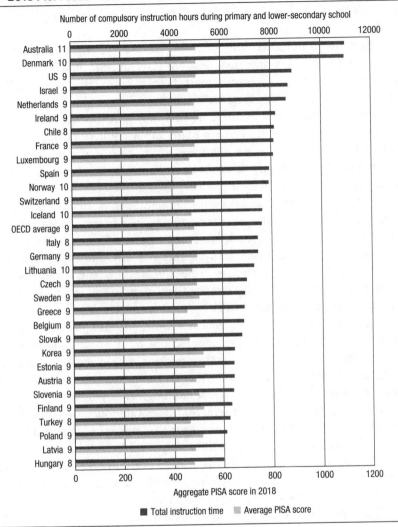

Source: OECD (2019a, 2019d).

Figure 2.14. A Typical 4th-Grade School Day in a Primary School in Finland

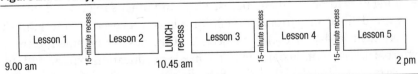

part of learning time in school for students. As we (Sahlberg & Doyle, 2019) describe in *Let the Children Play*, the more you play, the more you learn.

The Finnish paradox could also be: Test less, learn more. Finland is known for its very informal student-testing culture where census-based standardized tests don't exist before senior secondary school students show their readiness to higher learning in the Matriculation Examination that was explained in Chapter 1. Although students are not tested in Finland as they are in many other countries using frequent standardized tests, this does not mean that there is no assessment of students in Finland or any data about students' learning—quite the opposite. Teachers evaluate their students all the time.

In principle, student assessment in Finland can be divided into three categories. First is classroom assessment by teachers; this includes diagnostic, formative, and summative assessment of students as part of teaching and learning. In all schools, this is solely the responsibility of teachers. All teachers are prepared to design and use various assessment methods in their work. Classroom assessment occupies a significant amount of out-of-classroom working time for teachers.

The second category of student assessment is comprehensive evaluation of students' progress after each school term or semester. Students receive a report card that indicates their performance in academic and non-academic subjects as well as in behavior and engagement. Students' report cards are always a collective professional judgment by their teachers. It is up to the school to decide the criteria for this evaluation, based on national student assessment guidelines. This means that report cards issued by different schools are not necessarily fully comparable because they are not based on standardized and objective measures. Many teachers, however, believe that this is less of a problem than having standardized criteria and tests that would impersonalize schools and lead to "teaching to the test."

Third, progress of the education system toward its set goals is also assessed externally in Finland. Regular national assessments are carried out by the Finnish Education Evaluation Centre (FINEEC) using sample-based methodology that includes about 10% of an age cohort (e.g., 6th- and 9th-grade students). These assessments measure students' learning in reading, mathematics, science, and other subjects and themes that are defined in national evaluation plans approved by the Finnish government in 4-year cycles. Subjects and themes are included in these external assessments according to the needs of education experts and the requests by national authorities. Schools that are not included in these samples may purchase one or more of these tests from the FINEEC to benchmark their performance to that of other schools.

The key role of evaluation of the education system's performance and assessment of student learning is enhancement and positive change, rather than comparison and competition. The national quality assurance system in education that has evolved during the last 2 decades in Finland is an example of an enhancement-led evaluation paradigm that has become an integral part of the Finnish Model of education described in this book. The basic elements of the national education evaluation system are the field-specific goals laid down by law, the national core curricula for K–12 education, and practical implementation of school evaluations and student assessments at local levels and schools. The quality assurance policies also determine competence-based qualifications, operating licenses and authorizations to provide education, and the regulations for teachers' qualifications.

The Finnish Education Evaluation Centre (FINEEC), which is an independent expert organization responsible for developing and executing system-level evaluations of education, operates according to a 4-year National Education Evaluation Plan. The purpose of these evaluations is to provide reliable information for better decisionmaking and effective steering of the educational policy development on all levels of education. Education Evaluation Plans are formulated by an expert body called the Education Evaluation Council and approved by the Ministry of Education. The first National Education Evaluation Plan was for a 3-year period of 2009–2011. Since then the Evaluation Plans have been approved for 4-year periods. In the current Evaluation Plan of 2020–2023, the four focus areas are (Finnish Education Evaluation Centre, 2020a):

1. Development of learning and skills
2. Strengthening equity of education
3. Enhancement of functionality of the education system
4. Support to continuous development of education

It is important also to underline the core purposes of these educational assessments in Finland. In general terms, FINEEC conducts these evaluations primarily for monitoring the functionality of the education system. More specifically, the specific evaluations stipulated in the National Evaluation Plans are carried out to serve the following purposes (Finnish Education Evaluation Centre, 2016):

- *support* the local, regional, and national development and decisionmaking with regard to both the evaluation processes and the evaluation results;
- *improve* the quality of education, the learning of the pupils and students, and the work of the teaching staff; and
- *promote* the attainment of the goals set for the renewal of the educational system and enhance the monitoring of the development of learning results.

During the current planning period (2020–2023), the FINEEC will organize evaluations in mathematics and mother tongue in three transition points (Year 3, Year 6, and Year 9), in English language in Year 9, and in Finnish as a second language in Year 9. In addition to these assessments, evaluations cover Swedish language, history and civics, religious education and ethics, art, music, crafts, domestic science, and physical education in Year 9. All these evaluations are carried out as sample-based assessments and outsourced to Finland's research universities and institutions. International student assessment programs, such as the IEA studies (TIMSS, PIRLS, and ICCS) and OECD studies (PISA and TALIS) compliment the findings of the national education evaluations described above.

All above-mentioned educational evaluations are funded through the state budget directly to FINEEC. In 2020, for example, the total annual budget that includes FINEEC's staff costs and implementation of all evaluation projects from early childhood education to higher education is less than 3.6 million euros, or US$4.2 million. The Finnish government invests 10 times more annually in professional development of teachers and improving schools than testing and assessment.

Testing what students have learned in school is not a bad thing as long as it does not harm teaching and learning. Problems arise when tests become higher in stakes, when they are of poor quality, and when students' test scores are used to judge other things, such as the quality of teachers or schools. There are alarming reports from many parts of the world where high-stakes tests have been employed as part of punitive accountability policies in education (Amrein & Berliner, 2002; Au, 2009; Koretz, 2017; Nichols & Berliner, 2007; Popham, 2007; Ravitch, 2013). Evidence suggests that teachers tend to redesign their teaching according to these tests, give higher priority to those subjects that are tested, and adjust teaching methods to drilling and memorizing information rather than understanding knowledge. It is highly questionable how much educational value such standardized tests, which are high stakes for teachers and schools (linked to teacher evaluation, promotion, salary, reputation, or accreditation) and no stakes for students, add to student learning and school improvement. Since there are no standardized high-stakes tests in Finland before the Matriculation Examination that students take at the end of their upper-secondary education, teachers can focus on teaching and learning without the disturbance of frequent tests that have to be passed.

Other signs of weakening reliance on competition and testing in education come from recent policy changes in Scotland and Wales, the Netherlands and New Zealand, where some of the national standardized tests have been replaced by smarter ways of assessing students and schools. In Singapore, the government is reducing mandatory tests in schools. Since 2019, tests for the first two grades of primary school have been history. Furthermore, children are no longer ranked by using national test scores. In 2020 the COVID-19 pandemic made national standardized tests redundant in the United States and Australia among a number of other countries around the world.

Paradox 3: The More You Play, the More You Learn

In Finnish and Swedish languages there is a special word for childish play—*leikki* (Finnish) or *lek* (Swedish). There are different words for playing sports or musical instruments. When the word *leikkiä* is used as a verb to describe what someone is doing, there is no question about what that means. The word itself conveys a meaning that refers to an activity that is driven by a child's (or an adult's) intrinsic interest, entails active engagement and experimentation, and leads to joyful experience and emotions. In other words, children are playing.

Many people know Finland as a place where people take play very seriously. Most parents agree that free outdoor play during early childhood benefits children more than anything else. Most teachers agree that teaching and learning in primary school should be built on children's active engagement in playful activities rather than teaching different subjects in more traditional ways. Many secondary schools incorporate learning through play in their menus of teaching methods to engage students more in experimentation, exploration, and discovery across the curriculum.

There are several reasons why the adage "the more you play, the more you learn" fits well in the Finnish educational culture. First, children in Finland start formal schooling older than their peers in most other countries, at the age of 7. Finnish parents and educators value this extended childhood that allows children to play more and grow up in their own natural pace. Second, school days in primary school are relatively shorter in Finland compared to most other countries. Schools' daily schedules must include regular play breaks between the lessons, and every school must include at least an hour each day for physical and play activities for all children as shown in Figure 2.14. This gives all children more time to play during the day. Finally, children in Finland have less regular homework compared to their peers elsewhere in primary and lower-secondary schools. Out-of-school time is generally considered as free time for children to play, attend hobbies, or spend time with family.

Free, unstructured play for younger children and learning through play in primary and secondary schools are strongly embedded in the daily work of Finnish schools. Play is considered as a basic human right of each and every child, and that right is mandated in national regulations that guide the work of schools. National authorities require that learning through play has a significant role in promoting children's well-being, interaction with others, and learning essential skills in kindergartens and preschools. The Finnish Parents' League, which is the national builder of cooperation between the home and the schools and nursery schools, advises parents about the important role of play in children's life:

> Play inspires children and provides joy. At the same time, children also learn new skills. They process matters that are important to them through play. Early Childhood Education and Care personnel ensure that each child has an opportunity to participate in a variety of play and shared activities. It is important for the personnel to also discuss the importance of play with the child's guardians. (Vanhempainliitto, 2017)

The National Core Curriculum for Early Childhood Education and Care in 2019 has a clear focus on play as described in Chapter 1. It states that "understanding the importance and pedagogical possibilities of play for the child in the promotion of wellbeing and learning is essential for early childhood education and care" (Finnish National Agency for Education, 2018). Learning through play is a common pedagogical approach during the first years of primary education and often included ingredient in teaching in secondary schools. It is evident that children in Finland play more in and out of school than children in other countries. In brief, many Finns are sure that the more children play, the more they learn.

Paradox 4: Better Quality by Stronger Equity

The main policy principle of Finland's comprehensive school reform of the 1970s was to provide equal educational opportunities for all, as was described in Chapter 1. This also included the idea that student achievement should be less determined by her home background and be evenly distributed across social groups and geographic regions. It is true that Finland long remained ethnically homogeneous. However, since it joined the European Union in 1995, cultural and ethnic diversification has progressed faster in Finland than in other European Union countries, especially in larger cities' districts and schools, where the proportion of the first- and second-generation immigrant population accounts for one quarter of the total population. Massive migration to Europe in 2015 from Middle East and northern Africa brought thousands of asylum seekers and foreign children to Finnish communities and schools. Table 2.4 shows how the number of first- and second-generation population in Finland has developed since 1990. In 2000, approximately 2.5% of inhabitants in Finland were foreign-born citizens, and most of them didn't speak any of the domestic languages (Finnish, Swedish, or Sami) at home. In the beginning of 2020 that number had exceeded 8%.

Finnish schools have had to adapt to this changing situation within a very short time. In the year 2000, there were about 100,000 foreign-language speaking residents in Finland. That number had grown to over fourfold by 2020, according to Statistics Finland (Table 2.4). As a consequence, some municipalities have introduced limits to the proportion of immigrant students who attend each school to avoid segregation. For

Table 2.4. Population With Foreign Background in Finland Since 1990

Year	Born Abroad	Born in Finland	Total
1990	32,804	4,814	37,618
1995	71,633	8,217	79,850
2000	98,977	14,268	113,245
2005	135,143	22,216	157,359
2010	202,443	34,623	237,066
2015	286,803	53,122	339,925
2020	351,721	71,773	423,494

Source: Statistics Finland database.

example, in the city of Espoo, there are schools with half of students with foreign background, while some schools have only a few. In 2020, for example, 18% of the 290,000 inhabitants in Espoo had foreign background and about one of five students in Espoo schools had foreign background. City authorities believe that a more even distribution of immigrant students in their schools would benefit both students and schools. However, school principals are doubtful about such forceful policies and their impact on communities. The proportion of immigrant children in primary and lower-secondary schools in Helsinki[4] is over 22%, and the number of languages spoken in these schools exceeds 40. This trend is evident in all major cities in Finland.

The Finnish education system follows the principles of inclusiveness and right to education in child's mother tongue (during the inception to school) regarding the treatment of students who have differing characteristics and needs. Students are placed in regular schools unless there is a specific reason to do otherwise. Therefore, in a typical Finnish classroom, one finds teachers teaching students with different abilities, interests, and ethnicities, often with the help of assistant teachers. Cultural heterogeneity in Finnish society would suggest that variance in student learning among schools may become wider. The most recent data shows that the actual performance differences between schools are getting bigger (Rautopuro & Juuti, 2018). In light of international comparisons, however, equity of education outcomes remains strong.

The Finnish sociocultural situation, which is experiencing a rapid diversification of schools and communities, offers an interesting case for research. Professor emeritus Jarkko Hautamäki has explored the influence of increased immigration on student learning in schools. Two interesting findings emerge. First, based on the PISA data, immigrant students in Finnish schools performed significantly better than immigrant students in many other countries in PISA before 2009 when foreign background student numbers were small (Hautamäki et al., 2008). Immigrant students in Finland scored on average 50 points higher than their peers in other countries. Second, since 2015 the performance differences between pupils with an immigrant background and those belonging to the native population have been the largest in the OECD countries. According to schools this is often linked to students' difficulties to learn Finnish (or Swedish) language and lack of capacities in schools to sufficiently help them catch up with language proficiency soon enough.

According to PISA 2018, students with immigrant background are falling behind. According to the Ministry of Education (2019), "The mean score of first-generation immigrant students in reading literacy was 107 points and the mean score of second-immigrant students was 71 points below the mean score of students in the majority population." These results follow the declining trend of reading literacy performance of the majority population. "However," the Ministry of Education (2019) says, "the link between an immigrant background and literacy proficiency outcomes is not very strong: In Finland's PISA 2018 data, the student's immigrant background explained 5% of the variations in reading proficiency." The proportion of foreign background students in the 2018 PISA sample was 5.8%, which was more than twice as much as in 2009. Still, the number of these students, about 300, is too small to explain all the trends in Finland's performance in PISA since then, but it is most likely linked to a growing number of low-performing students in Finnish schools since 2010. Helping immigrant students catch up in learning the Finnish language is one of the biggest challenges for larger urban school systems.

Poverty is another factor that affects teaching and learning in schools. The child relative income poverty rate refers to the percentage of children with household disposable income after taxes and transfers adjusted for household size below the poverty threshold of 50% of the median disposable income in each country. Based on that definition, according to the OECD Income Distribution Database (IDD), 3.6% of children in Finland live in poverty as shown in Figure 2.15. This is the smallest child poverty rate in the OECD. In Canada 11.6%, in the United Kingdom 12.9%, in Australia 13.3%, and in the United States 21.2% of children live in poverty.

Figure 2.15. Child Relative Income Poverty Rates in Rich Countries in 2017

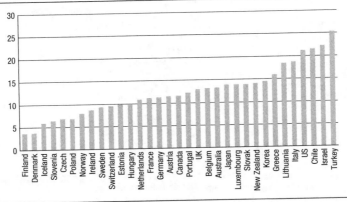

I have often been asked what is the best education system? Too often, I think, this question is answered simply by looking at the top country in the most recent international education league table. The quality of an education system depends on many more variables than students' test scores measured at one point of their schooling. In this chapter, education system "performance" is defined by the quality of learning outcomes, equity of education outcomes, and cost efficiency of education. All these dimensions need to be taken into account when answering that question above. There are other outcomes of schooling that can influence the overall quality of education in any given country. For example, student well-being, sense of belonging to school, engagement in learning, and happiness have lately become part of evaluating education systems' performance (UNICEF, 2020). Figure 2.16 shows how students' life satisfaction and their academic achievement were related in some OECD countries in 2018.

Life satisfaction measured in PISA is defined as an overall perception that an individual makes using her or his own criteria about the quality of life (OECD, 2019d). On average in the OECD countries two of three 15-year-old students reported being satisfied with their lives. In Finland, 43% of students said that they are very satisfied with their lives and just 10% were those who were not satisfied. Figure 2.16 shows that if life satisfaction is seen as happiness (there is a strong correlation between these two), then Finland is the only OECD country with happy high-achieving students as measured by PISA in 2018.

Figure 2.16. Students' Life Satisfaction and Academic Achievement in Some OECD Countries in 2018

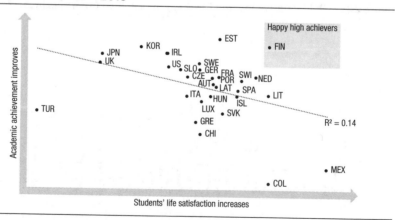

THE PERILS OF PISA

Since its inauguration in 2000, PISA has had a huge impact on global education reforms, as well as national education policies in the participating countries. It has become a significant pretext for educational development in Asia, Europe, and North America, and is gaining interest in the rest of the world. Large-scale education reforms have been initiated (in the United States, England, New Zealand, Germany, Korea, Japan, Australia, and Poland), new national institutions and agencies have been created, and thousands of delegations have visited well-performing education jurisdictions, including Finland, Estonia, Alberta, Ontario, Singapore, and Korea, to discover the "secrets" of good education. In most of almost 80 participating education systems or regions, PISA is a significant source of education policy development.

Perhaps it is surprising that Finnish educators are not as excited by OECD's PISA as foreigners would expect. Many Finnish teachers and school principals think that PISA measures only a narrow band of the spectrum of school learning and doesn't say anything about how children learn nonacademic competences that are often better predictors of success in life and further studies than what is included in PISA. There are also Finns who see that PISA is promoting the transmission of educational policies and "best practices" that are not transferable from one place to another. This will, they maintain, lead to a simplistic view of educational change and improvement. Like in sports, too strong an emphasis on international comparisons (or competitions) may lead to unethical means of temporarily boosting performance just to get a better position in the results tables. A good school system and high educational performance are much more than just measured academic scores. Some teachers in Finland are afraid that the current movement, which judges the quality of education systems by using academic units of measurement only, will eventually lead to narrowing curriculum and the dominance of the measured subjects at the expense of social studies, arts, sports, music, and whole-child development.

There is, indeed, an increasing debate about what these international tests really measure and whether PISA alone can be used to judge the quality of education systems. Some critics' and defending proponents' arguments are available in the educational literature (Adams, 2003; Bautier & Rayon, 2007; Bracey, 2005; Dohn, 2007; Engle & Rutkowski, 2020a; Fischman et al., 2019; Goldstein, 2004; Kreiner & Christensen, 2013; Mortimore, 2009; Prais, 2003, 2004; Riley & Torrance, 2003; Schleicher,

2007; Sellar et al., 2017). Many commentators on PISA, most of whom are internationally recognized scholars, have insisted that politicians and the public at large (including media) must understand better what PISA can and cannot do. Among them is David Spieghalter (2013) of the University of Cambridge, who wrote in the *Guardian*, "If PISA measures anything, it is the ability to do PISA tests. Aligning policy along a single performance indicator can be damaging. We need to look at the whole picture." Yong Zhao of the University of Kansas has argued that while the East Asian systems may enjoy being at the top of PISA tests, they are not happy at all with the outcomes of their education. "They have recognized," Zhao writes in his blog post, "the damages of their education for a long time and have taken actions to reform their systems." In his book *Who's Afraid of the Big Bad Dragon?*, Zhao (2014) offers a comprehensive summary of the most recent critique of PISA and concludes that the core of Chinese education, including Shanghai's high PISA scores, are the three basics: "Chinese families' high expectation, hard work and diligence, and the examination system" (2014, p. 187). Howard Gardner (2010) of Harvard University wrote in his commentary titled "The Ministers' Misconception" following the 2009 PISA results: "I am constantly surprised at the persistence, in ministerial talk and writing, of allegiance to the 'transmission theory' of education . . . and the notion that the best questions have a single correct answer and a resulting suspicion of multiple plausible answers, productive errors and creative leaps." Furthermore, Sam Sellar and Bob Lingard (2013) argue that "PISA, and the OECD's education work more broadly, has facilitated new *epistemological* and *infrastructural* modes of global governance for the OECD in education." In *Global Education Race: Taking the measure of PISA and international testing*, Sam Sellar and his colleagues provide an important and balanced description of what international students assessments like PISA can and can't do (Sellar et al., 2017). In the foreword for that book, David Berliner and I offer further ideas to be considered when the relevance, trustworthiness, and usefulness of PISA are debated (Berliner & Sahlberg, 2017).

First, we argue that PISA attempts to predict the quality of the workforce and the knowledge and skills required in the future economies from the test scores of 15-year-old students in school. The problem is to predict something as uncertain and complex as economic competitiveness and a nations' economic performance over time. The global pandemic in 2020 is a good example of how quickly and unexpectedly many of these predictions can collapse. Another notion using data from PISA and from global economic competitiveness indexes is that there is only a weak positive association between national economic performance and student achievement internationally.

Second, we argue that the scores on PISA assessments are much less a function of the schools that students go to and much more explained by the social conditions of students' schools and communities. This means that PISA results are more strongly linked to the social conditions and economic circumstances that affect the children than they are to the nation's education system or its schools.

Third, PISA has accelerated the shift to "back-to-basics" in school curricula, which means giving priority to reading, mathematical, and scientific literacies before other subjects or topics in teaching and learning. We argue that there are many other important things that children need to learn to be "well educated" and to succeed in life. It is unfortunate that in the United States, for example, civics, arts, music, and physical activity have been the victims of these curricular transitions in schools that are more caused by wrong-headed accountability policies and faith in high-stakes standardized testing than international assessments.

PISA has affected other national education systems in similar ways (Fischman et al., 2019). All things considered, it is important to be aware of these and other possible flaws of PISA and other large-scale international student assessments before making any conclusions based on the findings in these assessments. Closer analysis of the data from 2018 PISA (OECD, 2019a), for example, reveals that two of three students in OECD countries did not try their best on the PISA tests, as mentioned earlier in this chapter. This figure was 63% in the United States, 70% in Finland, 73% in Australia, and 79% in Canada, respectively. Such a high proportion of students who may not have made their full effort in taking the PISA test has potentially huge implications for the validity of international comparisons of students' learning in reading literacy, mathematics, and science. Indeed, it may be that students' lack of motivation to do their best in PISA tests explains more of the country's overall measured performance than many of us think.

Another common and rather serious myth about the power of PISA is the positive link between improved PISA test scores and the nation's economic growth. The logic behind this belief is that students' skills measured by PISA predict and help to improve the workforce's skills in the future that, in turn, contributes to the future economic growth. In the OECD (2010) report "The High Cost of Low Educational Performance— The Long-Run Impacts of Improving PISA Outcomes" in 2010, the organization claims that a targeted education reform agenda that would aim at a 25-point increase in PISA scores would add 30% to the nation's GDP by the end of this century. Although these kinds of optimistic arguments about how knowledge capital can boost economic growth have been shown to be wrong by several studies (Komatsu & Rappleye, 2017, 2020; Ramirez et al., 2006), the same arguments seem to prevail over and again also in the strategies of the World Bank, the European Union, and a number of neoliberal think tanks. In 2019, the European Commission hired Eric Hanushek from the Hoover Institute (Stanford University) and Ludger Woessmann from the Centre for Economics of Education (University of Munich) to advise European countries about their future education system reforms. The report titled "The Economic Benefits of Improving Educational Achievement in the European Union: An Update and Extension" (Hanushek & Woessmann, 2019) repeats the same claim the OECD made in its 2010 report mentioned above: By improving PISA scores, the member states could expect significant gains in their national economies. Not only that these promises are based on flawed economic analysis and possibly incorrect measures of students' skills, but they also can be dangerous for those governments who take them to heart. For example, prime ministers of Australia and Denmark went on, encouraged by these false promises, to set their national education goals by expecting their countries should be on the top 5 in PISA in the early 2020s. Sam Sellar and colleagues also warn the education system leaders not to fall into the global education race trap. There are successful education systems in Europe, like the Nordic countries, that have different education values and who define the purpose of schooling more broadly than the human capital advocates and some intergovernmental organizations mentioned above. Komatsu and Rappleye (2020) who have criticized the OECD and the World Bank for building their advice to the governments on flawed logic were surprised that the European Commission has turned to Hanushek and Woessmann, paying them hefty consultancy fees to write policy recommendations for Europe. They wondered: "Why does the EC Directorate for Education, Youth, Sport, and Culture need to turn to American think tanks to generate new policy ideas?" Indeed, there are much more interesting alternatives and research-based solutions around Europe than the economic models imported from a foreign continent that have proven to fit poorly to different European social, economic, and cultural landscapes.

There is also growing interest to investigate cost benefits of PISA and other large-scale student assessments. Surprisingly little is known about how much the governments actually pay to participate in OECD's PISA. In the article "Pay to Play: What Does PISA Participation Cost in the

US?" Laura Engel and David Rutkowski (2020) show that the annual fee paid to the OECD for PISA by the U.S. government is about US$1 million. Then there is about US$7 million cost line in the federal budget for the implementation of PISA. Perhaps the most puzzling finding that Engle and Rutkowski (2019) made in their investigation is that in the United States, schools and students are paid money to take part in the PISA test. Moreover, they discovered that even when offered money, many schools are not interested in having more testing of their students than they already do. Many schools, Engel and Rutkowski tell, declined the offer even when the fee to students and schools was doubled or tripled. They conclude, "This is a huge threat to the validity of comparing results between countries that pay their students and countries that do not." In another OECD country, students were served pizza and coke at school after successfully completing the 90-minute PISA test. When this bonus was discontinued after the 2008 financing crisis, the students swiftly responded: "No pizza, no PISA." And indeed, the country's PISA scores went to hell in a handbasket.

Are students in Finland paid to sit through the PISA tests? No, they are not. And as the OECD's data from 2018 PISA show (OECD, 2019a), most of them take the test rather frivolously.

These observations are good reminders that PISA is a good servant but a bad master. Even if it may be at the moment the best international assessment for comparing school systems, it nevertheless measures the best of the past. The global COVID-19 pandemic in 2020 has raised new questions about the kinds of competences young people need in the near future as the societies and economies come out of that crisis changed and financially crippled. Furthermore, there are many who are afraid that PISA, like many other social indicators, verifies Campbell's Law. Campbell's Law states that "the more any quantitative social indicator is used for social decision-making, the more subject it will be to corruption pressures and the more apt it will be to distort and corrupt the social processes it is intended to monitor" (Campbell, 1976, p. 49). OECD's own analysis shows how PISA has become an increasingly high-stakes social indicator for national policies and their implementation in several countries (Breakspear, 2012).

Many Finns—myself included—would like to see much lower stakes for these international student assessments and a much better understanding of what these tests are about among national policymakers. Surprisingly, Finnish educators and many authorities have been careful with making too many conclusions about education systems based on the international education league tables. I offer the following lessons from the Finnish experience:

- *The quality of education systems or their schools cannot be determined by international standardized test scores.* Since the beginning, Finnish scholars, authorities, and practitioners have maintained that an education system's success must include many other indicators than test scores in some academic subjects. For example, the purpose of school education in Finland is defined by social, cultural, and personal development, not just by economic or other instrumental rationales.
- *National education policies and reforms shouldn't be driven by international student assessments and hegemony of intergovernmental organizations.* Finland and other high-performing education systems rely first and foremost on their own data and research in determining the directions in educational development. PISA and other international data are used to verify the validity of these directions.
- *The national goal setting in education cannot be done by aiming at certain positions in PISA league tables or gains in PISA test score points.* Finland has never set any educational strategic goals using global learning metrics or wished to improve PISA scores even when its place in PISA comparisons has been declining. Finnish educators understand that gains or losses in standardized measures like PISA can happen for a range of reasons—many of them have only a little to do with actual quality of teaching and learning.

In this chapter and those that follow, I have used data from OECD's databases to illustrate some characteristics of Finnish education compared to other OECD countries. I would, therefore, urge readers to be mindful with possible limitations that these data may have. Correlations presented don't mean that there are causal links between these variables. Some data that are used in this book come from respondents' (teachers and students) self-reporting and opinions. Flaws in international student assessment data should also be noted here, especially when measured student learning outcomes are used as a variable in these correlations (e.g., Figures 2.4, 2.5, 2.8, 2.12, 2.15, and 5.1). Those interested in understanding in detail about how the data was collected and analyzed can find answers to these questions in the technical reports of the respective authorities.

CHAPTER 3

The Finnish Advantage

The Teachers

You have two ears and one mouth—use them in that same proportion.

—My grandmother's advice to me for being a good teacher

Many factors have contributed to Finland's educational system's development from mediocre to one of the world's leading systems, such as its 9-year comprehensive school (*peruskoulu*) for all children, whole-child focused curriculum and pedagogy, systematic care for students with diverse special needs, and trust in schools to find the best ways how to teach all children well. However, research and experience suggest that one factor is a necessary condition for all these mentioned success factors: the daily contributions of excellent teachers.

This chapter examines the central role that Finnish teachers play and describes how teacher education and a systematic focus on teacher professionalism are making major contributions to transforming Finland's educational system into a global subject of interest and an object of study. This chapter suggests, however, that it is not enough to improve teacher education or to have "the best and the brightest" teaching in schools. The Finnish experience shows that it is more important to ensure that teachers' work in schools is based on professional dignity, social respect, and collegiality so that they can fulfill their intention of selecting teaching as a lifetime career, together with their like-minded peers. Teachers' work should strike a balance between classroom teaching and collaboration with other professionals in school, as this chapter argues. This is the best way to create an image of teaching among young people that will attract young, talented professionals to choose teaching as their career. Before describing current principles and policies related to Finnish teachers and teacher education, it is useful to review some relevant cultural aspects of the teaching profession in Finland.

THE CULTURE OF TEACHING

Education has always been an integral part of Finnish culture and society. Although access to 6-year basic education became a legal obligation and right for all as far back as 1922, Finns have understood that without becoming literate and possessing broad general knowledge, it would be difficult to fulfill their lifetime aspirations. Before formal public schooling began to spread during the 1860s, cultivating public literacy was the responsibility of priests and other religious brethren in Finland as early as the 17th century. Catechist schools offered religious-oriented initial literacy education in Sunday schools and itinerant schools within villages and in remote parts of Finland. By tradition, the ability to read and write was required for legal marriage by the church for both women and men. Becoming literate, therefore, marked an individual's entry into adulthood and citizenship, with its associated duties and rights. Teachers gradually assumed these responsibilities as the Finnish public school system began to expand in the early 20th century. Primarily due to their high social standing, teachers enjoyed great respect and also uncontested trust in Finland. Indeed, Finns continue to regard teaching as a noble, prestigious profession—akin to medicine, law, or economics—driven mainly by moral purpose, rather than by material interest, careers, or rewards.

Until the 1960s, the level of Finnish educational attainment remained rather low, as Figure 2.1 showed. For example, in 1952, when Finland hosted the Summer Olympics, 9 out of 10 adult Finns had completed only 7 to 9 years of basic education. A university degree was regarded as an exceptional attainment at that time in Finland (Sahlberg, 2010a, 2015a). The Finnish educational level was close to that of Malaysia or Peru, and lagged significantly behind Scandinavian neighbors Denmark, Norway, and Sweden. In the 1960s, elementary school teachers were still prepared in 2- or 3-year teacher education seminars, not by academic institutions but rather by units that offered shorter, practical training in teaching. One graduate of a teacher preparation seminar in Oulu in the late 1950s, Martti Ahtisaari went from being a primary school teacher, to being an international diplomat, to being the president of Finland (1994–2000), and is now a Nobel Peace Prize laureate and praised global peacemaker. Today, when celebrating its educational achievements, Finland publicly recognizes the value of its teachers and implicitly trusts their professional insights and judgments regarding schooling. Stated quite plainly, without excellent teachers and a modern teacher education system, Finland's current international educational achievement would have been impossible.

The Finnish education system is distinctly different from public education in the United States, Canada, Australia, or England. Some differences are closely related to the work of teachers. For example, the Finnish education system lacks rigorous school inspection, and it does not employ external high-stakes standardized testing to inform the public about school performance or teacher effectiveness. Teachers also have more professional autonomy to create their own school-based work plan and curriculum. All education in Finland is publicly financed from preschool to universities, including teacher education in Finland's research universities.

Finnish teacher education today is fully congruent with these characteristics of educational policy in Finland. Five categories of teachers exist:

1. *Kindergarten teachers* work in early childhood education and care and are also licensed to teach preschool children.
2. *Primary school teachers* teach in grades 1 to 6 in 9-year comprehensive schools. They normally are assigned to one grade and teach several subjects.
3. *Subject teachers* teach particular subjects in the upper grades of basic school (typically grades 7 to 9) and in general upper-secondary school, including vocational schools. Subject teachers may teach one to three subjects—for example, mathematics, physics, and chemistry.
4. *Special education teachers* work with individuals and student groups with special needs in primary schools and the upper grades of comprehensive schools.
5. *Vocational education teachers* teach in upper-secondary vocational schools. They must possess at least 3 years of classroom experience in their own teaching field before they can be admitted to a vocational teacher preparation program.

In addition to these five teacher categories, teachers in adult education institutions are required to have similar pedagogical knowledge and skills. This chapter focuses on the education of primary and subject teachers in the K–12 part of the Finnish educational system (i.e., preprimary to upper-secondary school), which constitutes about two thirds of all teacher education students.

Teaching as a profession is closely tied to sustaining Finnish national culture and building an open and multicultural society. Indeed, one purpose of formal schooling is to transfer cultural heritage, values, and aspirations from one generation to another. Teachers are, according to their own opinions, essential players in building the Finnish welfare society. As in countries around the world, teachers in Finland have served as critical transmitters of culture. Through the centuries, Finland has struggled for its national identity, mother tongue, and its own values, first, during 6 centuries under the Kingdom of Sweden; next for more than a century under the Russian Empire; and then for another century as a newly independent nation positioned between its former patrons and the powers of globalization. There is no doubt that this history left a deep mark on Finns and their desire for personal development through education, reading, and self-improvement. Literacy is the backbone of Finnish culture, and reading for pleasure has become an integral part of the cultural DNA of all Finns.

It is no wonder, then, that teachers and teaching are highly regarded in Finland. The Finnish media regularly report results of opinion polls that document favorite professions among general upper-secondary school graduates. Surprisingly, teaching is consistently rated as one of the most admired professions, ahead of medical doctors, architects, and lawyers, typically thought to be dream professions (Liiten, 2004). Teaching is congruent with the core social values of Finns, which include social justice, caring for others, and happiness, as reported by the National Youth Survey (2010). Teaching is also regarded as an independent high profession that enjoys public respect and praise. It is particularly popular among young women—more than 80% of those accepted for study in primary teacher education programs are female, and 77% of all teachers and principals in basic schools (K–9) are women (Opetushallitus, 2017).

In a national opinion survey, about 1,300 adult Finns (ages 15 to 74) were asked if their spouse's (or partner's) profession had influenced their decision to commit to a relationship with them (Kangasniemi, 2008). Interviewees were asked to select 5 professions from a list of 30 that they would prefer for a selected partner or spouse. The responses were rather surprising. Finnish males viewed a teacher as the most desirable spouse, rated just ahead of a nurse, medical doctor, or architect. Women, in turn, identified only a medical doctor and a veterinarian ahead of a teacher as a desirable profession for their ideal husband. In the entire sample, 35% rated teacher as among the top five preferred professions for their ideal spouse. Apparently, only medical doctors are more sought after in Finnish mating markets than teachers. This clearly documents

BOX 3.1: WHY DO I WANT TO BE A TEACHER?

Becoming a teacher was easy for me. Actually, it was not a choice at all, but rather a process that grew from a childhood dream into a realistic goal as an adult. I have many educators in my family, and teaching is in my blood. My parents have encouraged me to take this direction. They helped me find summer jobs and hobbies where I had a chance to work with children. I always found those jobs rewarding, fun, and morally fulfilling. It was that fun aspect of working with children that influenced me when I graduated high school and moved on in my career.

During my part-time teaching in school and also currently in teacher education in the university, the rosy picture of teaching has from time to time been tarnished, but every time shines again. Now, when I am about to graduate and get my master's degree to teach in primary school, I have started to think about what it is to be a teacher. Why do I do this? First is the internal drive to help people discover their strengths and talents, but also to realize their weaknesses and inadequacies. I want to be a teacher because I want to make a difference to children's lives and to this country. My work with children has always been based on love and care, being gentle, and creating personal relations with those with whom I work. I think this is the only way I will attain fulfillment in my life.

But I also understand that in my work, I will face huge responsibility for a modest salary and heavy workload. I also know that shrinking financial resources for schools will continue and will influence my work in school. In Helsinki, the social problems that children increasingly face in their lives will also be part of my work in the classroom. I need to be able to observe diverse individuals and offer help in situations for which I am probably not yet prepared. I accept that my work is not only teaching the things I like but also working out conflict situations, working with colleagues who do not necessarily think the same way I do, and collaborating with different parents in educating their children. Without a doubt, I will continue to ask myself whether this work is really worth all that.

The well-known Finnish educator Matti Koskenniemi used the term "pedagogical love," which is also a cornerstone of my own theory of action as a teacher. Teaching is, perhaps more than any other job, a profession that you can successfully do only if you put your heart and personality into play. Each teacher has her own style and philosophy of teaching. There may be many motives for becoming a teacher. My own is that I want to do good for other people, to care about and love them. I do love them and thus I will be a teacher.

—Veera Salonen, Primary School Teacher, Helsinki

both the high professional and social status that teachers have attained in Finland—both in and out of schools.

BECOMING A TEACHER

Due to the popularity of teaching and becoming a teacher, only Finland's most passionate and committed are able to realize those professional dreams. Every spring, thousands of Finnish general upper-secondary school graduates, including many of the most talented, creative, and motivated youngsters, submit their applications to departments of teacher education in eight Finnish research universities. Thus, becoming a primary school teacher in Finland is highly competitive. It is normally not enough simply to complete general upper-secondary school successfully and pass a rigorous matriculation examination with high marks (see Chapter 1). Successful teacher education candidates must also possess moral purpose for the teaching profession, positive personalities, excellent interpersonal skills, and a commitment to work as a teacher in school, as my niece tells in Box 3.1. Annually, only about 1 of every 5 to 10 applicants will be accepted to primary school teacher education master's programs depending on which university they apply to. For example, 1,600 candidates applied to the primary teacher education program at the University of Helsinki in 2020. Only 121 of them were accepted, which is 7.6% of the applicants. The University of Helsinki is the most popular study place, and therefore acceptance rates are larger in other universities. Table 3.1 shows the total applicants to all kindergarten and primary teacher education programs in all Finnish universities and the number of accepted students since 2015.

Primary school teacher education candidates are selected in two phases: First, students take a written exam in early May that is the same for all eight universities that offer teacher education programs. This exam is based on a set of scientific and professional articles that are

Table 3.1. Number of Applicants to Kindergarten and Primary Teacher Education Programs in Finnish Universities (2015–2019)

	2015	2016	2017	2018	2019
Total applicants	10,058	9,511	8,400	8,179	7,218
Accepted	1,741	1,760	1,851	2,039	2,035

Source: University of Helsinki (2020).

announced and made available to students in late March. In 2014, there were six articles to be read for the exam, and they covered a wide range of issues, such as "Development and assessment of working memory in childhood," "Equality and justice in basic education placement and selectivity," and "Change in education policy and school's position in Europe." Based on students' performance in this exam, they are then invited to the second phase of the selection process, which varies from one university to another. It is worth noting that this first-phase exam puts all candidates behind the same line: Grades or merits do not matter in getting to the second phase, only the exam mark. Therefore, those who claim that Finland recruits its teachers from the top 10% of each cohort graduate from upper-secondary school are not exactly right. Nevertheless, it is safe to say that there is careful quality control at the entry into the teaching profession in Finland. It is difficult to get into teacher education without solid knowledge, skills, and moral commitment to teach.

The purpose of the second phase is to test the candidate's personality, knowledge, and overall suitability to become a teacher. Most universities require candidates to demonstrate how they can create ideas, plan, and work with other people. All candidates will go through individual interviews that, among other things, often ask candidates to explain their reasons for choosing to become a teacher. In their final selection of successful candidates, universities may take into account the results of the first phase of the exam, grades in the Matriculation Examination, and a student's diploma, as well as his or her merits in arts, sports, and any other activities that they see as relevant to the teaching profession.

As these two selection phases suggest, access to Finnish teacher education is highly competitive. Normally, at least some prior experience in teaching or working with children is required for successful candidates. In 2014, total applications to primary school teacher education programs reached 8,400, with candidates competing for only 800 available student positions in eight Finnish universities. In 2020, these numbers were 4,900 and 900, respectively. Figure 3.1 summarizes the trend in total annual applicants between 2001 and 2020, disaggregated by gender.

Two phenomena are apparent. First, the Finnish teaching profession in primary schools continues to be an attractive career choice for a large number of young Finns. Intake of new students in Finland's universities is determined by the Ministry of Education, and higher education is also fully paid by the government. The number of accepted students in teacher education programs is carefully forecasted by the government's

Figure 3.1. Total Annual Applicants and Accepted Students to Finnish Primary School Teacher Education Programs in 2001-2020

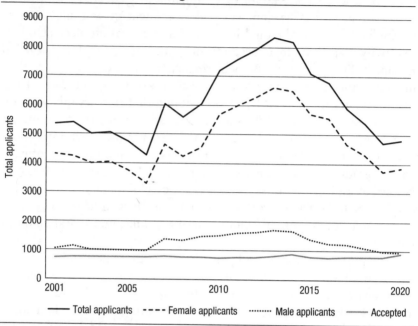

Source: VAKAVA database (www.helsinki.fi/fi/verkostot/kasvatusalan -valintayhteistyoverkosto/hakeminen/tilastoja).

labor market specialists, which means that practically all new graduates are able to find employment right after graduation. Second, there has been a notable decline in the number of applicants to primary teacher education, since 2013 when a total of 8,350 applications were recorded in all universities. In 2020, this number was just below 5,000, similar to the level before the first PISA study. In absence of research that would explain more precisely what accounts for this trend, I asked some leading teacher education experts what they think about this question. Their responses can be summarized in three possible factors.

One, interest in the teaching profession in Finland has returned back to the "normal situation" before the PISA era (Figure 3.1). The bubble in applications to primary teacher education that started in 2006 and was boosted by Finland's global fame in PISA is now gone. Teaching is still one of the most popular professions among young people, and the most recent statistics suggest that the downward trend in applications has stopped. Two, the image of the teaching profession has become more negative during the 2010s. Finnish media has been mostly reporting bad news about schools and teachers, which has made some young people think twice whether teaching is still such a good idea. Quite surprisingly, perhaps, there are no education reporters employed in Finnish media who would be experienced to write about current issues in education. And three, as a consequence of the 2008 global banking crisis that also hit Finland's economy, most municipalities had to cut their education budgets. This led to, among other things, reduced resources and teaching aids in schools. Teachers were not happy about these changes and, again, media was quick to share the bad news about worsened working conditions of schools, teachers' increased workload, and how parents were unhappy with what teachers were doing in schools.

Finland is one of the few nations able to select the most motivated and talented young people for primary school teacher education programs year after year. A similarly good situation exists in Singapore, South Korea, Canada, Ireland, and in some other countries where teacher education is based on high-quality and demanding academic study. This has created a strong moral and professional foundation for teaching in Finnish primary schools, where Finnish children spend their first 6 school years with able, knowledgeable professionals.

What Makes Teaching a Top Job?

If we use Finnish education as a reference, three conditions emerge for attracting the best young people into teaching and keeping them in schools. First, and most important, it is paramount that teachers' workplaces allow them to fulfill their moral missions. In Finland, as in many other countries, a teaching career is the result of an inner desire to work with people and to help both people and society through teaching. Second, teachers in Finland possess a strong sense of being esteemed professionals, similar to medical doctors, engineers, or lawyers. Teachers at all levels of schooling expect that they will be given the full range of professional autonomy they need to practice what they have been educated to do: to plan, teach, diagnose, execute, and evaluate. They also expect to be provided with enough time to accomplish all of these goals, both inside and outside of normal classroom duties. Third, as described in Chapter 2, teachers spend relatively less time teaching than their peers in many other countries do, as shown in Figure 2.12. For example, in the United States and Australia, teachers are engaged in teaching during the vast majority of their daily working time in school, which leaves little space for any other professional activities. The concept of the professional learning community (PLC) is often applied to the way teachers work in schools, frequently on their own time. However, in Finland, Korea, and Japan, for instance, schools are regarded as professional learning communities because of the inherent nature and balance of teachers' daily professional work.

I have talked with Finnish primary school teachers in order to understand what would prompt them to leave their chosen profession (Hammerness et al., 2017; Sahlberg, 2012, 2018). Interestingly, practically nobody cites salary as a main issue in teaching. Instead, many point out that if they were to lose their professional autonomy in schools and in classrooms, their career choice would be called into question. For example, if an outside inspector were to judge the quality of their work or if a merit-based compensation policy influenced by external measures were imposed, many would change their jobs.

Finnish teachers are particularly skeptical of using frequent standardized tests to determine students' progress in school. Many Finnish teachers have told me that if they encountered external pressure regarding standardized testing and high-stakes accountability, similar to what their peers in England or the United States face, they would seek other jobs. In short, teachers in Finland expect that they will experience professional autonomy, prestige, respect, and trust in their work.

First and foremost, the working conditions and moral professional environment are what count when young Finns decide whether they will pursue a teaching career or seek work in another field. Teacher education should be sufficiently competitive and demanding to attract talented young high school graduates. Teacher education attracts many of Finland's high school graduates because it constitutes a master's degree program and is therefore challenging enough for them. In addition, due to the high quality of Finnish students entering teacher education programs, the curricula and requirements have become very demanding, comparable to other degree programs offered by Finnish academic universities. Graduates who hold a master's degree can, without further work, apply for doctoral studies. That same degree also qualifies an individual to work in government or local administration, teach in the university, or compete with other master's degree holders in private sector employment. It has been questioned in Finland now and then whether primary school teachers necessarily need master's-level academic and research-based qualifications. However, Finnish experience suggests that if the primary school–teaching

Figure 3.2. Annual Actual Salaries of Teachers and School Heads in Public Institutions in 2017 (in Equivalent US$ Converted Using PPPs)

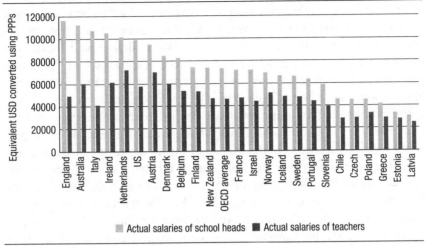

Source: OECD (2019d).

degree requirement were lowered, many potential teachers would seek studies in professional fields that would give them higher academic status and thus open more employment opportunities later in their careers. As mentioned earlier, the salary level is not the main motive to become a teacher in Finland. Teachers earn slightly more than the national average salary. The annual statutory teacher's salary in the lower-secondary school after 15 years of experience (in equivalent U.S. dollars, converted by using purchasing-power parity) in 2017 was about US$51,200, as shown in Figure 3.2. The comparable annual salary in the United States is US$55,000, and in Australia US$56,000 (OECD, 2019d).

Although making money is not the main reason for becoming a teacher, there should be a systematic way for salaries to increase. Finnish teachers climb the salary ladder as their teaching experience grows, reaching the peak after about 20 years of service. The same salary scheme is applied in all parts of the country and is determined in a national labor contract that the Trade Union of Education (OAJ) negotiates with the municipal employers' organization called KT (Local Government Employers) that promotes the interests of Finland's municipalities and joint municipal authorities on the labor market. However, there are a number of factors that affect the paycheck.

First, teachers' pay depends on the type of school (e.g., primary or upper-secondary school). Although teachers' pay in Finland is not linked to their students' achievement in any way, the salary structure is based on merit and performance. Then, basic salary includes the base pay determined in the labor contract and an addition determined locally depending on required particular skills, responsibilities, social skills, and working conditions that may vary greatly from school to school. Next, there is a personal bonus in each teacher's salary that depends on overall job performance (including feedback from parents, colleagues, and the principal), yet it is not measured by student achievement. There is also extra pay for additional hours on top of the minimum required teaching load together with other possible compensation. Three hours a week of collaboration, school improvement, or other collegial activities are included in each teacher's basic salary. Finally, teachers may receive a performance bonus awarded to their school or cluster of schools as a collective reward for especially successful work accomplished together. As a consequence, there may be variation in teachers' earnings even within the same school depending on seniority, the nature of their work, and overall performance that is normally judged by the principal.

RESEARCH-BASED TEACHER EDUCATION

Until the end of the 1970s, primary school teachers were prepared in teacher colleges or special teacher education seminars. Lower- and upper-secondary school subject teachers studied in specific subject-focused departments within Finnish universities. By the end of the 1970s, all teacher education programs became a part of academic higher education and, therefore, were only offered by universities. A master's degree became the basic qualification for teaching in Finnish schools. Simultaneously, scientific content and educational research advances began to enrich teacher education curricula. Finnish teacher education is now *academic*, meaning that it must be based on and supported by scientific knowledge and must be focused on the thinking processes and cognitive skills needed to design and conduct educational research (Hammerness et al., 2017; Jakku-Sihvonen & Niemi, 2006; Niemi, 2008). A particular principle of research-based teacher education in Finland is the systemic integration of scientific educational knowledge, didactics (or pedagogical content knowledge), and practice to enable teachers to enhance their pedagogical thinking, evidence-based decisionmaking, and

Table 3.2. Required Teacher Qualifications by Type of Finnish School

Type of School	Age of Pupils	Grades	Required Teacher Qualifications
Kindergarten	0–6		Kindergarten teacher (BA)
Preschool	6		Kindergarten teacher (BA)
			Primary school teacher (MA)
Comprehensive school (*peruskoulu*)	7–16	1–9	Comprehensive school teacher (MA)
Primary school	7–12	1–6	Primary school teacher (MA)
Lower-secondary school	13–15	7–9	Subject teacher (MA)
General upper-secondary school	16–18	10–12	Subject teacher (MA)
			Vocational teacher (BA)
Vocational upper-secondary school			Subject teacher (MA)
University	19–		Higher academic degree (MA/PhD)
Polytechnic			Higher education degree (MA/PhD)

Source: Sahlberg (2012).

engagement in the professional community of educators. Consequently, the basic requirement today for permanent employment as a teacher in all Finnish comprehensive and upper-secondary schools is the possession of a research-based master's degree, as shown in Table 3.2.

Teacher education is an important and recognized part of higher education in Finland. In many other nations, the situation is different: Teacher preparation is frequently viewed as semiprofessional training arranged outside of academic universities. In the Acts on Teacher Education in 1978–1979, the minimum requirement for permanent employment as a teacher was raised to a master's degree that includes an approved master's thesis with scholarly requirements similar to those in any other academic field. This legislative policy served as the impetus to transfer all teacher education programs from colleges to Finnish universities. The seeds were sown for believing that the teaching profession is based on scholarly research. An important side effect of this transition was the unification of the Finnish teaching cohort, which had become divided by the comprehensive school reform of the 1970s into primary school teachers and subject teachers working in lower- and upper-secondary schools.

The role of the Trade Union of Education in Finland (OAJ), established in 1973, has been both as a negotiator of the terms of teachers' employment contracts and an advocate for education (www.oaj.fi). The union represents teachers at various school levels and institutes, ranging from kindergarten teachers to instructors in vocational schools, and to school principals and lecturers in universities. More than 95% of teachers in Finland are OAJ members.

As mentioned above, all Finnish teachers must hold a master's degree. The major subject in primary school teacher education programs is *education*. In subject-focused teacher education programs, students concentrate within a particular subject—for example, mathematics or foreign languages. Subject-focused teacher candidates also study didactics, consisting of pedagogical content knowledge (subject didactics) within their own subject specialty. Today, successful completion of a master's degree—which includes a bachelor's degree—in teaching takes, in theory, 5 years, but in reality less than half of students reach that target, about two thirds of students graduate in less than 6 years, according to the Finnish Ministry of Education (Vipunen database[1]). There are no alternative ways to earn a teacher's diploma in Finland; only the university degree constitutes a license to teach. In the United States, for example, the Teach for America program admits college graduates, immerses them in pedagogy courses for several weeks over a summer, and then sends them to schools in need of teachers—where they often find classroom challenges to be exceedingly difficult. There are similar teacher certification initiatives in 53 countries within the Teach for All network in 2020, such as Teach First in the United Kingdom, New Zealand, Israel, and Norway, Teach for India, Teach for South Africa, Teach for China, and Enseña Chile, which promises to develop leadership in classrooms and communities for fixing educational inequalities in these countries. A lesson from Finland, however, suggests that a more sustainable way to ensure all children can fulfill their dreams and discover their talents is to have a more equal society overall, invest systematically in educational equity, and make teaching a high profession where there is now a need and place for unprofessional fast-track pathways to teach children in school.

Academic teacher education in Finland focuses on the balanced development of a prospective teacher's personal and professional competences. Particular attention is devoted to building pedagogical thinking skills, enabling teachers to manage instructional processes in accord with contemporary educational knowledge and practice (Hammerness et al., 2017; Toom et al., 2010; Westbury et al., 2005). In Finnish primary teacher education, this is characterized by the study of education as a main subject, composed of three thematic areas:

1. Theory of education
2. Pedagogical content knowledge
3. Subject didactics and practice

Finnish research-based teacher education programs culminate in a required master's thesis. Prospective primary school teachers normally complete their theses in the field of education. Typically, the topic of a master's thesis is focused on or is close to a student teacher's own school or classroom practice, such as mathematics teaching or learning. Subject-focused student teachers, in turn, select a thesis topic within their major subject. The level of scholarly expectations for teacher education studies is similar across all teacher preparation programs, from elementary to upper-secondary school.

Teacher education in Finland is aligned with the framework of the European Higher Education Area that is being developed under the on-going Bologna Process.[2] Currently, Finnish universities offer a two-tier degree program. First is an obligatory 3-year bachelor's degree program that qualifies students for a 2-year master's degree program that is the minimum qualification for a license to teach in Finland. These two degrees are offered in multidisciplinary programs consisting of studies in at least two subjects. Studies are quantified in terms of credit units within the European Credit Transfer and Accumulation System (ECTS) within 46 European nations. ECTS, which will become the guiding policy for the European Higher Education Area, is a student-centered system based on the student workload required to achieve program objectives.

The objectives are normally specified in terms of the learning outcomes and competencies to be acquired. ECTS is based on the assumption that 60 credits represent the workload of a full-time student over 1 academic year. The annual student workload for a full-time study program in Europe equals, in most cases, about 1,500 to 1,800 hours. Therefore, one ECTS credit represents about 25 to 30 working hours a week. Teacher education requires 180 ECTS credits for a bachelor's degree (which doesn't meet the qualifications for a teaching diploma or enable permanent employment as a teacher), followed by 120 additional ECTS credits for a master's degree.

A broad-based teacher education curriculum ensures that newly prepared Finnish teachers possess well-balanced knowledge and skills in both theory and practice. It also implies that prospective teachers develop deep professional insight into education from several perspectives, including educational psychology and sociology, curriculum theory, student assessment, special needs education, and didactics (pedagogical content knowledge) in their selected subject areas. It is noteworthy that contemporary Finnish teacher education has been strongly influenced by research and development in this field in American, Canadian, and British universities.[3] To illustrate what teachers study during their preparation program, Table 3.3 illustrates primary school teacher education topics with required credit units, as offered by the Department of Education at the University of Helsinki. All eight Finnish universities that offer teacher education have their own nationally coordinated teacher education strategies and curricula, ensuring coherence but encouraging local initiative to make the best use of each university's resources and nearby opportunities.

As a general rule, teacher education preparing teachers for the lower grades (typically, grades 1 to 6 of comprehensive schools) includes 60 ECTS credits of pedagogical studies and at least 60 additional ECTS credits for other courses in educational sciences. An integral part of these additional educational studies is a master's thesis requiring independent research, participation in research seminars, and defending of the completed educational study. The commonly assigned credit for this research work within all universities is 40 ECTS credits.

The revised teacher education curriculum in Finland requires primary school teacher candidates to complete a major in educational sciences and earn 60 ECTS credits in minor studies within subjects included in the National Framework Curriculum for Comprehensive School, which is regularly updated by the National Agency for Education and the Ministry of Education.

Most students in primary teacher education programs enter their studies with solid knowledge and skills in the range of subjects that are studied in upper-secondary school. In Finland, unlike in the United States or England, all upper-secondary school students are obliged to complete successfully a study program including up to 18 required subjects—such as physics, chemistry, philosophy, music, and at least two foreign languages in addition to two domestic languages. Normally, students accepted in Finnish primary school teacher education programs have earned higher than average grades in these subjects. For example, at the University of Helsinki, some 15% of students select mathematics as their minor subject, which earns them a license to teach mathematics as

Table 3.3. Summary of Primary Teacher Education Master's Degree Program at the University of Helsinki in 2018

Curriculum Component	Total Credits	BEd	MEd
Communication studies and orienting studies	25 cr		
Basics of Curriculum Planning	2 cr	1 cr	1 cr
Language and Communication Skills	14 cr		
Mother tongue			
Speech communication and interaction skills		*2 cr*	
Drama pedagogy		*3 cr*	
Scientific writing			3 cr
Foreign language		3 cr	
Second national language		3 cr	
Education and Social Justice	3 cr	3 cr	
Information and Communication Technology in Learning	3 cr	3 cr	
Introduction to Media Education	3 cr		3 cr
Main subject studies in education	140 cr		
Cultural Bases of Education	16 cr		
Introduction to educational sciences		3 cr	
Social, historical, and philosophical foundations of education		4 cr	
Facing specificity and multiplicity/education for diversities		6 cr	
Cultural diversity in schools			3 cr
Psychological Bases of Education	11 cr		
Introduction to educational psychology		5 cr	
Interaction and awareness of pupil		6 cr	
Pedagogical bases of education	23 cr		
Didactics		7 cr	
Theory and didactics of early childhood education		3 cr	
Evaluation and ethics of teaching and learning		3 cr	

(continued)

Table 3.3. (*continued*)

Curriculum Component	Total Credits	BEd	MEd
Curriculum theory and evaluation			3 cr
Pedagogical knowing and construction of personal practical theory			7 cr
Research Studies in Education	70 cr		
Introduction to educational research		3 cr	
Quantitative research methods		4 cr	
Qualitative research methods		3 cr	
Bachelor's thesis (incl. seminars, 4 cr)		10 cr	
Either practicing research methods (quantitative)			4 cr
or practicing research methods (qualitative)			4 cr
Method tray (two optional advanced method courses depending)			6 cr
Master's thesis			40 cr
Teaching Practice	20 cr		
Orienting practicum		3 cr	
Minor subject practicum			9 cr
Master practicum			8 cr
Minor subject studies—multidisciplinary studies and cross-curricular issues taught in comprehensive school	60 cr		
Mother Tongue and Literature Education	8 cr	8 cr	
Mathematics Education	7 cr	7 cr	
Arts and Skills Education	14 cr		
Visual arts education		3 cr	
Craft education		5 cr	
Didactics of physical education		3 cr	
Music education		3 cr	
Didactics in Humanistic Subjects	6 cr		
History education		3 cr	
either Lutheran religious education		3 cr	
or secular ethics education			3 cr

Curriculum Component	Total Credits	BEd	MEd
Didactics in Environmental and Science Subjects	12 cr		
Geography education		3 cr	
Biology education		3 cr	
Physics education		3 cr	
Chemistry education		3 cr	
Optional Courses	13 cr		
One of the following:			
Visual arts education, pedagogical orientation		4 cr	
Physical education, pedagogical orientation			4 cr
Music education, pedagogical orientation		4 cr	
Craft education, pedagogical orientation		4 cr	
One of the following:			
Visual arts education, sociocultural orientation		3 cr	
Physical education, sociocultural orientation		3 cr	
Music education, sociocultural orientation		3 cr	
Craft education, sociocultural orientation		3 cr	
One of the following:			
History education, optional studies		3 cr	
Religious education, Lutheranism, optional studies		3 cr	
Secular ethics education, optional studies		3 cr	
One of the following:			
Geography education, optional studies		3 cr	
Biology education, optional studies		3 cr	
Physics education, optional studies		3 cr	
Chemistry education, optional studies		3 cr	
Optional minor subject and optional studies	75 cr	40 cr	35 cr
Study points in the whole degree	300 cr		
1 ECTS credit = 27 hours of work			

subject teachers in grades 7 to 9 (Lavonen et al., 2007). Science education is also quite popular among primary school teacher students; each year approximately 10% take basic or advanced studies in science teaching. It is clear that primary school teachers in Finland, in general, possess strong mastery of the subjects that they teach because of their broadly based upper-secondary school studies and because primary teacher education programs build on that solid base.

Finnish subject teacher education follows the same principles as primary school teacher education but is arranged differently. There are two main pathways to becoming a subject teacher. Most students first complete a master's degree in their academic programs with one major subject, such as the Finnish language, for example, and one or two minor subjects, such as literature and drama. Students then apply to the university's Department of Education for their subject teacher education program. In pedagogical studies, the main focus is on subject-oriented teaching strategies equivalent to 60 ECTS credits and requires 1 academic year to complete. The other pathway to becoming a subject teacher is for students to apply directly to teacher education to pursue a major subject in their selected academic program. Normally, after 2 years of subject studies, students start their pedagogical studies in their university's faculty of education. The curriculum for this second pathway is identical to that of the first route, only it is scheduled differently within the bachelor's and master's tracks, typically over four academic terms, as illustrated by the program at the University of Helsinki shown in Table 3.4.

Prospective subject teachers decide to major in fields that they will be teaching, such as mathematics or music. For major subjects, advanced studies involving 90 ECTS credits are normally required. In addition, 60 ECTS credits are required in a second subject that will be taught in schools. Generally, departments of teacher education organize courses in pedagogical studies in collaboration with subject-matter departments in their universities. Each subject-matter department is also responsible for the teacher education of students seeking certification in that particular subject. Exceptions include teacher education for some subjects that are included in the National Curriculum core for basic education, such as textile work and crafts, special education, student counseling, and music, which are organized within departments of education. Teacher education for music, arts, and physical education usually occurs in separate departments or institutes within a university. It is also internationally unique that Finnish academic subject faculties—not the department of

Table 3.4. Structure of the Pedagogical Component of the Subject Teacher Education Program at the University of Helsinki in 2016

Bachelor's Level (25 European Credit Transfer and Accumulation Credits)	Master's Level (35 Credits)
FIRST TERM (18 CREDITS)	THIRD TERM (17 CREDITS)
Developmental psychology and learning (4)	Social, historical, and philosophical foundations of education (5)
Special education (4)	Evaluation and development of teaching (7)
Introduction to subject didactics (10)	Advanced teaching practice in teacher training school or field school (5)
SECOND TERM (7 CREDITS)	FOURTH TERM (12 CREDITS)
Basic teaching practice in teacher training school (7)	Research seminar (teacher as a researcher) (4)
	Final teaching practice in teacher training school or field school (8)
AS PART OF MASTER'S PROGRAM	
Research methodology (6)	

teacher education—issue master's degrees for subject teachers and thus play important roles in Finnish teacher education.

TEACHERS AS RESEARCHERS

Instruction in Finnish teacher education departments is arranged to support pedagogical principles that newly prepared teachers are expected to implement in their own classrooms. Although all university teachers have full pedagogical autonomy, every department of teacher education in Finland has a detailed and often binding strategy for improving the quality of teacher education programs. Subject-focused pedagogy and research in science education within Finnish universities, for example, are regarded as advanced by international standards (Lavonen et al., 2007). Moreover, cooperative learning, problem-based learning, reflective practice, and computer-supported education are now implemented—at least to some extent—in all Finnish universities. A Finnish higher education evaluation system that offers public recognition of and financial prizes for effective, innovative university teaching practice has served as an important driver of these positive developments.

Research-based teacher education means that the integration of educational theories, research methodologies, and practice all play important roles in Finnish teacher education programs (Box 3.2). Teacher education curricula are designed so that they constitute a systematic continuum from the foundations of educational thinking, to educational research methodologies, and then on to more advanced fields of educational sciences. Each student thereby builds an understanding of the systemic, interdisciplinary nature of educational practice. Finnish students also acquire the skills of designing, conducting, and presenting original research on practical or theoretical aspects of education. An integral element of Finnish research-based teacher education is practical training in schools—a key component of the curriculum, as documented in Tables 3.2 and 3.3.

There are, in principle, two kinds of practicum experiences within Finnish teacher education programs. A minor portion of clinical training occurs in seminars and small-group classes within a department of teacher education (part of a faculty of education), where students practice basic teaching skills with their peers. Major teaching practice experiences occur mostly within special teacher training schools governed by universities, which have curricula and practices similar to those of ordinary public schools. Students also use a network of selected field schools for practice teaching. In primary school teacher education, students devote approximately 15% of their intended study time (e.g., in the University of Jyväskylä, 40 ECTS credits) practice teaching in schools. In subject teacher education, the proportion of teaching practice in schools constitutes about one third of the curriculum.

The Finnish teacher education curriculum, as summarized in Tables 3.3 and 3.4, is designed to integrate teaching practice in theoretical and methodological studies systematically. Teaching practice is normally divided into three phases over the 5-year program: basic (orientation) practice, advanced (minor subject) practice, and final (master) practice. During each phase, students observe lessons by experienced teachers, complete practice teaching observed by supervisory teachers, and deliver independent lessons to different pupil groups, all evaluated by supervising teachers and department of teacher education professors and lecturers. Evaluations of Finnish teacher education have repeatedly identified the systematic nature of teacher education curricula as a key

BOX 3.2: Research-based Teacher Education

In my long career as a teacher educator, the most significant policy change was the requirement that all teachers must hold an academic master's degree in education or in the subject they teach in school. It launched a development chain that elevated all teachers as professionals who, among other things, are able to understand teaching holistically and improve their own work continuously. In Finland, it took more than 20 years to build common understanding among teacher educators, university professors, and practitioners about the complexity of the teaching profession. Research-based teacher education has the following three key principles:

- Teachers need a deep knowledge of the most recent advances of research in the subjects they teach. In addition, they need to be familiar with the research on how something can be taught and learned.
- Teachers must adopt a research-oriented attitude toward their work. This means learning to take an analytical and open-minded approach to their work, drawing conclusions for the development of education based on different sources of evidence coming from the recent research as well as their own critical and professional observations and experiences.
- Teacher education in itself should also be an object of study and research.

Many people ask why Finnish students perform so well in school and why many young Finns choose teaching as their career. There is no regular standardized testing, school inspection, teacher evaluation, or ranking of schools in Finland. Public education has a central role in enhancing equality and well-being in Finnish society. High-quality academic teacher education ensures readiness to work in many other areas of the Finnish labor market. Most important, in Finland teachers and schools enjoy strong public confidence. Parents trust teachers the way that they trust their dentists. Parents do not need to worry about finding a good school for their children. Many think that the nearest school in their community is good enough. I believe that because teachers—as a result of their academic education—have clear moral purpose and independent professional ethos, they are trusted. Research-based teacher education is essential in making that possible.

—Hannele Niemi, Professor emerita of Education, University of Helsinki strength and a characteristic that distinguishes Finnish teacher education from that of many other nations (Darling-Hammond, 2006; Darling-Hammond et al., 2017; Jussila & Saari, 2000; Saari & Frimodig, 2009).

The Finnish teacher education program represents a spiral sequence of theoretical knowledge, practical training, and research-oriented inquiry into teaching. Teacher education responsibilities are integrated within the activities of academic university units. At the University of Oulu, three faculties—science, humanities, and education—deliver teacher education courses for their students. They include staff (normally university lecturers and professors) who specialize in subject-oriented teaching methodologies. Their curricula are coordinated with the Faculty of Education, which is responsible for the overall organization of teacher education.

Although teacher training schools constitute the main portion of the network within which Finnish students complete their practice teaching, some ordinary municipal public schools (called municipal field schools, or MFS) also serve the same purpose. Teacher training schools where practice teaching occurs have higher professional staff requirements; supervising teachers must prove their competency to work with student teachers. Teacher training schools (but not MFS) are also expected to pursue research and development roles in teacher education in collaboration with the university's department of teacher education, and sometimes also with the academic units' teacher education staff. For example, at the University of Oulu, the Faculty of Science and the Faculty of Humanities assume teacher education roles and support appropriate staff. All teacher training schools can, therefore, introduce sample lessons and alternative curricular designs to student teachers. These schools also have teachers who are experienced in supervision, teacher professional development, and assessment strategies. There are no specific qualifications to be designated as such a teacher—it is each individual's responsibility to build the needed knowledge and skills required for employment in a teacher training school.

PROFESSIONAL DEVELOPMENT

Because teaching is a much-desired profession in Finland, most new graduates seek immediate school employment. During their studies, students develop their impressions of what school life from a teacher's viewpoint may be like. However, graduates do not necessarily acquire experience participating in a community of educators, assuming full responsibility for a classroom of students, or interacting with parents. All these considerations are part of the curriculum, but many licensed graduates discover that there is a chasm between lecture-hall idealism and school reality.

Induction of a new teacher into a first classroom assignment is relatively less developed in Finland than in the United States or England, although research and development work on teacher induction is rather active (Jokinen & Välijärvi, 2006; OECD, 2014b; OECD, 2019f). It is up to each school and municipality governing these schools to incorporate new teachers' needs for induction or mentoring into their teaching responsibilities. Thus, practices regarding Finnish teacher induction are, admittedly, diverse. Some schools, as part of their mission, have adopted advanced procedures and support systems for new staff, whereas other schools merely bid new teachers welcome and show them to their classrooms. In some schools, induction is a well-defined responsibility of school principals or deputy principals, while in other schools induction responsibilities may be assigned to experienced classroom teachers. Teacher induction is an area that requires further development in Finland.

It is recognized that professional development and in-service programs for teachers are not aligned with initial teacher education and often lack focus on essential areas of teaching and school development. Perhaps the main criticism deals with weak coordination between initial academic teacher education and the continuing professional development of teachers (Hammerness et al., 2017; Ministry of Education, 2009). Municipalities, as the overseers of primary and lower- and upper-secondary schools, are responsible for providing teachers with opportunities for professional development or in-service training, based on their needs. According to the employment contract, there are 3 mandatory professional development days annually in which all teachers must take part that are offered by the local education authorities. It is up to individual teachers or school principals to decide how much time beyond those 3 days and what type of professional development is needed, and whether such interventions, in fact, can be funded.

In Finland, a significant disparity exists among municipalities' and schools' ability to finance professional development for teachers. The main reason for this situation is the way that education is financed. The central government has only a limited influence on budgetary decisions made by municipalities or schools. Therefore, some schools receive significantly more allocations for professional development and school improvement than do others, particularly during times of economic downturn when professional development budgets are often the first to vanish.

Governance of Finnish education is inconsistent throughout the nation. Some schools experience relatively high autonomy over their operations and budgeting. Others do not. Therefore, Finnish teacher professional development appears in many forms. Ideally, the school is the prime decisionmaker regarding the design and delivery of professional development. Schools may also be motivated to lower operating expenses, such as for textbooks, heating, and maintenance, and may divert those funds to teacher development priorities. However, some Finnish municipalities still organize professional learning programs uniformly for all teachers and allow little latitude for individual schools to decide what would be more beneficial for them. According to OECD's TALIS 2013, four of five Finnish lower-secondary teachers had engaged in professional development during the past 12 months; that means that 20% of teachers in Finnish schools do so only occasionally. The next TALIS in 2018, which included 31 OECD countries (Figure 3.3), found out that 93% of lower-secondary school teachers in Finland participated in professional development 12 months prior to the survey (OECD, 2019f). In this comparison Finland is behind most other OECD countries, and this is considered one area that requires urgent improvement in Finland.

The Finnish state budget allocates normally about 30–40 million U.S. dollars each year to the professional development of teachers and school principals through various forms of university courses and professional learning activities. The main purpose of this investment is to ensure equal access to further training, particularly for teachers who work in more disadvantaged schools. This professional development support is contracted to service providers on a competitive basis. The government initially determines the focus of the desired training, based on current national educational development needs. Local education authorities that own the schools and also employ all the teachers make an investment of similar scale in the professional development of their education personnel each year.

Finnish teachers possessing a master's degree have the right to engage in doctoral studies to supplement their normal professional development opportunities. Primary school teachers can easily begin their further studies in the faculty of education; their PhD dissertations will then focus on a selected topic in the educational sciences. Many primary

Figure 3.3. Percentage of Lower-Secondary School Teachers Who Participated in Professional Development Activities in 2018

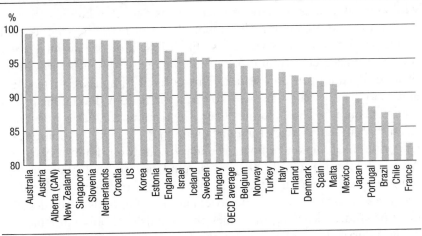

Source: OECD (2019f).

school teachers take advantage of this opportunity, often while simultaneously teaching in schools. Doctoral studies in education for subject teachers who have their previous degrees in some other academic field require more work. These teachers must first complete advanced studies in the educational sciences because the main subject requires a shift from a student's initial academic major—for example, chemistry—into education, so that students are qualified to complete their research in education.

TEACHERS ARE LEADERS

Teaching is commonly viewed in Finland as a demanding profession that requires superior academic qualifications, even for teachers of very young students. Since teacher education became part of academic university studies in the 1970s, Finnish teachers' identity and sense of belonging to a highly regarded profession have gradually increased. During the course of Finland's education reforms, as explained in Chapter 1, teachers have demanded more autonomy and responsibility for curriculum planning and student assessment. The professional context of teaching in Finland differs significantly from that in other countries when it comes to the way teachers experience their work. The professionally respectful environment that teachers experience in Finland is an important factor not only for teacher education policies but also for explaining why so many young Finns regard teaching as a much-admired career.

Curriculum planning is the responsibility of teachers, schools, and municipalities, not the state. Most Finnish schools today have their own customized curriculum that is coordinated with and approved by their local education authorities. This correctly implies that teachers and school principals have key roles in curriculum development and school planning. The National Core Curriculum for Basic Education (Finnish National Agency for Education, 2016) and the National Core Curriculum for General Upper Secondary Education (Finnish National Agency for Education, 2020) provide guidance and necessary regulations that each school must keep in mind in its curriculum development activities. However, there are no strict national standards for or descriptions of student learning outcomes that Finnish schools must include in their curriculum, as is true in the United States, Great Britain, or Canada, for example. That is why Finnish curriculum planning and the curricula that result from it can vary from school to school. The teachers' key role in pedagogical decisionmaking clearly requires teacher education to install in all prospective teachers well-developed knowledge and skills related to curriculum development, student assessment theory and practice, and teacher leadership. Moreover, it has shifted the focus of Finnish teacher professional development from fragmented in-service training toward more systemic school improvement that builds better ethical and theoretical grounding for effective teaching.

Another important teacher responsibility is student assessment. As mentioned earlier, Finnish schools do not employ census-based standardized tests to determine their progress or success. There are four primary reasons for this:

1. Education policy in Finland gives high priority to personalized learning and creative teaching as important components of schooling. Therefore, students' progress in school is primarily judged against their respective characteristics and abilities, rather than by a reliance on uniform standards and statistical indicators.

2. Education developers insist that curriculum, teaching, and learning are priority components in education that should necessarily drive teachers' thinking and school practice, rather than focusing on assessment and testing, as is the case in some

other education systems. Student assessment in Finnish schools is embedded in teaching and learning processes and is thereby used to improve both teachers' and students' work in school.

3. Determining students' personal and cognitive progress is regarded as a responsibility of the school, not of external assessments or assessors. Most Finnish schools acknowledge some shortcomings, such as comparability or consistency, when teachers do all student assessments and grading. At the same time, there is wide acknowledgment that the problems that are often associated with external standardized testing can be even more troublesome. These problems, according to teachers, include a narrowing curriculum, teaching to the test, and unhealthy competition among schools and teachers. Classroom assessment and school-based evaluation are therefore important and valued components of Finnish teacher education curricula and professional development.

4. The Finnish national strategy for student assessment is based on the principle of diversified evidence in which test-based performance data are just one part of the whole. Data regarding student achievement in various subjects are collected using sample-based standardized tests and thematic reviews. Municipalities are autonomously designing their quality assurance practices according to their needs and aspirations.

The only external standardized assessment of student learning is the National Matriculation Examination that students take at the end of upper-secondary school when they are 18 or 19 years old, as described in Chapter 1. It has exerted, many Finnish education specialists argue, a discernible effect on curriculum and teaching in general upper-secondary school.[4]

Although Finnish teachers' work consists primarily of classroom teaching, many of their duties are performed outside of class. Formally, teachers' working time in Finland consists of classroom teaching, preparation (in the case of lab-based subjects such as biology), and 3 hours weekly of planning and development work with colleagues. Unlike in many other nations, Finnish teachers do not need to be present at school if they do not have classes or if the school principal has not requested that they perform other duties.

Schools in Finland are autonomous in terms of scheduling their work, but they are required to have a 15-minute recess within every hour of instruction, which is often a welcome break for teachers as well.

Recently, schools have sought alternative arrangements to allow more time for teachers to collaborate—for example, combining lessons or classes into longer periods or larger groups and thereby providing more discretionary time during the school day for teachers.

Figure 3.4 reveals notable differences in the average net teaching hours of primary, lower-secondary, and upper-secondary teachers between Finland and some other OECD countries in 2018. Even if teaching time is adjusted to annual school days, it appears that teachers in Finland spend less time each day in teaching—about 100 hours less each year in any level of schooling compared to OECD countries on average, or an hour less daily in primary school compared to their peers in the United States.

A question arises: How do teachers in Finland spend their days at school? An important—and still voluntary—part of Finnish teachers' work is devoted to school improvement and work with the community. It is worth recalling that Finnish schools are responsible for the design and continuous development of their school curriculum. Students receive their grades from teachers whose duties include designing and conducting appropriate assessments and tests to monitor their students' progress in school. Finnish teachers have accepted curriculum development, experimentation with teaching methods, responsibility to engage in student welfare support, and collaboration with parents as important aspects of their work outside of classrooms. These are also some of the most essential elements of teacher leadership in Finnish schools.

Foreign visitors to Finnish schools often ask how teacher effectiveness is determined. They are also curious to know how administrators know which are effective teachers and where bad teachers are. The overall answer is simple: There are no formal teacher evaluation measures in Finland. Because there are no census-based standardized test data about student achievement available, it is not possible to compare school performance or teacher effectiveness in the same ways that it is measured in the United States or Australia. The only exception is the use of matriculation examination results by certain media every spring to rank Finnish high schools according to their students' grades on the exams. That annual early summer news rarely gets any significant attention from parents or schools.

The questions of teacher effectiveness or the consequences of being an ineffective teacher are not relevant in Finland. As described earlier, teachers have time to work together during the school day and to understand how their colleagues teach. This is an important condition for reflecting on teachers' own teaching and also for building a sense of professional leadership and shared accountability between teachers. The

Figure 3.4. Average Net Teaching Time in Hours per School Year in Some OECD Countries in 2018

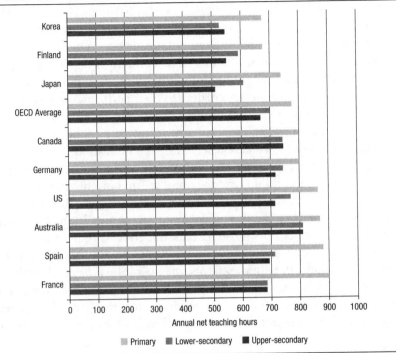

Annual net teaching hours

■ Primary ■ Lower-secondary ■ Upper-secondary

Source: OECD (2020); data for the United States are from Abrams (2015).

school inspection system that previously provided external feedback and evaluation of how teachers taught and schools operated was abolished in the early 1990s. Today, school principals, aided by their own experience as teachers, are able to help their teachers recognize strengths and areas of work that need improvement. The basic assumption in Finnish schools is that teachers, by default, are well-educated professionals and are doing their best in schools. In real professional learning communities, teachers trust one another, communicate frequently about teaching and learning, and rely on their principals' guidance and leadership.

Internationally, identifying teacher effectiveness has become a new trend in finding ways to improve education. Novel statistical techniques, called value-added modeling (VAM), are intended to resolve the problem of socioeconomic and other differences by adjusting for students' prior achievement and demographic characteristics. Although VAM approaches are fairer comparisons of teachers than judgments of their students' test scores, closer analysis of VAM results has led researchers to doubt whether this methodology can identify good or bad teachers as well as its designers claim (Baker et al., 2010). It is safe to believe that such quantitative measures are rarely the sole or even the primary factor when it comes to identifying a good or poor teacher. Even some management experts from the business world warn against using such measures for making salary or bonus decisions, as has been done, for example, in paying teachers according to their performance merits (using student test scores as the main source of evidence). "In both the United States and Great Britain," reports a review of the problems with using student test scores to evaluate teachers by the Education Policy Institute, "governments have attempted to rank cardiac surgeons by their patients' survival rates, only to find that they had created incentives for surgeons to turn away the sickest patients" (Baker et al., 2010, p. 7). Paying teachers based on their students' standardized test scores is an alien idea in Finland. Authorities and most parents understand that caring for and educating children is too complex a process to be measured by quantitative metrics alone. In Finnish schools, the operational principle is that the quality of teaching and of the school is defined through the mutual interaction between the school and the students, together with their parents. These are also the essential ingredients of teacher leadership in Finland.

SCHOOL LEADERS ARE TEACHERS

Regardless of how well teachers are trained in any education system, consistent high educational performance requires good professional leadership at the school level. Some countries allow their schools to be led by noneducators, hoping that business-style management will raise efficiency and improve performance. Similarly, local education authorities and administrators are sometimes persons without experience in teaching or leading schools. In Finland, educational leadership in municipal education offices is without exception in the hands of professional educators who have experience in working in the field of education. This is an important factor in enhancing communication and building trust between schools and educational administration.

In Finland, school principals have to be qualified to teach in the schools that they lead, and they must have strong track records as teachers. They also must have successfully completed academic studies on educational administration and leadership offered by universities in Finland.

This means that a corporate CEO or a retired military chief without these merits would not be qualified to lead a school in Finland. Without an exception the school principal is an experienced teacher with proven leadership competencies and a suitable personality. In many schools, principals also have a small number of classes that they teach themselves each week. According to TALIS 2018, three out of four lower-secondary school principals in Finland have teaching duties in school, compared to just one third of principals with teaching responsibilities in TALIS countries on average (OECD, 2019e). Pedagogical leadership is one of the key areas of professional school leadership in Finland. Teachers rely on their leaders' vision, and the principal understands and trusts the teachers' work. Therefore, leadership and management in Finnish schools are informal but effective, as foreign observers have witnessed (Hargreaves et al., 2008).

Before the 1990s, becoming a school principal was often a reward for successful service as a teacher. In some cases, however, a rather young teacher was appointed as a school leader. Leadership experience or qualities were rarely examined when filling an open principal's post in schools. Nor did school principals need to be experts in administration, financial management, or political lobbying as they must today. In the early 1990s, this situation rapidly changed. One driver of this change was the sudden decentralization of public sector management and educational administration in Finland at that time. A new financing scheme that increased the autonomy of the municipalities immediately affected schools in most parts of the country. School principals offered to control their school budgets; in some cases, that included teachers' salaries and all recurrent costs.

Second, and a related driver of change, was an unexpected financial crisis that hit Finland harder than many other Western countries in the early 1990s. School principals became the operational arms of the municipalities in deciding how forthcoming budget cuts, which were typically double-digit in magnitude, would be managed. Finnish school principals found themselves in a situation similar to that of corporate CEOs who had to adjust their firms into shrinking markets. The nostalgic image of the head of the school had changed. Major educational changes—such as the curriculum reforms of 1994—have been implemented successfully primarily due to the professional attitude and pedagogical leadership of school principals. Ever since, this leadership community in Finland has served as a critical voice in shaping education policies and steering school improvement based on the needs of teachers, students, and society. Based on these experiences, it is difficult to imagine that market-based education reforms, which often undermine the central role of pedagogical leadership, could have been implemented in Finland. School principals have been the first to stand between these intentions and the well-being of schools.

GOOD TEACHERS, GREAT SCHOOLS

What else have OECD's TALIS surveys revealed about Finland's lower-secondary teachers? The following are some of the main conclusions (OECD, 2014b, 2019e). First of all, about three out of five teachers feel that their profession is valued in society, which is well above the average of 32% in the other 45 countries that took part in TALIS in 2018. Survey data show that when schools provide staff with the opportunity to participate in school decisionmaking, teachers are more likely to feel that teaching is a valued profession. Second, the vast majority of teachers in Finland report being satisfied with their work. More specifically, 92% of teachers report that the advantages of being a teacher outweigh the disadvantages; this is well above the average of 75% in the other countries surveyed. Similarly, 79% of Finnish lower-secondary school teachers would choose the profession again and just 7% of teachers regret becoming a teacher, compared with the averages of 76% and 10%, respectively, in other countries. Finally, about 90% of teachers in Finland report that they are satisfied with their jobs.

However, TALIS 2018 (OECD, 2019e) also casts some worrying shadows on teachers and the teaching profession in Finland. Compared to TALIS 2013 (OECD, 2014b) there has been a slight decline in Finnish lower-secondary teachers' job satisfaction and how they perceive their work in school. First, 74% of lower-secondary school principals in Finland said that there were no mentoring programs available for the teachers in their school. Less than one of five principals said that mentoring is available for all new teachers in their school. Only 4% of teachers had assigned mentor in Finland, according to TALIS 2018. Second, peer learning or observation is not a common practice among lower-secondary school teachers in Finland. Just 14% of teachers said that that have taken part in formal peer learning with colleagues compared to almost 50% in other countries taking part in TALIS 2018. Third, Finnish teachers report that there are more issues with classroom discipline compared to previous TALIS in 2013. One third of teachers strongly agreed or agreed that "when the lesson begins, the teacher has to wait quite a long time for students to quieten down" and that "there is much disruptive noise in this classroom." It is necessary to remember when interpreting these changes in Finnish schools that they are based on teachers' personal perceptions of the classroom disciplinary climate and therefore may reflect various factors as much as real changes in students' behaviors.

In summary, what are the relative strengths of teacher education in Finland, based on international perspectives? Although the Bologna Process directs overall European higher education structures and policies, it doesn't stipulate how signatory nations should design curricula or arrange their teacher education. There are, and will continue to be, significant differences in national teacher education policies and practices among European education systems. Within this mosaic of European teacher education systems, Finland has three peculiarities.

1. Talented and motivated individuals go into teaching. Since it shifted primary school teacher education to the universities and upgraded teacher diplomas to a required master's degree in the late 1970s, Finland has attracted some of its most multi-talented and motivated youth to become teachers. As described earlier, there is a strong cultural influence in the career planning of young Finns, but that alone does not explain the sustained popularity of teaching. Two other salient factors may be identified. First, the required master's degree in educational sciences provides a competitive professional foundation, not only for becoming employed as a primary school teacher but also for many other careers, including education administration and work in the private sector. All graduating teachers are fully eligible to enroll in doctoral studies, which are still tuition-free in Finland. Second, many young Finns select teaching as their primary career because work in schools is perceived as an autonomous, independent, highly regarded profession, comparable to working as a medical doctor, lawyer, or architect, for example. Increased external control over teachers' work in schools through test-based accountability or centrally mandated regulation would likely deflect more bright young people to other professional careers where they have freedom to make use of their own creativity and initiative.

2. There is close collaboration between subject faculties and teacher education in Finnish research universities. Subject teacher education is organized collaboratively and is coordinated to ensure both a solid mastery of the subjects to be taught and state-of-the-art pedagogical competences for all graduates. Faculties in Finnish universities perceive teacher education as an important component of their academic programs. Lecturers and some professors in the subject faculties have specialized in the teaching of their own disciplines, which has enhanced cooperation among teacher educators. Faculties of education and various subjects within the university are also positively interdependent: They can achieve sustainable success only when all of them do their best.

3. Teacher education is research-based. Teacher education in Finland is also recognized because of its systematic and research-based structure. All graduating teachers, by the nature of their degree, have completed research-based master's theses accompanied by rigorous academic requirements of theory, methodology, and critical reflection equal to any other field of study in Finnish universities at that level. Research orientation to teacher education prepares teachers, at all levels, to work in complex, changing societal and educational environments. Research-based academic training has also enabled the implementation of more radical national education policies. For example, enhanced professional competencies have led to putting increased trust in teachers and schools regarding curriculum planning, student assessment, reporting of student performance, and school improvement. Finland has successfully integrated research, knowledge of content and didactics, and practice into its teacher education programs.

Indeed, this research focus carries a twofold significance for teacher education. Research findings establish the professional basis for teachers to teach and work effectively within a complex knowledge society. Teacher education—within any society—has the potential to progress as an effective field of professional activity only through and from robust contemporary empirical, scientific inquiry. *Professionalism* as the main characteristic of teaching requires teachers to be able to access and follow ongoing developments in their own profession and to freely implement new knowledge within their own instructional work. Thus, further development of Finnish teacher education must necessarily be built on ongoing, high-quality, internationally relevant research and development achievements.

4. Teacher education includes learning through clinical practice. Teacher training schools are an integral part of the initial preparation of teachers and active hubs of research on teaching and learning in Finland (Hammerness et al., 2017). Teacher education is based on contemporary research on issues that cover a wide range of topics and disciplines combined with clinical practice that supports professional growth of new teachers. Clinical training refers to learning about school and how to teach in real classroom settings under the supervision of experienced teachers and educators, similar to how medical students are taught in university's teaching hospitals.

There are 11 teacher training schools with nearly 9,000 students in Finland that operate and are governed by the universities.[5] They include primary schools and lower- and upper-secondary schools, and are funded from the state budget and belong to the category of public independent schools in Finland. Teacher training schools typically have the following tasks: general education to children in their catchment area, supervision of student teachers studying in the university, participation in and supporting research done in the university, and professional development of teachers.

What can we learn from Finland's teacher policies? Education reformers often argue that the way to improve schools is simply to have better teachers. The Finnish experience suggests that real life in schools is more complicated than that. Drawing from what Finland and other high-performing school systems have done to get the most out of their schools, two conditions must exist regarding teachers.

First, teachers and students must teach and learn in an environment that empowers them to do their best. When teachers have more control over curriculum design, teaching methods, and student assessment, they are more inspired to teach than when they are pressured to deliver prescribed programs and must submit to external standardized tests that determine progress. Similarly, when students are encouraged to find their own ways of learning without fear of failure, most will study and learn more than when they're driven to achieve the same standards under the pressure of regular testing.

I've argued elsewhere (Sahlberg, 2013a) that if education policies prevent teachers and students from doing what they think is necessary for good outcomes, even the best teachers will not be able to make significant improvements. Competition among schools over enrollment, standardized teaching and learning, and test-based accountability are the most common toxic aspects of today's school systems globally. These are the wrong means for sustainable improvement, and they are often the main reason why so many teachers leave the profession earlier than planned.

Second, teaching is a complex profession that requires advanced academic education. Current trends in many parts of the world suggest just the opposite: If you're smart, the thinking goes, you can teach because teaching is not rocket science; with clear guidelines and specific standards in hand, almost anyone can teach. In some countries, for example, retired military personnel are being converted into teachers and principals to address the teacher shortage caused by teachers who leave the profession early. In some other countries, teachers are licensed to teach through online courses or fast-track arrangements that give them only limited involvement in real classroom life or work in school prior to their employment.

Teaching will become a more popular career choice among young people if the basic qualification to become a teacher is elevated to a master's degree on a par with what is needed for other esteemed professions. Professional leadership will flourish among teachers only if they have the autonomy to influence what and how they teach and to determine how well their students are performing. Achieving these essential elements requires a scientific approach to teacher education, in which curriculum, pedagogy, assessment, school improvement, professional development, and systematic clinical practice play an integral part. This is the first lesson that can be learned from Finland.

Many visitors to Finland wonder why the Finnish education system hasn't been infected by the market-based reform ideas that are so prevalent around the world. The answer is simple: Teachers in Finland are prepared to resist these ideas because of their advanced academic education and the collaborative nature of their profession, just as medical doctors would reject any suggested cure for a disease if it were not based on reliable experiments and research. Not only are better-educated teachers more effective in the classroom, but they're also better equipped to keep their education systems healthy and free from reform ideas that are harmful to both teachers and children.

Finnish teacher education's greatest potential lies in the diversity of hundreds of talented and motivated young people who, year after year, seek enrollment in teacher education programs. This is a crucial factor for the continued and future success of teacher education in Finland. Young Finns gravitate toward teaching because they regard it as an independent, respected, and rewarding profession within which they will have freedom to fulfill their aspirations. However, general upper-secondary school graduates also weigh the quality of teacher education programs when they make decisions about their future career. It is therefore paramount that Finnish teacher education continues to develop in order to ensure that, in the future, it remains an attractive and competitive option for highly able young people.

Teachers' professional status in Finnish society is a cultural phenomenon, but how teachers become prepared to teach in classrooms and work collaboratively in professional communities is attributable to systematically designed and implemented academic teacher education. For other nations, imitating the Finnish curriculum system or organizational aspects of schools may not be a wise strategy. However, a positive lesson that Finns themselves have learned by raising the level of teacher education on par with other academic pursuits certainly merits closer examination. A critical condition for attracting the most able young people year after year to teacher education is that a teacher's work should represent an independent and respected profession rather than merely focusing on the technical implementation of externally mandated standards, endless tests, and administrative burdens. Indeed, teaching is not rocket science—it is much harder than that. This is the second lesson that Finland can offer to others.

WHAT IF FINLAND'S GREAT TEACHERS TAUGHT IN YOUR SCHOOLS?

I have been privileged to meet and host scores of foreign education delegations to Finland in recent years in their quest to build higher-performing school systems in their own countries. What most of these visitors take away is that Finland has a highly standardized teacher education system that requires all teachers to hold master's degrees that can be only earned in the country's research universities. Therefore, competition in these teacher education programs is tough. A visit to any of the Finnish universities reveals that Finland, just like Singapore, South Korea, and Japan, has strict control over the quality of applicants at their entry into teacher education and only the best candidates will be accepted. The number of accepted students accurately corresponds with the needs in the labor market after their graduation. Many guests realize that allowing "bad" teachers to enter teaching in Finnish schools rarely happens.

As a consequence of these lessons from Finland, I have often heard people wondering if the quality of their own schools and entire education system would improve if only they had teachers like the Finns have—just as having good teachers has improved schools in Finland, Singapore, and South Korea, for example. There has been a global movement to turn attention to teacher quality and how it might be improved. Indeed, the desire to enhance teacher quality comes from the lessons learned from education systems that score high on international student assessments. Each of these successful systems has managed to create a situation where teaching is regarding by young people as an interesting career choice. Most teachers in these countries spend most of their working lives serving schools. From the international perspective, however, there are three myths related to teacher quality and school improvement that often steer education policies in the wrong direction in countries where the teaching profession has declined in status (Sahlberg, 2013b).

The first myth is that *the most important single factor in improving quality of education is teachers*. This is what the former Washington, DC, school chancellor Michelle Rhee said in *Waiting for "Superman"* in 2010 and what many other "Reformers" repeat in their change rhetoric. If this wasn't a myth, then the power of a school would indeed be stronger than children's family background or other out-of-school factors, and all children would achieve more if only there were good enough teachers in all schools. This myth has often led to the conclusion that what needs to be done first is to get rid of poorly performing teachers. However, there are two points of evidence that show this notion is indeed a myth.

First, since the Coleman Report in 1966 (Coleman et al., 1966), several studies have confirmed that a significant part of the variance in student achievement can be attributed to out-of-school factors such as parents' education and occupations, peer influence, and students' individual characteristics. Half a century later, research on what explains students' measured performance in school concludes that only a small part of the variance in measured student achievement can be attributed to classrooms—that is, teachers and teaching—and a similar amount of the variance comes from factors within schools—that is, school climate, facilities, and leadership (see Figure 3.5 below). In other words, most of what explains student achievement is outside the school gate and therefore beyond the control of schools.

Second, over 30 years of systematic research on school effectiveness and school improvement reveals a number of characteristics that are typical of more effective schools (Teddlie, 2010). Although school effectiveness research shows mixed findings, most scholars agree that effective leadership is among the most important characteristics of effective schools, equally important as effective teaching. Effective leadership includes leader qualities, such as being firm and purposeful, having a shared vision and goals, promoting teamwork and collegiality, and frequent personal monitoring and feedback. Several other characteristics of more effective schools include features that are also linked to the culture of the school and leadership:

maintaining focus on learning, producing a positive school climate, setting high expectations for all, developing staff skills, and involving parents. In other words, school leadership matters as much as teachers do.

The second myth is that *the quality of an education system can never exceed the quality of its teachers*. This statement became known in education policies through the influential McKinsey & Company report titled *How the World's Best Performing School Systems Come out on Top* (Barber & Mourshed, 2007, p. 40). The same argument appears in OECD's influential PISA reports and was repeated in a recent column by Andreas Schleicher (2019). Although these writings take a broader view on enhancing status of teachers by paying them better and by selecting initial candidates for teacher education programs more carefully, the impact of this statement is that the quality of an education system is a simple sum of the efforts of its individuals—in other words, of its teachers. By saying this, they assume that teachers work independently from one another and that what one teacher does doesn't affect the work of the others. This is a narrow human capital view to change. However, in most schools today, in Finland, the United States, and elsewhere, teachers work as teams, and the outcome of their work is a joint effort of the whole school. This myth therefore undermines the impact of teamwork and the social capital that it creates in most schools today.

This myth has found its way into several national education policy documents and reform programs today. However, there are studies on team-based school culture and the role of collegiality in school that show how enhanced social capital through professional collaboration in school can increase teachers' effect on students' learning in school (Quintero, 2017). This is the main principle of *Professional Capital* (2012), an award-winning book by Andy Hargreaves and Michael Fullan. The role of an individual teacher in a school is like that of a player on a football team: All teachers are vital, but the collegial culture and teachers' professional judgment in the school are even more important for the quality of the school. Team sports offer numerous examples of teams that have performed beyond expectations because of leadership, commitment, and spirit. Take the U.S. ice hockey team in the 1980 Winter Olympics, when a team of college kids beat both the Soviets and Finland in the final round to win the gold medal. The overall quality of Team USA certainly exceeded the quality of its individual players. They succeeded because the team spirit, perseverance, leadership, and genuine willingness to help one another be better than they would be alone. The same can be said for schools in the education system.

The third myth is that *if any children had three or four great teachers in a row, they would soar academically, regardless of their socioeconomic background, while those who have a sequence of weak teachers will fall further and further behind.* This theoretical assumption appeared in an important policy recommendation called *Essential Elements of Teacher Policy in ESEA: Effectiveness, Fairness and Evaluation* (Center for American Progress & The Education Trust) presented to the U.S. Congress in 2011. Great teachers and great teaching here, again, are measured by the growth of students' test scores on standardized measurements.

The assumption that students would perform well if they simply had more great teachers presents a view that education reform alone could overcome the powerful influence of family and social environment mentioned earlier. It means that schools should get rid of low-performing teachers and hire only great ones. This myth has the most practical difficulties. The first one is related to what it means to be a great teacher. Even if this were clear, it would be difficult to know exactly who is a great teacher at the time of recruitment. Becoming a great teacher normally takes 5 to 10 years of systematic practice, and to reliably determine the "effectiveness" of any teacher would require at least 5 years of consistent, accurate data. This would, in general, be practically impossible as Stanford's Edward Haertel (2013) says.

We should also keep in mind what the American Statistical Association (ASA) that is the world's largest independent community of statisticians found out about the effect teachers have on student learning compared to out-of-school factors. They said that most "studies find that teachers account for about 1% to 14% of the variability in test scores, and that the majority of opportunities for quality improvement are found in the system-level conditions" (ASA, 2014). According to Haertel (2013), research shows that about 20% of variance in measured student achievement in school is explained by in-school factors, the size of unexplained variation is about the same, and up to 60% is associated to factors outside the school (Figure 3.5). This doesn't mean that teachers have little effect on students' learning. Instead, ASA states that "*variation* among teachers accounts for a small part of the variation in scores. The majority of the variation in test scores is attributable to factors outside of the teacher's control such as student and family background, poverty, curriculum, and unmeasured influences."

Let's return to the question in the heading of this section. Imagine that we could transport Finnish teachers and school principals who all hold master's degrees and have been through highly regarded teacher

Figure 3.5. Variance in Student-Measured Achievement Explained by Different Factors

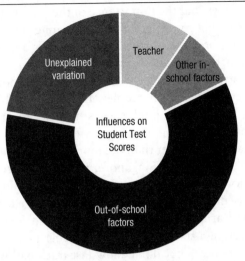

Source: Haertel (2013).

preparation to teach in, say, Indiana in the United States. Indiana's own teachers and principals would go and work in Finnish schools. (Imagine that there would be no language barriers.) After 5 years—assuming that education policies in both Indiana and Finland would continue as they have been going—we would check what had happened to students' test scores on mandatory student assessments. I argue that if there were any gains in Indiana students' achievement, they would be only marginal. Why? Education policies in Indiana and in many other states in the United States create a professional and social context for teaching that would limit the Finnish teachers when it comes to using their knowledge, experience, and passion for the good of their students' learning. I have met some experienced Finnish teachers who teach in the United States, and they confirm my earlier hypothetical reasoning. Based on what I have heard from some of them, it is also probable that many of those transported Finnish teachers would already be doing something else other than teaching by the end of the 5th year—like their American peers. The other question is: Would Finnish school ratings collapse as a consequence of American teachers teaching in its schools? Most likely not. The educational culture in Finland would try to assist any teachers who cannot perform according to expectations. Less time in the classroom would provide these foreign teachers with more time to work with their colleagues and find better ways to help their students become successful.

Everybody agrees that the importance of the teaching profession and the quality of teaching in contributing to learning outcomes is beyond question. It is therefore understandable that teacher quality is often cited as the most important in-school variable influencing student achievement. But just having better teachers in schools will not automatically translate into better learning outcomes. Lessons from high-performing school systems, including Finland, suggest that we must reconsider the way we think about teaching as a profession and what the role of the school is in our society. Rather than dreaming about having teachers like those in Finland, Canada, or Singapore, national policymakers should consider the following three aspects affecting the teaching profession.

First, teacher education should be more standardized, and at the same time teaching and learning should be less standardized. Singapore, Canada, and Finland all set high standards for their teacher preparation programs in academic universities. They don't allow fast-track pathways into teaching or alternative training that doesn't include studying theories of pedagogy and related clinical practice. All these countries make it a priority to have strict quality control before anybody will be allowed to teach.

Second, the toxic use of accountability for schools should be redesigned. Current practices in many countries that judge the quality of teachers by counting their students' measured achievement alone is in many ways inaccurate and unfair. It is inaccurate because most schools' goals are broader than just good performance in a few academic subjects. It is unfair because most of the variation in student achievement on standardized tests can be explained by out-of-school factors. In education systems that score high in international rankings, teachers feel that they are empowered by their leaders and other teachers. In Finland, the TALIS 2018 survey shows that teachers find their profession rewarding because of professional autonomy and the social prestige that comes with it.

Third, changing teacher policies is not enough to make the teaching profession attractive—other school policies must be changed, too. The experiences of those countries that do well in international rankings suggest that teachers should have autonomy in planning their work, freedom to use teaching methods that they know lead to best results, and authority to influence the assessment of the outcomes of their work. Schools and teachers must also be trusted in these key areas of teaching for the teaching profession to really become an attractive career choice for more young people.

CHAPTER 4

The Finnish Way

Competitive Welfare State

Real winners do not compete.

—Samuli Paronen, Finnish author, 1917–1974

What makes Finnish education unique is its steady progress from a system that was barely at international averages to one of the rare strong public educational performers today. Equally important, Finland has been able to create a network of schools where the best school is the neighborhood public school. Simultaneously, participation in and graduation from upper-secondary education in Finland—both upper-secondary and higher education—have increased significantly. The success of Finnish education has been frequently noted by global media and various education development agencies. This exceptional development was not accomplished by following the same education reform principles that are dominant in the United States, England, Australia, and much of the rest of the world.

Finland has a competitive national economy, low levels of corruption, a good quality of life, a strong sustainable-development lifestyle, gender equality, and therefore, the happiest people in the world. These qualities make Finland also one of the most prosperous nations. The success of Finland as a small, remote northern European nation has been built on flexibility and a solution orientation in all aspects of society. In Finland's education system, these principles have enabled schools to experiment with creativity and take risks while seeking to reach set goals, whether these goals represent effective teaching or productive learning. This is in harmony with policies and strategies in other areas of the public sector. Especially interesting has been the close interplay between education policies and economic strategies since the early 1990s.

This chapter discusses in more detail how education policies in Finland have responded to international educational reform ideas and how they are linked to the overall development of the knowledge economy and welfare state. It describes the increased interdependency among public sector policies in Finland since 1970 and presents a tentative typology to compare education reform principles and economic development policies in Finland. The main point of this chapter is that education policies for system excellence need to be based on a systems view of policymaking and sustainable leadership that does not undermine complex relationships between different public sector policies in these societies.

THE POWER OF GLOBALIZATION

Internationalization has shaped Finland and the lives of its people during the past 3 decades. Membership in the European Union and an active role in the OECD have increased individual mobility and the exchange of policies between Finland and the rest of the developed world. Finnish people, however, remain divided regarding globalization. Many think that globalization has led to a diminishing role for nation-states and the loss of their sovereignty, as a result of the emergence of global hegemony of transnational money, media, and entertainment corporations. Others argue that standardization in economies, policies, and cultures has become a new norm for competitive corporations and nations, thus diminishing Finnish customs and traditions. Changes in global culture also deeply affect educational policies, practices, and institutions. It is obvious that there is no straightforward view of the consequences of the globalization process on educational policies.

Globalization is a cultural paradox: It simultaneously unifies and diversifies people and cultures. It unifies national education policies by integrating them with broader global trends. Because problems and challenges are similar from one education system to the next, solutions and education reform agendas are also becoming similar. As a result of the international benchmarking of education systems by using common indicators and international comparisons of student achievement, the distinguishing features of different education systems are becoming more visible. For example, PISA has mobilized scores of politicians and education experts to visit other places, especially Finland, Canada, Singapore, Shanghai, and Korea, in order to learn how to redefine their own education policies and improve schools. As a consequence, globalization has also accelerated international collaboration, the exchange of ideas, and the transfer of education policies among education systems.

Analyzing global policy developments and education reforms has become a common practice in many ministries of education, development agencies, and consultant firms. Therefore, the world's education systems are beginning to share some core values, functions, and structures, and, evidently, they look alike. The question arises whether increased global interaction among policymakers and educators, especially the benchmarking of education systems through agreed-on indicators and the borrowing and lending of educational policies, has promoted common approaches to education reform throughout the world.

"Change knowledge," as Michael Fullan calls it, in education has been created in and disseminated predominantly by English-speaking countries. The United States, Canada, and the United Kingdom in the West and Australia, New Zealand, and Singapore in the Asia-Pacific region have become the centers of gravity for research and debate on school improvement, school effectiveness, and educational change. Two academic journals, *School Effectiveness and School Improvement* (established in 1990) and the *Journal of Educational Change* (established in 2000), are the key forums within which contemporary educational change knowledge is communicated.[1] Beyond the Anglo-Saxon world, the Netherlands, Sweden, Spain, and Norway have engaged most actively in international dialogue and research on educational change. Surprisingly, Finland, Korea, and Japan—all countries with high-performing and equitable education systems—have had only a modest role in the generation of global knowledge about change. Each of these countries has relied heavily on the research and innovation from the United States, the United Kingdom, Australia, and Canada.

In the business of global education development, it is important to be a critical consumer of the available evidence and research. Indeed, rather than shifting emphasis toward standardized knowledge of content and mastery of routine skills, some advanced education systems are focusing on flexibility, risk taking, creativity, and problem solving through modern methods of teaching combined with community networks and smart technologies. The number of examples is increasing, including China, an economic power that is loosening its standardized control over education by gradually making school-based curriculum a national policy priority (Zhao, 2014). Singapore is adopting the idea of "less is more" in teaching in order to make room for creativity and innovation, as Pak Tee Ng eloquently describes in his book *Learning From Singapore* (Ng, 2018). One of the highest-performing Canadian provinces, Alberta, loosened its grip on schools by removing standardized provincial assessments and creating more intelligent accountability policies, which focus on authentic learning and variety of student assessment methods. Wales has done this already. Scotland is also building smarter curriculum and accountability practices by staying away from heavy-handed external testing and school inspection. Even in England, once the most test-intensive education system in the world, the government is putting an end to all standardized testing in primary schools.

As a reaction to the overemphasis on traditional content-focused teaching and test-based accountability, authorities around the world are considering more dynamic forms of curriculum, introducing intelligent forms of accountability, and enhancing leadership in education in order to find alternative instructional approaches that promote the deeper, productive learning required in knowledge economies. Instead of focusing on single institutions, education reforms are beginning to encourage networking of schools and communities. At the core of this idea is *complementarity*—that is, cooperation between schools and districts and striving for better learning in the network. Clustering and networking also appear to be core factors in the nations' economic competitiveness and efforts to cope with globalization.

Although the improvement of education systems is a global phenomenon, there is no reliable, recent comparative analysis about how education reforms in different countries have been designed and implemented. However, the professional literature indicates that the focus on educational development has shifted from structural reforms to improving the quality and equity of education (Fullan, 2016; Hargreaves et al., 2010; Schleicher, 2018). As a result, curriculum development, student assessment, teacher evaluation, integration of information and communication technologies into teaching and learning, and proficiency in basic competencies (reading literacy, mathematical literacy, and scientific literacy) have become common priorities in education reforms around the world. In order to bring about these changes in schools, governments employ often outdated and bad management models from the corporate world, such as competition between schools, standardization of teaching and learning, punitive test-based accountability, performance-based pay, and data-driven decisionmaking. I call this the Global Educational Reform Movement (Sahlberg, 2006, 2007, 2010a, 2016a).

THE GLOBAL EDUCATIONAL REFORM MOVEMENT

The idea of the Global Educational Reform Movement, or simply GERM, evolves from the increased international exchange of policies and practices. It is not a formal global policy program, but rather an unofficial educational agenda that relies on a certain set of assumptions to improve education systems (Fullan, 2011; Hargreaves et al., 2001; Hargreaves & Shirley, 2009; Sahlberg, 2016a). GERM has emerged since the 1980s and is one concrete offspring of globalization in education. It has become accepted as "a new educational orthodoxy" within many recent education reforms throughout the world, including reforms in the United States, Australia, Canada, the United Kingdom, some Scandinavian countries, and an increasing number of countries in the developing world.[2]

Tellingly, GERM is promoted through the strategies and interests of multinational private corporations, supranational development agencies, international donors, private foundations, and commercial consulting firms through their interventions in national education reforms and policymaking processes around the world. In developing countries, global and regional development banks; in industrial nations, OECD and the International Monetary Fund (IMF); in the United States, wealthy corporations and private philanthropy have been the advocates of corporate models to national education policymakers. Diane Ravitch (2013, 2020) has described how venture philanthropy injects billions of dollars into public education systems in the United States—and, to a lesser extent, in some other countries—and often insists on employing business management concepts and principles in the school systems. By doing so, it promotes the viral spread of GERM not only within the United States but globally. There are only a small number of private foundations that provide funds to public education in Finland, and they have to operate under the close supervision of the authorities. Their influence on education policies or the direction of education reforms is next to none.

The inspiration for the emergence of GERM comes from three primary sources. The first is the new paradigm of learning that became dominant in the 1980s. The breakthrough of cognitive and constructivist approaches to learning gradually shifted the focus of education reforms from teaching to learning. According to this paradigm, the intended outcomes of schooling emphasize greater conceptual understanding, problem solving, emotional and multiple intelligences, and interpersonal skills, rather than the memorization of facts or the mastery of irrelevant skills. At the same time, however, the need for proficiency in literacy and numeracy has also become a prime target of education reforms.

The second inspiration is the public demand for guaranteed, effective learning for all pupils. The global campaign called Education for All, which was adopted by the Dakar Framework in April 2000 at the World Education Forum, was influential in shifting the policy focus in education from teaching of some to learning for all. Inclusive education arrangements and the introduction of common learning standards for all have been offered as a means to promote the ideal of education for all. This has led, generally speaking, to raising expectations for all students through national curricula and common programs.

The third inspiration is the privatization movement in education that has accompanied the global wave of decentralization of public services. Making schools and teachers compete for students and resources and then holding them accountable for the results (i.e., student test scores), this movement has led to the introduction of education standards, indicators, and benchmarks for teaching and learning, aligned assessments and testing, and prescribed curricula. As James Popham (2007) has noted, various forms of test-based accountability have emerged where school performance and raising the quality of education are closely tied to the processes of accreditation, promotion, sanctions, and financing. In other words, education has become a commodity where the efficiency of service delivery ultimately determines performance.

Since the 1980s, at least five globally common features of education policies and reform principles have been employed in attempts to improve the quality of education, especially in terms of raising student achievement. The first is increasing *competition* among schools. Almost all education systems have introduced alternative forms of schooling to offer parents more *choice* regarding their children's schooling. The voucher system in Chile in the 1980s and in Sweden in the 1990s, charter schools in the United States in the 2000s, and secondary academies in England in the 2010s are examples of faith in competition as an engine of betterment of education (Adamson et al., 2016). At the same time, the proportion of more advantaged students studying in private schools or independent schools has grown. In Australia, for example, every third primary and secondary school student studies in nongovernmental private or Catholic school (Jensen et al., 2013; OECD, 2020a). Ranking schools based on their performance on national standardized assessments has further increased competition between schools. OECD data show that according to school principals across OECD countries, more than three quarters of the students assessed by PISA attend schools that compete with at least one other school for enrollment (OECD, 2020b), in Australia it is almost every child. Finally, students—especially in many Asian countries—experience stronger pressure to perform better against their peers due to tough competition for entry into the best high schools and universities (Ng, 2018; Zhao, 2014).

The second is *standardization* in education. Outcomes-based education reform became popular in the 1980s, followed by standards-based education policies in the 1990s, initially within Anglo-Saxon countries. These reforms, quite correctly, shifted the focus of attention to educational outcomes—that is, to student learning and school performance. Consequently, a widely accepted—and generally unquestioned—belief among policymakers and education reformers is that setting clear and sufficiently high performance standards for schools, teachers, and students will necessarily improve the quality of desired outcomes. The enforcement of external standardized testing and school evaluation systems to judge how these standards have been attained emerged originally from these standards-driven education policies. Standardization draws from an assumption that all students should be educated to the same, ambitious learning targets. This notion, in turn, has led to the prevalence of prescribed curricula and homogenization of curriculum policies worldwide. The National Curriculum in England in the 1990s, the New National Education Standards in Germany in the 2000s, and the Common Core State Standards in the United States and the Australian Curriculum in the 2010s are examples of attempts to bring coherence and quality to teaching and learning in all schools.

The third common feature of the Global Educational Reform Movement is *focus on core subjects* in the curriculum, such as literacy and numeracy. Basic student knowledge and skills in reading, writing, mathematics, and natural sciences are elevated as prime targets and indices of education reforms. Due to the acceptance of international large-scale student assessments (ILSAs) such as OECD's PISA and IEA's TIMSS and PIRLS as metrics of educational performance, these core subjects have now come to dominate what pupils study, teachers teach, schools emphasize, and national education policies prioritize in most parts of the world. According to the OECD and research in a number of countries, national education policies are increasingly being influenced by the international student assessments, especially PISA. In our own research on what impact ILSAs have had on national school reforms, we concluded:

> Perhaps the most significant finding associated with the use of ILSAs in the literature we reviewed is the way in which new conditions for educational comparison have been made possible at the national, regional, and global levels. On the one hand, ILSAs have the potential to provide governments and education stakeholders with useful and relevant modes of comparison that purportedly allow for the assessment of educational achievement both within cities, states, and regions, and between countries. On the other hand, a common approach to analyze ILSAs' results—the good, the bad, and the ugly—without considering the strong influence of unequal educational opportunities in various contexts or acknowledging the broader political or economic agendas driving the production and use of ILSAs in education is dangerous. (Fischman et al., 2018, pp. 542–543)

Literacy and numeracy strategies that increased instruction time for so-called core subjects in England and Ontario are concrete programmatic examples of the GERM. In the United States, the No Child Left Behind legislation led most school districts to steal teaching time from other subjects—especially from social studies, arts, and music—and playtime from children by abolishing recess in many schools so students would be better prepared for state tests that measured student performance in literacy and mathematics (Jennings & Stark Rentner, 2006; Robert Wood Johnson Foundation, 2010; Sahlberg & Doyle, 2019). At the same time, however, to be successful in life and employment requires young people who are curious, who know how to work with other people, who can solve difficult problems, and who master leadership.

The fourth characteristic is *test-based accountability*—holding teachers and schools accountable for students' achievement through external standardized tests. School performance—especially raising students' measured achievement—is intimately tied to the processes of evaluating, inspecting, and rewarding or punishing schools and teachers. Performance-based pay, data walls in teachers' lounges, and school rankings in newspapers are examples of new accountability mechanisms that often draw their data primarily from external standardized student tests and teacher evaluations. The problem with test-based accountability is not that students, teachers, and schools are held accountable per se, but rather the way accountability mechanisms affect teachers' work and students' studying in school. Whenever school accountability relies on poor-quality and low-cost standardized tests, as is the case in many places, accountability becomes what is left when responsibility is subtracted.

The fifth globally observable trend in educational reform is *school choice*. Parental choice is an idea that became commonly known as a consequence of Milton Friedman's economic theories in the 1950s. Friedman and many of his disciples and advisees—including President Ronald Reagan—believe that parents must be given the freedom to choose their children's education, thereby encouraging healthy competition among schools so that they better serve families' diverse needs. Typically, school choice manifests itself through the emergence of private schools where parents pay tuition for their children's education. Today, there are scores of various types of alternative schools other than fee-based private schools to expand choice in education markets. Charter schools in the United States, free schools in Sweden, upper-secondary school academies in England, independent schools in Australia, and religious schools in the Netherlands are examples of mechanisms to advance parental choice. School choice ideology maintains that parents should be able to use the public funds set aside for their children's education to choose the schools—public or private—that work best for them.

In 2009, the U.S. Department of Education launched a competitive grant program named Race to the Top (RTTT), which was intended to encourage and reward states that are creating conditions for innovation and reform. With its US$4.35 billion budget, this program was designed to spur reforms in state and local district education by developing teacher and principal evaluation systems that substantially relied on measures of student achievement and growth. It encourages competition among states and also between districts as they seek more effective practices and practitioners. According to the Education Policy Institute's evaluation conducted by their partner organization "Broader, Bolder Approach to Education" in 2013, RTTT policies had fallen short in terms of teacher improvement and had failed to address the core drivers of opportunity gaps. Furthermore, RTTT's shortcomings have spurred state–district and union–management conflicts that hinder progress. The evaluation (Weiss, 2013, p. 8) concludes that "overall, this assessment finds that the key tenet of Race to the Top—that a state hold teachers and schools accountable before helping them establish foundations for success—is deeply flawed." Among other experts, Diane Ravitch (2020) has made similar conclusions about this federal reform program. Table 4.1 also illustrates how education policies in Finland since the 1980s have been almost the opposite those suggested by RTTT.

There are others who have analyzed global educational change efforts. Andy Hargreaves and Dennis Shirley (2009) have described global educational change by using the metaphor of "Ways" in their book *The Fourth Way*, to which I will return later in this chapter. Michael Fullan (2011) has used the term "drivers of change," such as education policy or strategy levers, which have the best chances of catalyzing intended change in education systems. "In the rush to move forward," writes Fullan (2011, p. 5), "leaders, especially from countries that have not been progressing, tend to choose the wrong drivers." These include accountability (versus professionalism), individual teacher quality (versus collegiality), technology (versus pedagogy), and fragmented strategies (versus systems thinking). These ineffective elements of education reform, which resonate closely with the aspects of GERM discussed above, have fundamentally missed the targets and continue to do so, according to Fullan. In his analysis of whole-system reforms in the United States and Australia, he goes even further:

> There is no way that these ambitious and admirable nationwide goals will be met with strategies being used. No successful system has ever led with these drivers. They cannot generate on a large scale the kind of intrinsic motivational energy that will be required to transform these massive systems. The US and Australian aspirations sound great as goals but crumble from a strategy or driver perspective. (Fullan, 2011, p. 7)

None of the elements of GERM shown in Table 4.1 have been adopted in Finland in the ways that they have been within the education policies of many other nations. This, of course, does not imply that there is no educational standardization, learning of basic skills, or accountability in Finnish schools (Sahlberg, 2015b). Nor does it suggest that there is a black-and-white distinction between each of these elements in Finland vis-à-vis other countries. But, perhaps, it does imply that a good education system can be created using alternative policies that are the opposite of those commonly found and promoted in global education policy markets.

A number of foreign scholars and journalists have stressed the notion that Finland's success, at least to a certain extent, is a result of being able to resist fashionable global trends summarized in Table 4.1. For some, Finland stands as an example par excellence in implementing smart business ideas in its education system. Dr. Sam Abrams who leads the

Table 4.1. Global Educational Reform Movement and the Finnish Model of Educational Change

Global Educational Reform Movement (GERM)	The Finnish Model
Competition between schools	*Collaboration among schools*
The basic assumption is that competition works as a market mechanism that will eventually enhance quality, productivity, and efficiency of service. When public schools compete over enrollment with charter schools, free schools, independent schools, and private schools, they will eventually improve teaching and learning.	The basic assumption is that educating people is a collaborative process and that cooperation, networking, and sharing ideas among schools will eventually raise the quality of education. When schools collaborate, they help one another and help teachers create a culture of cooperation in their classrooms.
Standardized learning	*Personalized learning*
Setting clear, high, and centrally prescribed performance targets for all schools, teachers, and students to improve the quality and equity of outcomes. This leads to standardized teaching through externally designed curriculum to ensure coherence and common criteria for measurement and data.	Setting a clear but flexible national framework for school-based curriculum planning. Encouraging school-based and individual solutions to national goals in order to find the best ways to create personalized learning opportunities for all. Using individualized learning plans for those who have special educational needs.
Focus on literacy and numeracy	*Focus on the whole child learning and well-being*
Basic knowledge and skills in reading, writing, mathematics, and the natural sciences serve as prime targets of education reform. Normally, instruction time of these subjects is increased at the expense of other subjects (such as arts and music).	Teaching and learning focus on deep, broad learning, giving equal value to all aspects of the growth of an individual's personality, moral character, creativity, knowledge, ethics, and skills. Play is the right of each and every child.
Test-based accountability	*Trust-based responsibility*
School performance and raising student achievement are closely tied to processes of promotion, inspection, and ultimately rewarding	Gradually building a culture of responsibility and trust within the education system that values teacher and principal professionalism in

(*continued*)

Table 4.1. (*continued*)

Global Educational Reform Movement (GERM)	The Finnish Model
schools and teachers. Teacher pay and school budget are determined by students' test scores. Sanctions often include terminating employment or closing down the school. Census-based student assessment and data are used to inform policymaking.	judging what is best for students. Targeting resources and support to schools and students who are at risk to fail or to be left behind. Sample-based student assessments and thematic research are used to inform policymaking.
Excellence through choice	*Equity of outcomes*
Basic premise is that parents must be given the freedom to choose their children's education, while encouraging competition among schools to better serve families' needs. Ideally, parents should be able to use the public funds set aside for their children's education to choose the schools—public or private—to improve quality of learning outcomes.	Basic premise is that all children should have equal prospects for educational success in school. Because school learning is strongly influenced by children's family background and associated factors, equity of outcomes requires that schools are funded according to their real needs to cope with these inequalities. Equitable education is seen as the key to system excellence.

National Center for the Study of Privatization in Education in Columbia University sees distinct difference in the Finnish Way of applying strategies from the business world in education. In his book *Education and the Commercial Mindset*, Abrams (2016) makes an eloquent comparison between Sweden and Finland by claiming that whereas Finland followed the Swedish example in the 1960s and the 1970s in rebuilding the structure and philosophy of its basic school, it never followed Sweden in their commercially minded education policies in the 1990s. Abrams notes that when Sweden allowed for-profit operators to establish and run schools, the Finns did a better job of adopting ideas from the corporate world. He refers to Finland's decision to systematically invest in teacher and leader professionalism within the ranks of the teaching profession rather than opening school gates to businessmen to lead and noneducators to teach in schools. Abrams (2016, p. 288) writes:

> Less obvious manifestations of business strategy include the decisions by
> Finnish authorities to abolish their school inspectorate in 1991 and never

follow their Nordic neighbors and much of the rest of the world in administering standardized exams to all students. In this regard, the Finns applied a far more subtle business lesson. In administering exams to small samples of students rather than employing universal assessments, Finnish authorities conferred on principals and teachers more autonomy and thus ownership.

GERM has had significant consequences for teachers' work and students' learning in schools wherever it has been a dominant driver of change (Sahlberg, 2016a). The most notable impact is the standardization of educational and pedagogical processes. Performance standards set by educational authorities and consultants have been brought into the lives of teachers and students without a full understanding that most of what pupils need to learn in school cannot be formulated as a clear standard. New forms of student assessments and testing that have been aligned to these standards are often disappointments and even bring new problems to schools. However, because the standardization agenda promises significant gains in efficiency and quality of education, it has been widely accepted as a basic ideology of change, both politically and professionally.

The voices of practitioners are rarely heard in the education policy and reform business. The educational change literature is primarily technical discourse created by academics or change consultants. Therefore, I devote space here to a school improvement practitioner from Scotland. This example is particularly relevant because Scotland is currently recovering from a rather serious GERM infection that occurred a decade back. The symptoms included top-heavy planning, rigid curriculum, fixed measures through audits, external snapshot inspection, and externally judged accountability. Many of these problems are now gradually fading away and giving room to teacher professionalism, more intelligent curriculum and evaluation policies, and deeper system-wide collaboration. Niall MacKinnon (2011), a Scottish educator, makes a compelling appeal for "locally owned questions and purposes in realizing practice within the broader national policy and practice frameworks." He gets right to the point of how GERM affected teachers and schools that time:

> There is the real practical danger that without an understanding of rationale and theoretical bases for school development, practitioners may be judged by auditors on differing underlying assumptions to their own developmental pathways, and the universalistic grading schemas come to be applied as a mask or front giving pseudoscientific veneer to imposed critical judgments

which are nothing more than expressions of different views and models of education. Through the mechanism of inspection, a difference of conceptual viewpoint, which could prompt debate and dialogue in consideration of practice, is eliminated in judgmental and differential power relations. One view supplants another. Command and control replaces mutuality, dialogue and conceptual exploration matched to practice development. Those who suffer are those innovating and bringing in new ideas. (p. 100)

GERM has gained global popularity among policymakers and change consultants because it emphasizes some fundamental new orientations to learning and educational administration. It suggests strong guidelines to improve quality, equity, and the effectiveness of education, such as putting making learning a priority, seeking high achievement for all students, and making assessment an integral part of the teaching and learning process. However, it also leads to the privatization of public education. GERM assumes that external performance standards, describing what teachers should teach and what students should do and learn, lead to better learning for all. By concentrating on the basics and defining explicit learning targets for students and teachers, such standards place a strong emphasis on mastering the core skills of reading and writing and mathematical and scientific literacy. The systematic training of teachers and external inspection are essential elements of this approach.

Is there any evidence of how GERM has affected student learning? Some evidence comes from OECD's PISA since 2000. None of the countries that were infected by the GERM—the United States, England, Australia, New Zealand, the Netherlands, or Sweden—has been able to significantly improve students' learning to the point that their education system would be considered "high-performing" by the OECD. Further evidence of the impacts of GERM in Sweden, Chile, and the United States is described in book edited by Frank Adamson, Björn Åstrand, and Linda Darling-Hammond in 2016 titled *Global Education Reform* (Adamson et al., 2016). In 2019, the *Educational Review* journal dedicated an entire special issue to the analysis of GERM and its consequences. In the introduction article of that journal, Kay Fuller and Howard Stevenson (2019) summarize the problematic consequences of GERM in different countries (e.g., Chile, England, and China) and state that "many of the articles point to the possibilities of hope and resistance as students and educators seek to speak back to a system that is visibly "cracked."

In 2012, when the OECD collected the data for that study from 65 education systems, the OECD (2013b) made this determination:

- Since the early 1980s, reforms in many countries have granted parents and students greater choice in the school the students will attend (p. 54).
- Between 2003 and 2012, there was a clear trend toward schools using student assessments to compare the school's performance with district or national performance and with that of other schools (p. 159).
- On average across OECD countries with comparable data from 2003 to 2012, students in 2012 were 20 percentage points more likely than their counterparts in 2003 to attend schools where the use of tests or assessments of student achievement are used to monitor teacher practice (p. 160).

Many countries have carried out their own studies to understand how market mechanisms affect the quality of their education systems. Wiborg (2010) studied the impact of 20 years of the free-school system (government-funded private schools) in Sweden and drew the following conclusion:

> [T]he Swedish experiment (using for-profit private providers) has proved expensive and has not led to significant learning gains overall. At the same time the Swedish reforms, albeit on a small scale, appear to have increased inequality, even in the context of this very egalitarian system. (p. 19)

The Australian Grattan Institute examined how market mechanisms, especially school competition, choice, and autonomy, impact schools' performance. The conclusion was that relying on markets is not the best way to improve student learning. The report stated that:

> [b]y increasing competition, government policies have increased the effectiveness of many sectors of the economy. But school education is not one of them. (Jensen et al., 2013)

Do PISA data suggest that the notions behind GERM are correct? There are three distinct findings in PISA since 2012 that are worth noting in order to see how the elements of GERM are associated with successful reforms worldwide.

The first finding is that education systems that give schools autonomy over their own curricula and student assessments often perform better than schools that do not (OECD, 2013b). This contradicts the basic premise of GERM, which assumes that externally set teaching standards and aligned standardized testing are preconditions for success. PISA shows that success is often associated with balanced professional autonomy and a collaborative culture in schools. Evidence also shows that high-performing education systems engage their teachers in setting their own teaching and learning targets, crafting productive learning environments, and designing multiple forms of student assessments to best support learning and school improvement.

The second finding is that high average learning outcomes and system-wide equity are often interrelated (OECD, 2018, 2019b). Equity of outcomes in education means that students' socioeconomic status has less impact on how well they learn in school. Equity is high on the agenda in all successful school systems. A focus on equity gives high priority to universal early childhood programs, comprehensive health and special education services in schools, and balanced curriculum that weighs arts, music, and sports, and academic studies equally. Fairness in resource allocation is important for equity, too. PISA 2018 (OECD, 2019b, 2019e) shows that fair resourcing is related to the success of the entire school system: High student performance tends to be linked to more equitable resource allocation between advantaged and disadvantaged schools.

The third finding is that school choice and competition do not improve the performance of education systems (OECD, 2011, 2019e). In the OECD countries, school choice and competition between schools are related to greater levels of segregation in the education system. That, in turn, may have adverse consequences for equity in learning opportunities and outcomes. Indeed, successful education systems do better than those that have expanded school choice. All successful school systems have a strong commitment to maintain their public schools and local school control. The PISA data show that the prevalence of charter and free schools, and the related competition for students, have no discernible relationship to improving student learning.

Table 4.1 suggests that the Finnish Model of educational change is radically different from GERM's. A typical feature of teaching and learning in Finland is high confidence in teachers and principals regarding curriculum, assessment, organization of teaching, and evaluation of the work of the school. Another feature is the way schools encourage teachers and students to try new ideas and approaches—in other words, to make school a creative and inspiring place to teach and learn. Moreover, teaching in schools aims to cultivate renewal while respecting schools' pedagogic legacies. This does not mean that traditional instruction and school organization are nonexistent in Finland; in fact, it is quite the opposite. What is important is that today's Finnish education policies are a result of 3 decades of systematic, mostly intentional development that has created a culture of diversity, trust, and respect within Finnish society in general and within the education system in particular.

I have named this alternative approach to the Global Educational Reform Movement the *Finnish Way*. A similar attempt in the development of an information society and economic system is called the *Finnish Model* (Castells & Himanen, 2002; Dahlman et al., 2006). What distinguishes Finland from most other nations is the proven level of performance of the education system that has occurred simultaneously in learning outcomes and equity in education. These are both the next-generation applications of the Third Way, or radical centrism, which became well known in the 1990s through the leadership of Tony Blair, Bill Clinton, and Gerhard Schröder. In education, the Finnish Way seems to have strongly inspired the Fourth Way (2009):

> The Fourth Way is a way of inspiration and innovation, of responsibility and sustainability. The Fourth Way does not drive reform relentlessly through teachers, use them as final delivery points for government policies, or vacuum up their motivations into a vortex of change that is defined by short-term political agendas and the special interests with which they are often aligned. (Hargreaves & Shirley, 2009, p. 71)

The Finnish Way is a professional and democratic path to improvement that grows from the bottom, steers from the top, and provides support and pressure from the middle. "Through high quality teachers committed to and capable of creating deep and broad teaching and learning," as Hargreaves and Shirley describe the Fourth Way, "it builds powerful, responsible and lively professional communities in an increasingly self-regulating but not self-absorbed or self-seeking profession" (Hargreaves & Shirley, 2009, p. 107). In the Finnish Way, teachers design and pursue high standards and shared targets, and improve their schools continuously through professional collaboration and networks, from evidence, and from literature in their trade.

The Finnish Way is an antidote to toxic neoliberal education agenda. Neoliberalism is an ideological foundation of GERM. It believes that allowing individuals to act in their own self-interest is the best way to economic prosperity and a good life for all. It, therefore, favors small government and encourages privatizing public services, especially education, health, and social protection, to provide people with choice and competition between different service providers. But for most parents of young children education as "a private marketplace" is an illusion. An Australian federal education minister recently instructed parents who are unhappy with their current early childhood provider to "shop around" to make sure they get the best value for their money. In the United States the Trump administration called school choice the civil rights statement of the year 2020. The list of similar examples doesn't end here. Neoliberalism is indeed alive and well in many other countries as well. But change may come.

In the midst of the COVID-19 pandemic governments around the world are negotiating their 2021 budgets or amendments in their current ones. The U.S. government is preparing a US$2 trillion coronavirus relief package to save businesses, employers, and citizens from a total catastrophe. Australian government's 2021 budget projects a deficit of AU$213.7 billion (US$155 billion). The British government's pockets are also empty: In the second half of 2020, the COVID-19 boosted borrowing and pushed national debt to a record £2 trillion (US$2.6 trillion). The treasuries' balance sheets in most other countries follow the same pattern. Where do governments get all that money to fix the growing budget deficits? As loans and credits from banks and international money markets.

In such a deep fiscal trouble caused by the coronavirus pandemic, neoliberal governments and private businesses that support them now turn to public spending, public institutions, and government regulation for help. They may hate the nanny state when business is as usual, but they need it when plans fail. Neoliberal governments criticize the Nordic social democratic welfare states for high taxes and big governments that waste taxpayers' money on expensive public services, such as early childhood education and care, healthy school lunches for all children, and publicly funded higher education for every student. Here is a possible silver lining as a lesson from the pandemic: The coronavirus pandemic will probably reveal how the governments that have invested in social inequality, built strong public service networks for health, social protection and education, and maintained public ownership of some key industries, such as telecommunication, postal services, and transportation, are more successful in protecting their citizens, educating their children, and protecting their businesses than others. In the middle of the crisis these governments invest in the essential aspects of their societies, such as free child care, public education, and renewable energy, rather than cut spending on them or ignore them altogether.

The United States has chosen a very different strategy in coping with the COVID-19 crisis. The 2-trillion-dollar relief package, which American children one day have to pay back, will not make the future any brighter if the money is spent unwisely. In democracy it is up to the people to decide how the borrowed public money will be spent. COVID-19 has taught that public spending and government regulation are powerful ways to keep us safe and improve our lives when done wisely. In August 2020, the new Finnish government led by Sanna Marin introduced the 2021 state budget with a projected 7 billion euro deficit (US$8.2 billion). The government decided to borrow that money to enhance employment, to secure better public services to all citizens, and to strengthen early childhood education, secondary education, and universities as essential investments for the future. Political leadership like that is not unique in Finland; it has happened before, as I will show next.

AN INNOVATION ECONOMY

The major economic transformation and need for sophisticated knowledge and skills in new high-tech industries provided the Finnish education system with unique opportunities for radical renewal in the 1990s. This happened at the same time that three significant economic and political processes were unfolding: the collapse of the Soviet Union (1989–1991), a deep and severe economic recession triggered by a Finnish banking crisis (1990–1993), and integration with the European Union (1992–1995). Each of these changes influenced the Finnish education sector either directly or indirectly.

By the middle of the 1990s, a clear Finnish consensus emerged that mobile communication technologies would eventually foster the transformation to a knowledge economy and that this was perhaps the best way out of the economic crisis and into the heart of European power (Halme et al., 2014). It was also realized that the knowledge economy is not only about preparing human capital for higher know-how; it is also about having highly educated and critical consumers who are able to benefit from innovative technological products in markets that require better technological literacy.

At the beginning of 1993, Finland was in the most severe economic recession since the 1930s. Unemployment was reaching 20%, gross domestic product volume had declined 13%, the banking sector was collapsing, and public debt had gone through the roof. The government led by the new, young prime minister, Esko Aho, responded to this national crisis in an unexpected way. First, investments were heavily targeted toward innovation instead of toward promoting a range of traditional activities. The survival strategy addressed diversification away from timber and conventional industries and toward high-technology and mobile communication. It introduced a new national competitiveness policy and accelerated the privatization of some government-owned companies and public agencies. It also accelerated the liberalization of fiscal markets and foreign ownership in Finland. The key assumption was that the facilitation of private sector innovation and reciprocal collaboration between public and private actors would be superior to traditional direct intervention and investment in broader research and development policy. Overcoming the crisis was mainly a result of the strong concentration on the telecommunication industry and the support of the Nokia Corporation in particular. Nokia gave birth to a completely new electronics industry in Finland, which was an essential part of the successful Finnish economic comeback in the 1990s.

Second, knowledge accumulation and development became the key turnaround feature in pulling Finland up from depression. Without many natural resources to rely on, Finland's main determinants for growth strategies became knowledge and the active internationalization of its economy and education. In 1998, the World Economic Forum (WEF) ranked Finland 15th in its global economic competitiveness index. By 2001, Finland had climbed to the top position in this influential ranking that covers more than 130 economies of the world (Alquézar Sabadie & Johansen, 2010; Sahlberg, 2006). Gross expenditure on research and development, commonly used as a proxy for competitiveness in knowledge-based economies, increased from 2.0% in 1991 to 3.9% in 2010, at the same time that the OECD average was fluctuating between 2.0% and 2.3% (Statistics Finland, n.d.b). The number of knowledge workers in the Finnish labor force also increased significantly. The total research and development labor force in 1991 was exactly at the OECD average at that time—slightly more than 5 per 1,000 workers. By 2003, this number had climbed to 22 per 1,000, almost three times higher than the concurrent OECD average.

The transformation of the Finnish economy into a knowledge economy is described as "remarkable, not only in light of its earlier economic difficulties . . . [but because] it is interesting to see that a knowledge economy can be built successfully in a small and comparably peripheral country" (Dahlman et al., 2006, p. 4). Trust and increased investment in innovation resulted in education policies in the 1990s that focused on better knowledge and skills, along with creativity and problem solving. The strong focus on mathematics, science, and technology contributed markedly to the growth of Nokia as a world leader in mobile communications and Stora Enso in paper manufacturing. Several Finnish universities were closely connected to research and development in these firms. Indeed, governmental innovation agencies actively facilitated innovation as a third element in the Finnish knowledge and innovation triangle. Finnish economists who endorsed the importance of innovation and education in national development policy also played an important role. Education was seen as necessary and as a potential investment—not just an expenditure—in helping to develop innovation and adopting more innovation throughout the economy. Highly educated people are certainly "irreplaceable for the implementation of new technologies from home and abroad" (Asplund & Maliranta, 2006, p. 282).

The information society and knowledge economy have been important contextual factors for educational change in Finland since the 1970s. The economic sector in Finland has expected the education system to provide skilled and creative young people who have the competencies businesses need to deal with rapidly changing economic and technological environments. In their call for raising standards of knowledge and skills, Finnish employers, for example, were reluctant to advocate for narrow specialization and early selection to schools, unlike many other countries at that time. Although Finnish industry actively promoted better learning of mathematics, sciences, and technology, it also supported rather innovative forms of school–industry partnerships as part of the formal curriculum. The rapid emergence of innovation-driven businesses in the mid-1990s introduced creative problem solving and innovative cross-curricular projects and teaching methods to schools.[3] Some leading Finnish companies reminded education policymakers of the importance of keeping teaching and learning creative and open to new ideas, rather than fixing them to predetermined standards and accountability through national testing.

Membership in the European Union in 1995 marked a mental challenge and change for, and within, Finland. The Soviet Union had disappeared only a few years earlier, an event that boosted the consolidation of Finland's identity as a full member of western Europe. The accession process of becoming a European Union member state was as important as attaining actual membership in 1995. As a new Finnish identity emerged during the years of accession to the European Union, the Finnish people were motivated to ensure that they and their institutions, including schools, were up to the level of other European nations. In fact, the poor reputation of mathematics and sciences in Finnish schools, compared with their European peers in the 1970s and the 1980s, became a reason to try harder to improve Finnish educational performance to the European level. Although education is not included in formal European Union membership requirements or common directives, the accession process nonetheless had a tangible positive impact on strengthening public institutions, including the education system in Finland, especially in the midst of the worst economic recession, described earlier in this chapter. Moreover, Finnish educators became increasingly aware of various European education systems. This certainly drove the ongoing education reform and the adoption of new ideas as more information became readily available about practices within other systems.

History and the personal mindset of Finns suggest that they are at their best when faced with these kinds of global challenges. For example, experiences such as the war against the Soviet Union (1939–1944), the 1952 Olympics, and the deep economic recession of the early 1990s provide good evidence of the competitive and resilient Finnish spirit, or *sisu*, as the Finns say. These educational and cultural attitudes were complemented by key economic, employment, and social policies that evolved since the 1970s, while the establishment of a welfare state and its institutions and policies was completed by the end of the 1980s. Survival has always been the best source of inspiration and energy for the Finns to go beyond expectations.

Analysis of educational change often includes speculation about the basic nature of change—that is, whether it is evolutionary or revolutionary. These terms refer to change as being either continuous, with smooth development from one stage to another, or a radical transition, where entirely new institutions and rules are created. Educational change in Finland has displayed periodic evolution, meaning that the nature of educational change has changed during these times. What is important to realize, as shown in Table 4.2, is that 1990 marks an important watershed in history that distinguishes two periods in Finnish education. The time prior to 1990 was characterized by the creation of institutions and frameworks for a welfare-based education system. The years since 1990 have been more concerned with interests, ideas, and innovations that have formed the education system as an integral part of a complex social, economic, and political system. Part of the success of the Finnish Way emerges from an ability to create punctuated equilibrium between these two periods of educational change.

Two simultaneous processes have played an important role in developing the education system in Finland since 1970. On the one hand, increased interaction among various public sector policies has strengthened the coherence of economic and social reforms and, therefore, created conditions for what Andy Hargreaves and Dean Fink (2006) term "sustainable leadership" in education. This increased coherence enables a systematic commitment to longer-term vision and intersector cooperation among different policies and strategies. On the other hand, internationalization and Finland's integration into the European Union have harmonized and intensified the consolidation and development of public institutions and their basic functions. In this light, three conclusions can be drawn regarding how Finnish educational success can be understood from an economic and political perspective:

1. The success of Finnish education reform is mainly based on institutions and institutional structures established in the 1970s and the 1980s, rather than on changes and improvements implemented from the 1990s. The state-generated social capital that is created through government regulations and motivated by the responsibility to provide basic conditions of well-being for all has provided a favorable social context for educational achievement.
2. Changes in Finnish primary and secondary education after 1990 have been more about interests, ideas, and innovations than about new institutional structures. Institutional changes in the 1990s have been smaller, except in higher education, where a new polytechnic system was introduced. Nonetheless, directions remain clear and are based on earlier policies.
3. The emphasis on national competitiveness that has been a key driving force in most public sector policies in the European Union has not been converted to clear targets or operations in Finnish public policy sectors during the 1990s and the 2000s. At the same time, equality and equity principles promulgated in the early 1970s have gradually lost influence in these policies.

To sum up, since 1970 there have been two differing yet interconnected educational change periods, which are distinguished in terms of the theories of change and sources of ideas and innovation that drive them. On the one hand, education reform principles have increasingly

Table 4.2. Increased Interdependency Among Public Sector Policies in Finland Since 1970

Strategy	Economic Policies	Employment Policies	Social Policies	Education Reform Principles
1970s: Institutionalization Consolidation of the pillars of welfare state and strengthened state-driven social capital. Fostering conventional industrial production structures.	Small, open economy that depended on exports and was state-regulated. Investments mainly in physical capital.	Establishing active employment policies and unemployment benefit system. Strengthening direct training for labor markets.	New risk-management systems for adults. Systems for unemployment, work–life balance, access to further education and housing.	Emphasis on equity and equal access to good primary and secondary education for all. Securing public provision of education.
1980s: Restructuring Welfare state completed. Restructuring economic regulations, information technology infrastructure, and public administration.	Rapid public sector growth. Industrial production concentrates on metal and wood sectors.	Restructuring unemployment benefit system. Using early retirement as part of new employment policies.	Student welfare services and medical care system. Student loan and social benefit systems. Restructuring unemployment legislation.	Restructuring upper-secondary education to increase access for all students. Transferring upper-secondary schools to municipal authority.

Establishment of institutions

Sector policies strengthen

196

1990s: Ideas and Innovation Public sector liberalization. Diversification of exports through innovation-driven markets and dissemination of ideas through a network society.	Public sector growth halts and starts to decline. Private service sector starts to grow, and new ICT industries emerge. Investments in R&D increased. Restructuring of banking sector.	Recession cuts employment benefits. New labor market benefit system to encourage employment. Employment policy system reform.	Fixing social consequences of Big Recession, especially for in-debt and long-term unemployed. Retraining and further education of unemployed.	Empowering teachers and schools through school-based curricula, coordinated innovations, and networking schools and municipalities for sharing ideas and change. Expansion of higher education sector.
2000s: Renewal Strengthening well-performing parts of economy and renewing social policies (further privatization) to match financial realities.	Focus on services increases. Central administration loses its role and productivity of public sector is emphasized.	Aging population casts a shadow on employment. Accent on rights and obligations of unemployed. Cross-sector approach emphasized.	Renewing immigration legislation. Adapting social system for further diversification.	Renewing education legislation, strengthening evaluation policies, and tightening state control over schools and productivity in education sector. Sizes of schools increase.

Interests, ideas, and innovation

Interdependency between public

Source: Sahlberg (2010b).

been created interdependently with other public policy sectors, following a *complementarity* principle. On the other hand, ideas for educational change—particularly for improving teaching and learning in schools—have been built on past good practices and traditions in Finland. This has sometimes been labeled *pedagogical conservatism* and has created a pedagogical equilibrium between progressivism and conservatism through learning from the past and teaching for the future (Simola, 2005, 2015). A common conclusion about the role of social and economic policies in building the education system in Finland since the 1970s is that it demonstrates how context makes a difference in educational achievement. In other words, it shows that individual well-being, equitable distribution of income, and social capital can explain student learning in international comparisons.

Let's take a closer look at how social policies and the welfare state are linked to performance in Finland's education system.

WELFARE, EQUALITY, AND COMPETITIVENESS

Social policy decisions in the 1950s and the 1960s in Finland underscored the economic importance of farms run by families. However, the general perceived image of Finland remained agrarian despite rapid industrialization and agriculture's declining contribution to the GDP over the second half of the 20th century. Regardless of drastic changes in the way of life and emerging cosmopolitanism among Finnish people, traditional social values endured. According to Richard Lewis (2005), who has studied the Finnish culture closely, these values included such cultural hallmarks as a law-abiding citizenry, trust in authority including schools, commitment to one's social group, awareness of one's social status and position, and a patriotic spirit. Policies that guided education reforms since the 1970s relied on these cultural values and principles of consensus building that have been distinguishing characteristics of Finnish society.

Finland followed the main postwar social policies of other Nordic countries. This led to the creation of a type of welfare state where basic social services, including education, became public services for all citizens, particularly for those most in need of support and help. It increased the level of social capital, as did national government policies that affected children's broader social environment and improved their opportunities and willingness to learn. Martin Carnoy (2007) calls this "state-generated social capital"—that is, the social context for educational achievement created by government social policies. The influence of social restructuring and educational reform in Finland was profound and immediate. Eager to improve their children's economic and social opportunities, Finnish parents turned to the education system, which has served as an equalizing institution in Finnish society.

Income inequality is often claimed to affect people's lives in more ways than just how much they can afford to spend on their living. Are education systems in more equal societies performing better than elsewhere? Richard Wilkinson and Kate Pickett (2009) argue in their book *The Spirit Level* that indeed these systems are doing better in more ways than one. Actually, Wilkinson and Pickett show how income inequality is related to many other issues in our societies as well. Income inequality, which can be measured in different ways, calculates the gap between the wealthiest and poorest quintile in each country. In Figure 4.1, I use the data from the OECD's database to construct a relationship between income inequality and child poverty in OECD countries. It appears that there is a strong positive relationship between wealth distribution and number of children suffering from economic and social disadvantage: In more equal societies children also benefit from a fairer share of common wealth. Furthermore, in their latest book *The Inner Level* (2018) Wilkinson and Pickett show how more equal societies reduce stress, restore sanity, and improve everyone's well-being. All these inequalities are closely linked to teaching and learning outcomes in school.

A conclusion using data from international student assessments is that students' home country and family income are equally important for predicting students' test scores in these tests. That is also what Dev Patel and Justin Sandefur (2019) found out when they researched how much do differences in human capital explain patterns of economic growth, trade, and inequality around the world. The *Economist* (2020), which is an international weekly newspaper, phrased it bluntly: "It's better be a poor pupil in a rich country than the reverse." It is noteworthy, however, that international tests don't necessarily indicate what students actually know or are able to do because they often don't show their best efforts in these tests, as was explained in Chapter 2.

It is understandable that income inequality, child poverty, and lack of appropriate pupil welfare in schools all play an important part in improving the quality of education systems. This has been well understood in Finland during the past half century. Complimentary healthy school lunches, comprehensive welfare services, and early support to

Figure 4.1. Income Inequality (Gini) and Child Poverty in OECD Countries in 2018

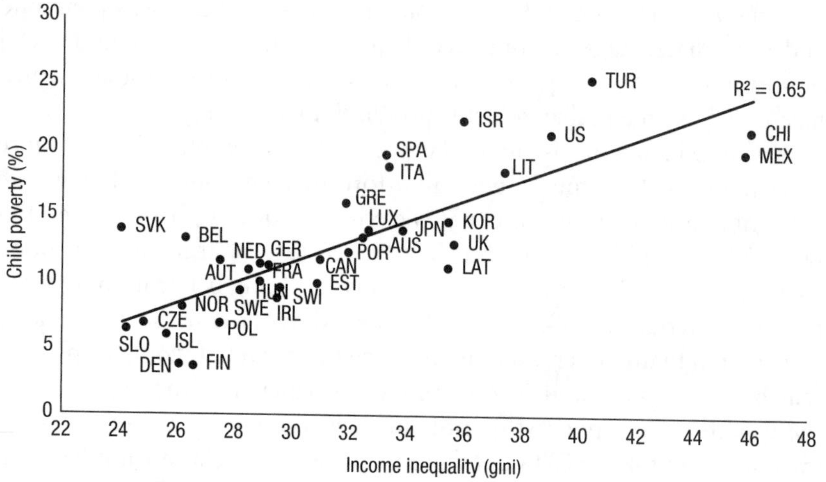

Source: OECD database.

those who are in need have been made available for all children in all Finnish schools—free of charge. Every child has, by law, a right to these welfare services in their school.

This chapter suggests that educational progress in Finland should be viewed within the broader context of economic and social development and renewal, both nationally and globally. Interestingly, the growth of the Finnish education sector coincided with an impressive economic transformation from an agrarian, production-driven economy to a modern information society and knowledge-driven economy. Indeed, Finland has transformed itself into a modern welfare state with a dynamic knowledge economy in a relatively short time. The Finnish experience of the 1990s represents one of the few documented examples of how education and therefore knowledge can become driving forces of economic growth and transformation. During that decade, Finland became the most specialized economy in the world in telecommunications technology and thus completed its transition from being a resource-driven country to a knowledge- and innovation-driven economic and educational system.

In the 2000s, Finland consistently scored high in international comparisons of national economic competitiveness, transparency and good governance, gender equality, technological advancement, innovation, implementation of sustainable development policies, and, surprisingly, happiness of the people. Finland was ranked as the most competitive economy several times in the first decade of the 21st century by the World Economic Forum's Global Competitiveness Index.[4] This is significant, given that Finland experienced a severe economic crisis in the early 1990s. Becoming a competitive knowledge economy, a leader in innovation and research, and the first country to make broadband Internet connection a human right for all citizens required a major restructuring of the Finnish economic system. Moreover, Finland has a reputation for rule of law and, as a consequence, enjoys a low level of corruption, which plays an important role in economic development and the performance of public institutions.

After the historic economic crisis of the 1990s, good governance, strong social cohesiveness, and an extensive social safety net provided by the welfare state made exceptionally rapid economic recovery possible. A similar turnaround of Finnish economic progress was recorded after the global financial crisis in 2008. One of the strategic principles used in pulling the Finnish economy out of a downturn has been continuous high levels of investment in research and development, as described earlier in this chapter. Despite severe cuts in public spending, both in the early 1990s and after the most recent fiscal crisis, the Finnish belief in knowledge generation and innovation has remained strong. In 2018, due to stagnated economic growth, Finland spent 2.7% of its GDP on research and development—that is above the average of the OECD countries.

Gender equality is an important value in Finnish society. In December 2019 the new government that took the power was led by five female ministers, including a prime minister, a finance minister, an education minister, and an interior minister who were younger than 35 years old. Finland's first female president, Tarja Halonen, led the country from 2000 to 2012, and an increasing number of women are now also in top positions in the corporate world. Laws and regulation require that all common issues in the society must be discussed and decided by experts and authorities representing equally both genders. Several political initiatives regarding education—for example, early childhood education as a right of every child—have been initiated by female politicians. Interestingly, of the current 200-strong Parliament in Finland, 23 have a teaching background and 7 others come from the education sector. In 2019, general elections brought a record number of women to the Parliament, 93, which is 47%. Figure 4.2 shows the percentage of women in national parliaments in OECD countries in 2019.

Figure 4.2. Percentage of Women in National Parliaments (or Similar) in OECD Countries in 2019

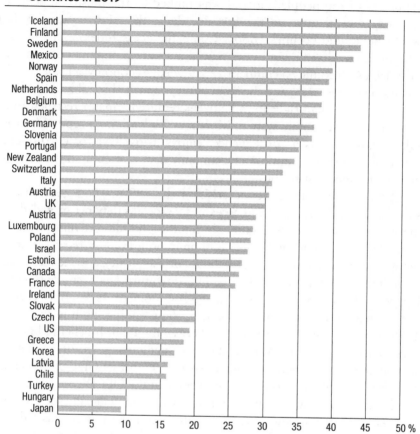

Source: OECD database.

As noted, this chapter asserts that education system performance has to be seen within the context of other systems in the society—for example, health, environment, rule of law, governance, economy, and technology. Not only does the education system operate well in Finland, but it is part of a well-functioning democratic welfare state. Attempts to explain the success of the education system in Finland should be put in the wider context and seen as a part of the overall function of democratic civil society. Economists have been interested in finding out why Finland has been able to become the most competitive economy in the world. Educators are trying to figure out the secret of Finland's good educational performance. The quality of a nation or its parts is rarely a result of any single factor. The entire society needs to perform harmoniously. This can be called system excellence.

Four common features are often mentioned as contributing factors for positive educational and economic progress. First, policy development has been based on integration rather than exclusive subsector policies. Education sector development is driven by medium-term policy decisions that rely on sustainable basic values, such as equal opportunities for good education for all, the inclusion of all students in mainstream publicly financed education, and strong trust in public education as a civil right rather than an obligation. These medium-term policies integrate education and training, and involve the private sector and industry in the creation and monitoring of their results. Similarly, economic and industrial policies have integrated science and technology policies and innovation systems with industrial clusters. Integrated policies have enhanced systemic development and the interconnectedness of these sectors and have thus promoted more sustainable and coherent political leadership for their successful implementation.

Second, strategic framework development and change have been built on a longer-term vision. National development strategies, such as the Information Society Program in 1995, the National Lifelong Learning Strategy in 1997, and the Ministry of Education Strategy 2020, have served as overarching frameworks for the sector strategies. These and other strategies have emphasized increasing flexibility, coherence among various sectors, and the development of local and regional responsiveness and creativity in institutions.

Third, the roles of government and public institutions have been central in policy developments and the implementation of both education and economic reforms. Good governance, high-quality public institutions, and the rule of law play important roles in policy development and the implementation of planned changes. Evaluation approaches in both sectors are development-oriented, and various players in the system are held accountable for process and outcomes. Specific institutions, such as the Parliamentary Committee for the Future, are shared by private and public representatives as well as by the key stakeholders of the society for consensus-building purposes.

Fourth, a highly educated and skilled labor force and broad participation in education at all levels guarantee the stock of *human capital* that is necessary (but not sufficient) for both a good education system and economic growth. For instance, all teachers are required to hold a master's degree, and most workers are encouraged to participate in continuous professional development as part of their work. Teachers are considered professionals in their schools and are therefore actively involved in planning and implementing changes in their work.

Flexibility is one of the key denominators of education and economic development in Finland. The education system went through a major transformation in the early 1990s when most state regulations were abolished, and pathways to education opportunities were dramatically increased. Similarly, private sector regulations became looser and more flexible standards were introduced, especially to foster networking among private companies, universities, public research, and development institutions.

Strong integrated policy frameworks and longer-term strategic visions have enhanced sustainable leadership in education and private sector developments. Because of this sustainability factor, the education system has been resistant to the market-oriented principles of the Global Educational Reform Movement. Frequent and open dialogue between private business leaders and the public education sector has increased mutual understanding of what is important in achieving the common good and promoting the development of a knowledge economy. Indeed, active cooperation between education and industry has encouraged schools to experiment with creative teaching and learning practices, especially in nurturing entrepreneurship and building positive attitudes toward work. Most important, the main principle in the development of Finnish society has been encouraging intellectual growth and the learning of each individual. Developing cultures of growth and learning in education institutions as well as in workplaces has proved to be one of the key success factors. That is why every school principal in Finland is also a teacher, as explained in Box 4.1.

FOREIGN INNOVATION, FINNISH IMPLEMENTATION

Many foreign observers have been surprised that they see only a few originally Finnish innovations practiced in classrooms. A closer look at the origin of Finland's current pedagogical models, school improvement practices, and education innovation in general reveals another intriguing characteristic of Finland's schools: Many of the innovations that have made Finnish schools blossom can be traced back to other countries, often to the United States. This is surprising given Finland's strong position as one of the most innovative societies and knowledge economies in the world.

Another observation is that all successful education systems have derived critical lessons and practical models from abroad. Singapore,

BOX 4.1: LEADERSHIP IN FINNISH SCHOOLS

School sizes in Finland are increasing. One hundred fifty years ago, when the Finnish public school was born, most schools had only one teacher. Today, these schools do not exist. In today's schools, teachers have to be able to work together in shared spaces and also educate students together. Each teacher has to adjust his or her pedagogical thinking and principles to those of other teachers. It is therefore essential that the school has a common culture that enables consistent teaching and learning for shared purposes. This is why a principal is needed in each school.

The Finnish school principal is always also a teacher. Almost all Finnish principals teach some classes each week. Finnish school principals have an increasing amount of administrative duties. Many complain that the workload is becoming too heavy. The principal needs a good theory of leadership in order to cope successfully with all tasks and responsibilities in school. I would say that principals should also have a vision of what a good school is and should know how leadership can help achieve that vision.

In my work as a principal, I made basic values the foundation on which I laid my leadership. In good schools, daily routines work well, and teaching is effective. My task was to help my teachers do their best, and I make the necessary decisions so that my school operates well. I worked hard to create a good atmosphere in school and to inspire teachers and students. As a leader of my own school and as part of the network of other public schools in my district, I must know national and local-level policies. It was important to guarantee that public money was wisely spent in all schools, including mine. That's what makes a good school principal.

I strived to be a good principal in my school. It means that I had to do my best as a manager, leader, director, and pedagogic guide for teachers and students: In other words, I wanted to be a good and trusted person. The biggest challenge for me was to combine all these aspects of my work. Being a school principal is not like being an administrator or the coach of a sports team. A school principal is in charge of the part of a complex social system that is continuously changing. Without experience as a teacher, this work would be very difficult to carry out successfully.

—Martti Hellström, School Principal Emeritus of Aurora School, City of Espoo.
Lecturer in the University of Helsinki.

one of the most successful reformers and highest performers in educa-tion, has been sending students to study education in American and British universities and encouraged their own university professors to collaborate in teaching and research with foreign colleagues. Japan, Hong Kong, and South Korea have done the same. More recently, China has also benefited from education innovation imported from the United States and other Western education systems.

Finland is no exception to this trend. The most successful practices in pedagogy, student assessment, school leadership, and school improve-ment in Finland are predominantly foreign. In their preparation for work in school Finnish teachers and principals study educational psychology, teaching methods, curriculum theories, assessment models, and classroom management researched and developed in American universities and re-search institutions. Primary school teacher education curriculum (see Table 3.2) in Finnish universities includes textbooks and research articles with models, methods, and theories written by international scholars. Professional development and school improvement courses and longer programs often include guest speakers from abroad to share their knowl-edge and experience with Finnish educators. So common is the reliance on American ideas in Finland that some have come to call the Finnish school system a large-scale laboratory of American education innovation.

The relatively low overall rating of "innovation in education" in the United States in the OECD's innovation-in-education ranking (in which Finland did not participate) in 2014 (OECD, 2014b) raises an inter-esting question: Why don't current education policymakers and system leaders in the United States make better use of the American education innovations that other countries have been able to utilize to improve the performance of their school systems during the last century? According to the OECD, the United States exhibits only modest innovation in its education system, but, at the same time, it is the world leader in produc-ing research, practical models, and innovation for other countries. The following five American educational ideas have been instrumental in ac-celerating Finland's success in education.

1. John Dewey's philosophy of education. The roots of Finland's pedagogi-cal ideas date back to the 1860s, when Uno Cygnaeus, who was a room-mate of my grandfather's grandfather Reinhold Ferdinand Sahlberg during their student years at the University of Helsinki in the 1830s and a fellow passenger to Sitka, Alaska, in the 1840s, created a masterplan for the Finnish folk school. Cygnaeus, who is sometimes referred to as the father of public education in Finland, said that in an ideal classroom, pupils speak more than the teacher. He was also a proponent of practical aspects of education and insisted that both boys and girls must learn all the practical skills that people need in everyday lives. It is understandable that the pragmatic, child-centered educational thinking of John Dewey has been widely accepted among Finnish educators. Dewey's philosophy of education forms a foundation for academic, research-based teacher education in Finland and influenced also the work of the most influential Finnish scholar, Matti Koskenniemi, in the 1940s. All primary school teachers read and explore Dewey's and Koskenniemi's ideas as part of their courses leading to the master's degree. Many Finnish schools have adopted Dewey's view of education for democracy by enhancing students' access to decisionmaking regarding their own lives and studying in school.

2. *Cooperative learning.* Unlike in most other countries, cooperative learning has become a pedagogical approach that is widely practiced throughout the Finnish education system. Finland's 9-year comprehensive school, launched in the early 1970s, was built on an idea of regular small-group learning of students with diverse backgrounds. But it was the national curriculum reform in 1994 that brought cooperative learning as it is known now to all Finnish schools. Before that, cooperative learning researchers and trainers, including David Johnson, Roger Johnson, Elizabeth Cohen, and Yael and Shlomo Sharan, had visited Finland to train trainers and teachers on their methods of teaching. Their books and articles were translated into Finnish and shared with all schools. The 1994 national curriculum included a requirement that all schools design their own curricula in a way that would enhance teaching and learning according to constructivist educational ideas. Although cooperative learning was not mentioned as an obligatory pedagogical practice in schools, there were several recommendations for teachers to include elements of cooperative learning into their regular teaching. Ever since, cooperative learning has become an integral part of initial teacher education in Finland and one of the most popular themes in professional development of teachers and school leaders in Finland. National Core Curricula for Basic School in 2014 and General Upper Secondary School in 2021 emphasize the importance of collaboration in both teaching and learning in school.

3. *Multiple intelligences.* The spirit of the 1970s school reform in Finland included another idea that derives from American universities and scholars: development of the whole child. The overall goal of

schooling in Finland was to support a child's holistic development and growth by focusing on different aspects of talent and intelligence. After abolishing all streaming and tracking of students in the mid-1980s, both education policies and school practices adopted the principle that all children can learn, that children have different kinds of intelligences, and that schools must find ways to cultivate these different individual aspects in balanced ways. Howard Gardner's theory of multiple intelligences (Gardner, 1983, 2020) became a leading idea in transferring these policy principles to school practice. Again, the 1994 national curriculum emphasizes that school education must provide all students with opportunities to develop all aspects of their minds. As a consequence, that curriculum framework required that all schools have a balanced program, blending academic subjects with art, music, crafts, and physical education. This framework, moreover, mandated that all schools provide students with sufficient time for their self-directive activities. Gardner's influence has also been notable in the Finnish system by conferring a broader definition of "talent." Today, Finnish teachers believe that over 90% of students can learn successfully in their own classrooms if given the opportunity to evolve in a holistic manner.

4. Alternative classroom assessments. Without a system of frequent standardized and census-based testing, the Finnish education system relies on local monitoring and teacher-made student assessments. A child-centered, interaction-rich, whole-child approach in the national curriculum requires that different student assessment models be used in schools. Furthermore, primary school pupils don't get any grades in their assessments before they are in 4th grade. It was natural that Finnish teachers found alternative student assessment methods attractive. And it is ironic that many of these methods were developed at American universities and yet are far more popular in Finland than in the United States. These methods include portfolio assessment, performance assessment, self-assessment and self-reflection, and assessment for learning methods. Teacher education programs in Finland that have been influenced by works of Linda Darling-Hammond, David Berliner, and others include elements of study of educational assessment and evaluation theories and also provide all students with practical knowledge and skills for how to use alternative student assessment methods in the classroom.

5. Peer coaching. Another surprising aspect of Finnish education is that it lacks much of the change knowledge that is normally expected to guide policymakers and education authorities in planning and implementing desired reforms in education. Research and development of system-wide educational reform and change hasn't belonged to the repertoire of Finnish academia. The number of research papers related to that field has therefore remained minimal. Instead, Finnish education experts have relied on foreign sources of expertise and knowledge. A good example of an innovation designed in the United States is peer coaching, which evolved in the 1980s and the 1990s as a result of the research and development work of Bruce Joyce and his colleagues (Joyce & Showers, 1995). Bruce Joyce also visited Finland in the 1980s to train trainers and education leaders on how the impact of professional development for teachers can be enhanced. Peer coaching—that is, a confidential process through which teachers work together to reflect on current practices; expand, improve, and learn new skills; exchange ideas; conduct classroom research; and solve problems together in school—have become normal practice in school improvement programs and professional development in Finland since the mid-1990s.

For many educators, including me, the United States is home to a great deal of educational change knowledge, research, and innovation. The question of why this doesn't show in international comparisons, like international student assessments or the recent review of innovation in education by the OECD, is an important one. Indeed, visitors to the United States often wonder why innovations that have brought improvement to all successful education systems in the world have not been practiced on a large scale in the United States school system. Lessons from Finland suggest that it may be that the work of the school in the United States is so much steered by bureaucracies, test-based accountability, and politics that schools are simply doing what they are forced to do in this awkward situation. Many visitors from the United States often note that what they see in Finnish schools reminds them of practices they had seen in many schools in the United States in the 1970s and the 1980s.

MYTHS ABOUT THE FINNISH SCHOOL

We have learned a lot about why some education systems—such as Alberta, Ontario, Japan, Estonia, and Finland—perform better year after year than others in terms of quality and equity of student outcomes. We also better understand now why some other education systems—for example, England, Australia, the United States, and Sweden—have not been able to improve their school systems regardless of politicians' promises, large-scale reforms, and truckloads of money spent on haphazard efforts to change schools during the past two decades.

Among these important lessons are:

- Education systems and schools shouldn't be managed like business corporations where tough competition, measurement-based accountability, and performance-determined pay are common principles. Instead, successful education systems rely on collaboration, trust, and collegial responsibility in and between schools.
- The teaching profession shouldn't be perceived as a technical, temporary craft that anyone with a little guidance can do. Successful education systems rely on continuous professionalization of teaching and school leadership that requires advanced academic education, solid scientific and practical knowledge, and continuous on-the-job training.
- The quality of education shouldn't be judged by the level of literacy and numeracy test scores alone. Successful education systems are designed to emphasize whole-child development, equity of education outcomes, well-being, and arts, music, drama, and physical education as important elements of curriculum.

The world has also learned many lessons about educational change in Finland about the rules to design an equitable and better education system for all. Besides these useful lessons about how and why education systems work as they do, there are misunderstandings, incorrect interpretations, myths, and even deliberate lies about how to best improve education systems (Sahlberg, 2018, 2019). Because Finland has been such a popular target of searching for the key to the betterment of education, there are also many stories about Finnish schools that are not true.

Part of the reason that reporting the Finnish story often fails to paint a bigger and more accurate picture of the actual situation is that most of the documents and resources that describe and define the Finnish education system are not available in English or other languages than Finnish and Swedish. Most foreign education observers and commentators are therefore unable to follow the conversations and debates taking place in the country.

For example, only very few of those who actively comment on education in Finland have ever read the laws and regulations, the national core curriculum for different levels of education, or any of thousands of curricula designed by municipalities and schools that explain and describe in detail what schools ought to do and why.

The other reason many efforts to report about Finnish education remain incomplete—and sometimes incorrect—is that education is seen as an isolated island disconnected from other sectors and public policies. It is wrong to believe that what children learn or don't learn in school could be explained by looking at only schools and what they do alone. This book has hopefully made it clear that everywhere, but especially in Finland, that what most children learn or don't learn in school is due to factors outside the school gate.

Most efforts to explain why Finland's schools are better than many others or why they do worse today than before fail to see these interdependencies in Finnish society that are essential in understanding education as an ecosystem. Almost without an exception the stories told about the Finnish Model have been silent about the role early childhood education and care, active engagement of the nongovernmental sector with its youth and sport services to children, or dense network of public libraries have had on students' performance in basic education. Too often the efforts to report the success and more recently the declining performance assume that certain in-school factors explain what is happening in Finnish schools. Most of these efforts end up being anything but myths that should be busted (Sahlberg, 2019).

Here are some of those common myths about Finnish schools.

First, in recent years there have been claims that the Finnish secret to educational greatness is that children don't have homework. This became clear in Michael Moore's documentary *Where to Invade Next* in 2015. Michael Moore was wondering how Finland was able to against all odds beat other countries to become number one in international education rankings. "That was the one question I wanted to answer to," he says in the movie while walking in the corridor leading to the office of the minister of education in Helsinki. "Before I could say anything," he says, "she blurted out their top secret." The minister said: "They don't have homework." So it happened and soon the media around the world reported that the Finnish miracle where all children achieve outstandingly was all about having short school days and no homework. Any Finnish teacher would contest that the former is true, but the latter is not. Children do have shorter school days than many other countries, as mentioned in Chapter 2, but they have homework, but not the same ways as their peers in other countries. In primary schools, homework is often done while students are still at school. High school students in Finland have often too much to study at home even to the point that it creates unnecessary stress and puts their mental health at risk.

Another commonly held belief is that Finnish authorities have decided to scrap subjects from school curriculum and replace them by interdisciplinary projects or themes. And a more recent notion is that all schools in Finland are required to follow a national curriculum and implement the same teaching method called "phenomenon-based learning" (that is elsewhere known as "project-based learning"). This is a myth, too.

In 2014, Finnish basic schools adopted new National Core Curriculum (NCC) that moved the 2004 curriculum framework to history (Finnish National Agency for Education, 2016). The core curriculum provides a common direction and basis for renewing school education and instruction. Only a very few international commentators of Finnish school reform are familiar with this central nearly 500-page-long document that describes the values, principles, and *modus operandi* of Finnish schools. Unfortunately, not many parents in Finland are familiar with it, either. Still, many people seem to have strong opinions about the direction Finnish schools are moving—the wrong way, they say, without really understanding the roles and responsibilities of schools and teachers in their communities, or what is really supposed to happen in Finnish schools and classrooms. Before making any judgments about what is great or wrong in Finland, it is important to understand the fundamentals of the Finnish school system. Here are some basics that were briefly mentioned in Chapter 1.

First, 310 local authorities (or municipalities) that are legally providing education and govern schools draw up local curricula and annual work plans on the basis of the NCC for early childhood education, basic education, and general upper-secondary education. Schools though actually take the lead in curriculum planning under the supervision of local education authorities.

Second, the national core curriculum documents provide local education authorities with fairly loose regulatory frameworks in terms of what schools should teach, how they arrange their work, and the desired outcomes. Schools have, therefore, a lot of flexibility and autonomy in curriculum design, and there may be significant variation in school curricula from one place to another.

Finally, because of this decentralized nature of authority in the Finnish education system, schools in Finland can have different profiles and practical arrangements, making the curriculum model unique in the world. It is incorrect to make any general conclusions about Finnish education based on what one or two schools do. At the system level, current school reform in Finland aims at those same overall goals that many students say are essential for them: to develop safe and collaborative school culture and to promote holistic approaches in teaching and learning. The NCCs are based on a pedagogical principle of transversal competences rather than traditional subject-based domains, and they state that the specific aim is that children would:

- understand the relationship and interdependencies between different learning contents;
- be able to combine the knowledge and skills learned in different disciplines to form meaningful wholes; and
- be able to apply knowledge and use it in collaborative learning settings.

All schools in Finland are required to revise their curricula according to these new common curriculum frameworks. Kindergartens and basic schools have done so already, and general upper-secondary schools will do so starting August 2021. Some basic schools have taken only small steps from where they were before, while some others went on with much bolder plans utilizing the professional autonomies that schools enjoy in Finland. One of those advanced schools is the Pontus Public School in Lappeenranta, a city in the eastern part of Finland.

The Pontus Public School is a new primary school and kindergarten for some 550 children from ages 1 to 12. It was built 3 years ago to support the pedagogy and spirit of the 2014 National Core Curriculum for basic school. The Pontus School was in international news in 2019 when the Finnish Broadcasting Company (YLE) reported that some parents have filed complaints over the "failure" of that new school—yet another example that the only breaking news about schools is bad news!

But according to Lappeenranta education authorities, there have been only two complaints by parents, both being handled by regional authorities. That's all. It is not enough to call that a failure. However, the damage to the school and its teachers was done, and fixing the moral harm and disappointment in school took a long time.

What we can learn from Finland, again, is that it is important to make sure parents, children, and media better understand the nature of current school reforms. "Some parents are not familiar with what schools are doing," said Anu Liljeström, superintendent of the education department in Lappeenranta. "We still have a lot of work to do to explain what, how and why teaching methods are different nowadays," she said to a local newspaper (cited in Sahlberg & Johnson, 2019). The Pontus School is a new school, and it decided to use the opportunity provided by new design to change pedagogy and learning. It takes more than a year to show what a new school can be.

Media around the world has claimed that traditional subjects in Finnish schools will be scrapped and students will study topics by projects instead. It is wrong to think that reading, writing, and arithmetic will disappear in Finnish classrooms. The fact is that for most of the school year, teaching in Finnish schools will continue to be based on subject-based curricula, including at the Pontus School. What is new is that now all schools are required to design at least one project for all students that is interdisciplinary and based on students' interests. Some schools do that better more often than others, and some succeed sooner than others.

Yes, there are challenges in implementing the new ideas. I have seen many schools succeed at creating new opportunities for students to learn knowledge and skills they need in their lives. But it is too early to tell whether Finland's current direction in education meets all expectations. All things considered, however, schools in Finland should take even bolder steps to meet the needs of the future as described in national goals and international strategies. Collaboration among schools, trust in teachers, and visionary leadership are those building blocks that will make all that possible.

CHAPTER 5

Is the Future Finnish?

A good hockey player plays where the puck is. A great hockey player plays where the puck is going to be.

—Wayne Gretzky, Hall of Fame Canadian hockey player

Finland has been engaged in comprehensive school reform since the 1970s. Research on specific features of *peruskoulu* led to the development of applied educational sciences, or subject didactics, in Finnish universities. However, more generic understandings of educational change remained relatively untouched until the early 2000s. Even today, research on educational change, school improvement, and school effectiveness in Finland is modest by international standards. Much more analytical and research work on the Finnish educational system is conducted on the country's educational policies at different phases of its history. It is somewhat paradoxical that even with undeveloped domestic educational change knowledge and research, Finland has been able to transform its education system in only about 2 decades, as this book describes. Models of change in Finland have often been borrowed from abroad, but educational policies, as discussed in the previous chapter, were crafted and then implemented according to the principles of the Finnish Way.

In early 2020, the world was hit by the worst health pandemic in a century. It came without much of early warnings—countries were not prepared for anything like that. In weeks it was clear that many societies must shut down their services and businesses, people were asked to work from home, teachers shifted to remote teaching when school buildings were closed, and millions lost their jobs altogether. It became clear early on in the COVID-19 pandemic that those nations that had strong public health care services, flexible employment policies, and credible leadership to encourage everyone to do their best to keep their communities safe would go through the crisis with less harm to their citizens and economies (Sahlberg, 2020c). Reports from around the world are now suggesting that self-organizing communities keep people safe in the age of the coronavirus pandemic better than those that act like bureaucracies or just comply with external orders.

The chapter next summarizes the key factors behind the educational success in Finland since the 1970s. These are often similar factors that have Finland a successful nation among all others in general. It then suggests that Finland needs to work out a bold new vision of the future that will inspire practitioners and communities to continuously renew teaching in schools and education in the communities. Ultimately, the core question considered is this: Will Finland be able to maintain its equitable and well-performing education system in the future?

SUCCESS BY BEING DIFFERENT

In April 2017, I spent 4 days with Sir Richard Branson at his home in the Caribbean. Necker Island in the British Virgin Islands has been his home since the 1980s. Sir Richard's education record is short and well known: He dropped out of school at the age of 16, established a student magazine and record company, later became the owner of Virgin Group and one of the Britain's most successful entrepreneurs. As dyslexic, Sir Richard doesn't have fond memories from his school years. That is why he hosted me and some other guests to learn more about what is wrong in education today and how that could be fixed.

He openly admitted that he doesn't know much about how education systems work or how they should be improved, but he has many interesting stories about his time as a businessman. One of the key reasons behind his continued success in the air travel industry, for example, is his way of approaching opportunities and challenges differently. Sir Richard told us that when many of his competitors sought faster growth and bigger profits, he turned to his people and asked them what makes them empowered and perform beyond expectations. His leadership principle is simple: Trust your frontline people and let them figure out how to best serve customers.

That same business idea rather than tough competition and race for higher test scores was adopted in Finland in the 1990s when teachers' and principals' expertise and professional wisdom to design the work of the schools so that it benefits all children became the main modus operandi in the education system. Now many Finnish educators contest that this leadership model worked and paved the way for future success.

In this book, I have conveyed my concern that an insistence on following bad business models and wrong education policy drivers may jeopardize schools' efforts to address children's individual interests and to teach them to live a good life that contributes to a sustainable future. It is common that district and whole system–level education reform interventions rely on strategic priorities borrowed from the suite of bad corporate ideas for setting higher expectations, strengthening accountability, increasing competition, expanding learning time, intensifying data-driven management, and investing only in human capital in schools. Evidence provided in the previous chapter suggests that GERM is the wrong way to improve educational performance—in other words, the quality and equity of educational outcomes—and there is no reason to believe that the system-wide change would succeed by relying on these principles anywhere. Forgoing the tenets of GERM, Finland has demonstrated sustained educational improvement and strong overall performance since the early 1970s. Finnish schools operate in congruence with an inclusive welfare state and a competitive knowledge economy, as was described in previous chapters. It is therefore useful to look at how that society has responded to the global challenge to transform national education systems to increase their overall effectiveness and relevance for 21st-century knowledge and skills that are required for a good life.

Finland's success as a nation owes much to being courageously different from most others. Whereas others have desired individual excellence, Finland has worked toward common good and equity. A most recent example is how the Finns responded to the global COVID-19 pandemic that forced schools to close their doors and lock citizens in their homes. A vast majority of people took the recommendations from health authorities and the government to heart not just for themselves but for others. With huge economic losses and personal sacrifice, people did what was necessary to keep the nation from going down to complete catastrophe. Finnish people have done that before, and they know the best way through the crisis is to trust one another and act for common good.

Finns have also a different way to think about teachers and teaching compared to most others. Many countries allow anybody into the teaching profession, but Finnish schools require higher professionalism from their teachers. When others have invested in having costly educational data-management systems, the Finns have focused on teaching and learning and created its own enhancement-led education assessment culture. Finnish educational reform principles since the early

1990s—when much of the public sector administration went through a thorough decentralization—have relied on developing professional responsibility by educators and encouraging learning among teachers and schools, rather than by applying bureaucratic, top-down account-ability policies. Therefore, sample-based testing of students, thematic evaluations of schools, reflective self-assessments by teachers, and an emphasis on creative learning have established a culture of mutual trust and respect within the Finnish education system. As this book has de-scribed, before the end of upper-secondary school in Finland no external high-stakes tests are employed. There is no inspection of teachers and only loose external teaching and learning standards to steer the schools. These practices leave teachers with the opportunity to focus on person-alized learning rather than be concerned about standardized outcomes, frequent testing, and the public rankings of their schools. Some policy-makers predicted in the mid-1990s that Finland would follow the school accountability policy models emerging in many other European coun-tries. But in a review of policy development in Finland a decade later, test-based accountability was not even mentioned (Laukkanen, 2008). Other Nordic countries have moved to adopt policies that are closer to GERM, and thus they have distanced themselves from their eastern neighbor and more Nordic traditions of trust-based responsibility and other forms of collaborative school cultures.

Explaining the educational success of nations or schools is by no means easy. Finland is said to have well-prepared teachers, pedagogi-cally designed schools, good school principals, an inclusive national edu-cational vision, and an emphasis on special education needs—each of these separately and collectively certainly help the Finnish educational system to perform well (Hautamäki et al., 2008; Kasvio, 2011; Matti, 2009; Rautopuro & Juuti, 2018; Simola, 2015; Välijärvi et al., 2007). Critics claim that because Finland is a small country that doesn't have a very diverse ethnic population that characterizes many other nations, its schools perform better. Others suggest that low levels of child poverty and a socially cohesive society can explain the good educational perfor-mance of Finnish students. I argue, however, that because Finland has kept its schools as centers of learning and caring, teachers can concen-trate on what is most important for every child's growth and well-being and what they can do best: helping children learn. They are not dis-turbed by frequent testing applied to schools, competition against other schools, or performance targets imposed by administrators. Since the beginning of the 1990s, Finnish schools have been systematically encouraged by educational authorities to explore their own conceptions of learning, develop teaching methods to match their own learning theories in action, and craft pedagogical environments to meet the needs of all their students. This is why many Finnish students learn well in all schools.

Finland is the land of nongovernmental organizations. There are 135,000 registered nongovernmental groups or societies in Finland, 70,000 of which are actively operational with a total of 15 million members. On average, each citizen belongs to three associations or societies. Young Finns are also actively involved in sports and youth associations that normally have clear educational aims and principles. They learn social skills, problem solving, and leadership when they participate in these associations. It is commonly accepted in Finland that these associations give a positive added value to the formal education offered by schools.

Finland's recipe for improving learning for all students differs from those found in many other countries:

1. Guarantee equal opportunities for good public education for all.
2. Strengthen the professionalism of and trust in teachers.
3. Engage teachers and principals in all central aspects of planning, implementation, and evaluation of education, including curriculum, assessment, and policy.
4. Facilitate network-based school improvement collaboration between schools and nongovernmental associations and local communities.

The key message of this book is that schools in competition-rich environments are stuck in a tough educational dilemma. The way forward requires brave, new thinking about the process of schooling. The current culture of toxic accountability[1] in the public sector, as it is employed in England, North America, and many other parts of the world, often threatens school and community social capital; it damages rather than supports trust (Sahlberg & Walker, 2021). As a consequence, teachers and school leaders are no longer trusted; there is a crisis of suspicion, as O'Neill (2002) has observed. Although the pursuit of transparency and accountability provides parents and politicians with more information, it also builds suspicion, low morale, and professional cynicism.

UNDERSTANDING THE FINNISH LESSONS

The history of education is full of stories about education reforms that have promised a lot but delivered a little. The reasons for these failures are many, but often the problem is in implementation. Even good ideas turn into disappointments when the complexity of educational change is underestimated. David Tyack and William Tobin wrote an essay about the "grammar" of schooling already a quarter of a century ago wondering why it is so hard to change. The grammar of schooling, according to Yong Zhao (2020), refers to behavioral and structural regularities that determine the culture of the school and the work of instruction. Tyack and Tobin (1994, p. 454) claimed that global education reforms have tried to change the structures and rules of schools in the following ways often without permanent success:

- To create ungraded, not graded, schools
- To use time, space, and numbers of students as flexible resources and to diversify
- Uniform periods, same-sized rooms, and standard class size
- To merge specialized subjects into core courses in junior and high schools or, alternatively, to introduce departmental specialization into the elementary school
- To group teachers in teams, rather than having them work as isolated individuals in self-contained classrooms

All these innovations that have been hard to make work elsewhere sound familiar to the Finnish teachers and educators as central elements of successful educational change in Finland since the 1990s. If this is true, it begs an intriguing question: Why has Finland managed to change education and the grammar of schools when others have found it much more difficult?

A typical feature of education in Finland is the way teachers and students are encouraged to try new ideas and methods, learn from innovations, and cultivate creativity in schools. At the same time, many teachers respect the traditions of good teaching. Education policies today are a result of 3 decades of systematic, mostly intentional, development that has created a culture of diversity, trust, and respect within Finnish society in general and within its education system in particular.

OECD's education chief suggests that one element of Finland's success has been "the capacity of policy makers to pursue reform in ways that went beyond optimizing existing structures, policies and practices, and moved towards fundamentally transforming the paradigms and beliefs that underlay educational policy and practice until the 1960s" (Schleicher, 2006, p. 9). Although education policy discourse in Finland changed dramatically during the 1990s as a consequence of new public sector management and other neoliberal policies, Finland has remained rather immune to market-based educational reforms. Instead, education sector development has been built on values grounded in equity and the equitable distribution of resources rather than on competition and choice. Importantly, the Trade Union of Education in Finland (OAJ) has consistently resisted adopting business management models in the education sector. Moreover, Finland is a society where achieving consensus on important social and political issues is not rare. Although education is politicized in Finland as it is everywhere, Finns have been able to get together across political party lines and reach agreements. *Peruskoulu* is a good example of that (see Box 1.1).

A question asked repeatedly is this: Why are Finnish students doing better in international comparison studies than many others? This book describes how Finland, by employing alternative approaches in education policies, has been able to improve student achievement, equity of education outcomes, and productivity of education.[2] Immediately after the first PISA results were released in 2001, Professor Jouni Välijärvi, who has worked with colleagues for several decades on international student assessments, observed that

> [F]inland's high achievement seems to be attributable to a whole network of interrelated factors in which students' own areas of interest and leisure activities, the learning opportunities provided by school, parental support and involvement as well as social and cultural context of learning and of the entire education system combine with each other. (Välijärvi et al., 2002, p. 46)

One accomplishment of the Finnish education system that is often overlooked is the especially high level of reading literacy that Finnish children possess at an early age. There are both educational and sociocultural reasons for this: Reading instruction in schools is based on individual development and pace rather than on standardized instruction. Finnish parents read a lot, books and newspapers are easily available through a dense library network, and children are exposed to subtitled television and movies at an early age. Good reading comprehension and the ability to understand texts fast is a great advantage in the mathematics and science sections of PISA tests, which are based on being able to understand descriptive tasks in all measured areas.

Another overlooked direction of Finnish educational development is the reform of school architecture along the guidelines set out by the National Core Curriculum and its pedagogical and philosophical principles. New school buildings are always designed in collaboration with teachers and architects, and they are thereby adapted to the teaching and learning needs of specific communities. The physical environment provides an important context for both students and teachers. "If the building is consciously viewed as an instrument of learning," reasons Kaisa Nuikkinen (2011, pp. 13–14), "the architecture itself can serve as an inspirational, tangible teaching tool, offering a living example of such things as good ergonomic design and the principles of sustainable development." The school building can create a sense of well-being, respect, and happiness—all hallmarks of Finnish schools.

The following is a summary of interrelated factors that are often mentioned when Finnish experts explain the reasons behind good educational performance internationally over time. All are related to education or school and should not suggest that social, community, physical environment, or family factors would not have important roles to play. It is important to understand the complex nature of all the interrelated factors that play a role in making the Finnish education system what it has been and what it is today.

Peruskoulu offers equal educational opportunities for all. All Finnish children start their formal schooling in August of the year they turn 7. Normally, class-based primary school lasts 6 years and is followed by 3-year lower-secondary school, although today *peruskoulu* is formally a unified 9-year school. Today it is widely recognized that the 6-year primary school provides a solid basis for the high-quality education system. Schools are typically small, with class sizes ranging from 15 to 25 students. In 2020, 15% of Finnish basic schools had fewer than 50 pupils, and 13% of schools had more than 500 pupils (Statistics Finland, n.d.a). In other words, Finnish schools are rather small by international standards. Primary schools (grades 1 to 6) typically have fewer than 300 pupils and often operate separately from the upper grades (7 to 9), although the unified *peruskoulu* is gradually bringing these two schools under the same roof. As a consequence of urbanization and tightening financial conditions in Finnish municipalities, about 700 basic schools have been shut down since 2010. Many of them were small rural schools.

Teaching as an inspiring lifelong career and profession. In Finnish society, the teaching profession has always enjoyed great public respect and appreciation, as explained in Chapter 3. Classroom teaching is considered an independent, respected profession that attracts some of the best upper-secondary school graduates each year. The main reason for the strong appeal of teaching as a career is the fact that a master's degree is the basic requirement for permanent employment as a teacher in Finnish schools, and having a master's degree opens the door to other future employment options. Therefore, individuals who choose teaching as their first career do not feel that their lives are limited to working in a school. Indeed, teachers with a master's degree often find interest in their credentials from human resource departments within the Finnish private sector and third-sector organizations. They also have access to doctoral studies in Finnish universities. During the past decade, Finnish schools have noted an upsurge in school principals and teachers who possess a PhD in education.

Researchers have pointed out that preparing teachers for a research-based profession has been the central idea of teacher education development in Finland since the mid-1970s (Hammerness et al., 2017; Sahlberg, 2012; Westbury et al., 2005). Teachers' higher academic qualifications have enabled schools to play an increasingly active role in curriculum planning, evaluating education outcomes, and leading overall school improvement. The OECD (2005) review on equity in education in Finland describes how Finland has created a virtuous circle surrounding teaching:

> High status and good working conditions—small classes, adequate support for counselors and special needs teachers, a voice in school decisions, low levels of discipline problems, high levels of professional autonomy—create large pools of applicants, leading to highly selective and intensive teacher preparation programs. This, in turn, leads to success in the early years of teaching, relative stability of the teacher workforce, and success in teaching (of which PISA results are only one example), and a continuation of the high status of teaching. (p. 21)

Today, the Finnish teaching profession is on par with other highly regarded professions; teachers can diagnose problems in their classrooms and schools, apply evidence-based and often alternative solutions to them, and evaluate and analyze the impact of implemented procedures. Parents trust teachers as professionals who know what is best for their children.

Trust-based professional responsibility. Finland has not followed the educational accountability movement that assumes that making schools and teachers more accountable for their performance is the key to raising student achievement. Traditionally, the evaluation of student outcomes has been the responsibility of each Finnish teacher and school. Due to the absence of census-based standardized tests, student assessment is based on teacher-created tests at the school level to report what students learn to parents and teachers, and on sample-based national assessments for monitoring educational progress for the authorities. Finnish pupils are not assessed using numerical grades that would enable a direct comparison of pupils with one another before 4th grade in primary school. Only descriptive assessments and feedback are employed, depending on how student assessment is described in the school curriculum or municipal education plan. Primary school is, to a large extent, a "standardized testing-free zone," and pupils are allowed to focus on learning to know, to create, and to sustain natural curiosity. Fear of learning and anxiety are not common in Finnish schools.

Educational accountability that in the Finnish education context is called professional responsibility preserves and enhances trust among teachers, students, school leaders, and education authorities and it involves them in the process, offering them a strong sense of professional responsibility and initiative. Shared responsibility for teaching and learning characterizes the way educational accountability is arranged in Finland. Parents, students, and teachers prefer trust-based responsibility that enables schools to keep the focus on learning and that permits greater freedom in curriculum planning, compared with the external standardized-testing culture that prevails in some other nations.

Enhancing equity of outcomes as the key education policy. The Finnish Dream was built on the idea that all children can learn and that they must be given equal opportunities to succeed in school. In the 1970s and the 1980s, many people in Finland feared that when equality and equity are the primary goals of education, the quality of learning outcomes suffer. The Finnish Way to enhance equity included adjusting school funding to the real needs of each school; making special education universal and flexible so that help is available early on; embedding health and well-being services in every school, for every child, every day; ensuring balanced curriculum throughout the school system that will serve multiple intelligences and different personalities evenly; and making sure that good teachers are employed in all schools. Only after the first PISA results became public in late 2001 did many admit that this Finnish strategy of driving quality gains by investing in equity in education was confirmed successful. Indeed, the most successful education systems are those that combine quality with equity. OECD (2012) concluded in its report *Equity and Quality in Education* that

> [s]chool choice advocates often argue that the introduction of market mechanisms in education allows equal access to high quality schooling for all. Expanding school choice opportunities, it is said, would allow all students—including disadvantaged ones and the ones attending low performing schools—to opt for higher quality schools, as the introduction of choice in education can foster efficiency, spur innovation and raise quality overall. However, evidence does not support these perceptions, as choice and associated market mechanisms can enhance segregation. (p. 64)

Figure 5.1 shows how equity (measured by economic, social, and cultural status) and quality (measured by learning outcomes in reading, mathematics, and science) are associated with one another. Following the definition of a successful (i.e., high achievement and high equity) education system,

Figure 5.1. Relationship Between Quality and Equity of Outcomes in OECD Countries in 2018

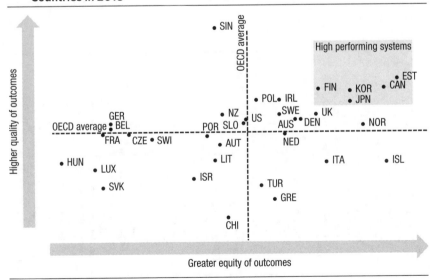

Source: OECD (2019b).

Figure 5.1 illustrates that the high-performing school systems in 2018 were Canada, Estonia, Finland, Japan, and Korea (in alphabetical order).

Another indicator of the equity of education systems is to measure how many students who come from disadvantaged home backgrounds can "beat the odds" and exhibit high levels of achievement in school. These students are called *academically resilient* because they overcome adversity and achieve academic success. The share of resilient students among all students can be calculated in different ways. According to OECD's PISA 2018 (OECD, 2019b, p. 66) survey defines that academically resilient students "are disadvantaged students who are in the bottom quarter of the PISA index of economic, social and cultural status (ESCS) in their own country but who score in the top quarter of reading in that country." By calculating the share of resilient students among all students in the education system, we'll get another indication of the equity of that education system. Across all OECD countries, 11.3% of the entire student population are academically resilient; in other words, they beat the socioeconomic odds that are stacked against them when compared with similar students in other countries. As Figure 5.2 shows,

Figure 5.2. Percentage of Disadvantaged Students Who Scored in the Top Quarter of Reading Performance in Their Own Country in 2018

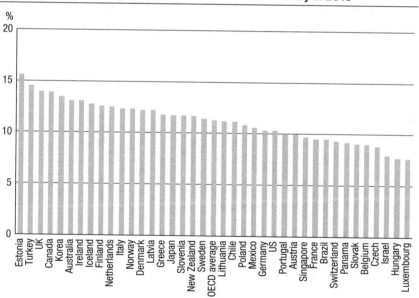

Source: OECD (2019b).

Canada has 13.9%, Australia 13.1%, Finland 12.6%, and the United States 10.3% resilient students. OECD (2019b, p. 66) reminds that "academic resilience is a relative measure, with both socio-economic disadvantage and performance thresholds defined within each country."

Data in Figure 5.2 indicate that academic resilience is a general feature of some disadvantaged students, their homes, communities, or the schools that enable them to overcome their social disadvantage and learn in school beyond expectations. The percentage of resilient students among all students therefore indicates something about the equity of education outcomes. All these different equity indices show that Finnish education policies have been successful in offering a good school for all students. It is noteworthy that even when Finland has been in a downward trend in international education rankings, the government policies have made it a priority to invest in various aspects of equity and equality in education (see Table 2.2) than simply addressing issues in teaching more literacy and numeracy in schools. The most significant factor behind Finland's declining educational performance is not curriculum or instruction but the widening gap between high- and low-performing students in schools. In 2006 Finland had the largest proportion of top-performing students and less low performers of any other OECD country.

Sustainable leadership. The success of Finnish education is not the result of any major national education reform per se. Instead, education development in Finland has been based on the continual adjustment of schooling to the changing needs of individuals and society. Risto Rinne and colleagues (2002) claim that although the emergence of the new public sector management meant revolutionary changes in Finnish educational discourse, the new rhetoric and practices have not been able to take root in education as easily as in other parts of society. As a consequence, the basic values and the main vision of education as a public service have remained unchanged since the 1970s. Governments from both the political left and right have respected education as the key public service for all citizens and have maintained their belief that only a highly and widely educated nation will be successful in world markets.

In education systems that undergo wave after wave of reforms, frequently the emphasis is on the implementation and consolidation of externally designed changes. The main result is frustration and resistance to change rather than the desire to improve schools. A steady political situation since the 1980s and sustained educational leadership have enabled Finnish schools and teachers to concentrate on developing teaching and learning. Rather than repeatedly allocating financial resources and time to implement new reforms, teachers in Finland have been given the professional freedom to develop pedagogical knowledge and skills related to their individual needs. After a decade of centralized professional development, following the launch of comprehensive school reform in the 1970s, the focus of professional development programs has shifted to meet the authentic demands and expectations of schools and individuals.

THE TRANSFER OF CHANGE KNOWLEDGE

Today, Finland is often used as a model of successful educational change. "As societies move beyond the age of low-skill standardization," writes Andy Hargreaves and colleagues (2008, p. 92), "Finland contains essential lessons for nations that aspire, educationally and economically, to be successful and sustainable knowledge societies." However, reform ideas and policy principles that have been employed in Finland since the 1970s will not necessarily work in other cultural or social contexts. For example, in Finland, as in other Nordic countries, people trust one another and therefore also trust their teachers and principals more than is the case in many other countries (OECD, 2008; Sahlberg & Walker, 2021). Similarly, there are other sociocultural factors that have been mentioned by some external observers, such as social capital, ethnic homogeneity, and the high professional status of teachers, that may play a key role when considering the transferability of education models and policies.[3]

Indeed, many want to learn how to develop a good education system from the Finns (Barber & Mourshed, 2007; Darling-Hammond & Lieberman, 2012; Hargreaves et al., 2008; Mortimore, 2013; Ofsted, 2010). Since the early 2000s, tens of thousands of visitors have traveled from great distances to learn Finnish lessons about successful educational improvement. Understanding Finnish educational success, however, needs to include an awareness of the sociocultural, political, and economic perspectives.

There is more to the picture than meets the eye. An external OECD expert review team that visited Finland observed that "it is hard to imagine how Finland's educational success could be achieved or maintained without reference to the nation's broader and commonly accepted system of distinctive social values that more individualistic and inequitable societies may find it difficult to accept" (Hargreaves et al., 2008, p. 92). Another visiting OECD team confirmed that the Finnish approaches to equitable schooling rely on multiple and reinforcing forms of intervention with support that teachers can get from others, including special education teachers and classroom assistants (OECD, 2005). Furthermore, Finland has shown that educational change should be systematic and coherent, in contrast with the current haphazard intervention efforts of many other countries. The conclusion was that "developing the capacities of schools is much more important than testing the hell out of students, and that some nonschool policies associated with the welfare state are also necessary" (Grubb, 2007, p. 112). Scores of news articles on Finnish education have concluded that trust, teacher professionalism, and taking care of those with special needs are the main (visible) factors that distinguish Finnish schools from most others.[4] There are also theories of change that represent very different paradigms from that of the Finnish Way.

These observations about the problem of the transferability of educational change knowledge contradict the thinking of those who claim that context, culture, politics, or governance are not very important to a school system and its leaders when seeking real improvement in educational outcomes. International consulting corporation McKinsey & Company analyzed education policies and practices in 25 countries hoping to find out how the world's best-performing school systems come out on top. Although acknowledging that the context determines the course the system leaders must follow for achieving real improvement in outcomes, McKinsey argues that culture, politics, or governance will not be as important to the school system and its leaders as the following educational reform principles:

1. The quality of an education system cannot exceed the quality of its teachers;
2. The only way to improve outcomes is to improve instruction; and
3. Achieving universal high outcomes is only possible by putting in place mechanisms to ensure that schools deliver high-quality instruction to every child (Barber & Mourshed, 2007, p. 40).

McKinsey's view of educational improvement is an example of a mechanistic and reductionist paradigm that is built on a classical theory of knowledge or human capital. Each of the three principles of McKinsey's theory of change is fragile in light of contemporary conceptions of systemic educational change. I already pointed out the weakness of McKinsey's first reform principle in Chapter 3. The second and third principles undermine the power of social capital and influence of out-of-school factors in explaining educational outcomes. Interestingly, the Finnish experience does not confirm the findings and recommendations of McKinsey & Company and similar suggestions made by the World Bank and some conservative Anglo-American think tanks.

Another example of educational change in contrast to the Finnish Way is the U.S. education reform legislation known as *No Child Left Behind* (NCLB). It was approved by both major political parties in 2002 and required states, school districts, and schools to ensure that all students are proficient in grade-level math and reading by 2014. Due to the fact that the federal role in education in the United States is limited, the states defined what grade-level performance means. According to this federal law, however, schools had to make "adequate yearly progress" so that proficiency rates increase in the years leading up to 2014. If one child in school didn't meet the proficiency target, the school was labeled as a low-performing school. The main mechanisms for achieving the intended change were accountability, standardized testing, school improvement, corrective actions, and restructuring. Failure to meet the adequate yearly progress goal caused losing students or even closing down the school. This legislation, according to many teachers and scholars, led to fragmentation in instruction, further interventions that were uncoordinated with the basic classroom teaching, and a larger number of poorly trained tutors working with students and teachers (Darling-Hammond, 2010; Ravitch, 2010). As a consequence, schools experienced too many instructional directions for any student, with an increase in unethical behaviors such as students cheating on tests and administrators manipulating student assessment protocols, as well as a loss of continuity in instruction and in systematic school improvement.

The perverse nature of NCLB became evident in Vermont, a small state in northern New England. In August 2014, the year when the reform should have led all students to be proficient in reading and mathematics, Vermont's secretary of education, Dr. Rebecca Holcombe, sent a letter to all parents and caregivers in her state. She wanted to inform citizens about the fact that in that year, every school whose students took the New England Common Assessment Program (NECAP) tests in the previous year was now considered a low-performing school by the U.S. Department of Education. Vermont is one of the highest-performing states in the United States in National Assessment of Educational Progress (NAEP), has the best graduation rate in the nation, and is ranked second in child well-being. In her letter the secretary also wrote that the

Vermont Agency of Education does not agree that all of their schools were low-performing schools. It is difficult to imagine an education reform that would be more distant from the Finnish Way—or education policies in any other high-performing country—than NCLB.

In 2012, I received an invitation from the White House in Washington, DC, to share my views about NCLB with President Barack Obama's education advisor. The meeting was held at the White House Mess, which is a small dining facility run by the U.S. Navy and located in the basement of the West Wing, next door to the Situation Room. We had a lively conversation about American education issues, including the NCLB, and whether that law would ever be able to change the American schools for better. My main suggestion to the president was that unless the federal and state education policies accept that there are countries that have been successful in building a world-class education system using very different theories of change than what he has also endorsed, and that there is a lot to learn from them, reform efforts here will most likely fail. The irony in me, a foreigner, saying this was that there were many much better-informed colleagues in the United States who could have told him the same thing with rigor and eloquence, such as Howard Gardner, Diane Ravitch, Sir Ken Robinson, and Linda Darling-Hammond, just to mention a few. That didn't happen during Barack Obama's time at the White House, which left many American teachers, educators, and parents disappointed and upset. I never met the president but was told that at the time of our breakfast conversation he was sitting just a few feet above me in the Oval Office.

The differences between these approaches to educational change and the Finnish Way described in this book are indeed notable: Rather than relying on data-driven bureaucratic delivery of education policies and reforms with detailed target-setting, the Finns have gradually built trust in schools and strengthened professional responsibility among teachers and leaders so that the education system works as a self-improving organization (Sahlberg & Walker, 2021). Rather than believing that standardized instruction and related testing can be brought in at the last minute to improve student learning and turn around failing schools, the Finns have worked systematically over the past 30 years to make sure that competent professionals who can craft the best learning conditions for all students are working in all schools. The rational and bureaucratic approaches to educational change above resonate with the key ideas of GERM and can be found in the educational policies of numerous nations and jurisdictions around the world, but not in Finland.

Importing specific aspects of the education system from Finland—whether those include curricula, teacher training, special education, or school leadership—is probably of little value to those who hope to improve their own education systems. The Finnish welfare system guarantees all children the safety, health, nutrition, and moral support that they need to learn well in school. As the passage from the novel *Seven Brothers* at the beginning of Chapter 1 illustrates, literacy and education in general have historically played a central role in what it means to be a full member of Finnish society. One lesson we can learn from Finland is, therefore, that successful change and good educational performance often require improvements in social, employment, and economic sectors. As described by complex systems researcher Stuart Kauffman (1995), the separate elements of a complex system rarely function adequately in a new environment and in isolation from their original system. Therefore, rather than only specific aspects or innovations from other education systems, it may be the features and policy principles of a larger, complex system—in this case, the Finnish Way—that should be borrowed. In a complex social system, interactions among elements of the system determine the behavior of that system as much as its individual elements alone. Some issues that should be considered when contemplating the transfer of ideas from the Finnish education system to other countries include:

1. *Technical drivers of good educational performance.* These
   include common comprehensive school for all, research-based
   teacher education, professional support for teachers, smart
   accountability policies, relatively small schools, and good
   educational leadership, especially within schools.
2. *Sociocultural factors.* These include a long reliance on the social
   value of literacy and education, strong professional ethics, trust
   in public institutions (including schools), and state-driven social
   capital created by a welfare state.
3. *Links to other public policy sectors.* The success of one
   sector depends on the success of all others. Therefore, good
   educational performance may only be explained through larger
   policy principles, including other public policies, such as health,
   youth, and employment policies.

Finnish people also need to be careful to avoid the illusion that the current methods of measuring the performance of education systems will last forever. Although there are some advantages to relying on global education indicators—especially those that are related to the economics of education—and student achievement numbers produced by PISA and other surveys, there will be a growing pressure in the coming years to develop educational units of measurement that better cover a broader range of learning and health outcomes of education, and acknowledge the changing face of future societies. PISA, which has been the main learning metric behind Finland's global fame, looks at just one part of the desired outcome of education. At the same time, as Peter Mortimore (2009) writes:

> PISA also suffers some limitations: It assesses a very limited amount of what is taught in schools; it can adopt only a cross-sectional design; it ignores the role and contribution of teachers; and the way its results are presented—in some, at least, of its tables—encourages a superficial, "league table" reading of what should be a more interesting but essentially more complex picture. (p. 2)

Many teachers and principals in Finland hold a skeptical view of how international measurements and benchmarking tools are used to rank countries and schools by standardized tests. Finnish educators perceive teaching and learning as complex processes and are aware that quantifying their effectiveness accurately is difficult, if not impossible.

All things considered, what can the world learn from educational change in Finland? I am not suggesting that other nations should adopt the Finnish education system or even its elements, such as *peruskoulu* or academic teacher education, as I have clearly pointed out throughout this book. However, there are many things that we can learn from one another in education. Although sensitivity to the problems of transferring educational ideas from one place to another is essential, I would propose that there are three main lessons from Finland that are relevant in trying to improve quality and equity of education in other places.

First, we should *reconsider those education policies that advocate choice, competition, and privatization* as the key drivers of sustained educational improvement. None of the best-performing education systems today currently rely primarily on them. Indeed, the Finnish experience shows that a consistent focus on equity and shared responsibility—not choice and competition—can lead to an education system in which all children learn better than they did before.

Second, we should *reconsider teacher policies by giving teachers a government-paid master's degree–level university education, providing better professional support in their work, and making teaching a respected profession.* As long as teachers' practice is not trusted and they are not respected as professionals, talented young people are unlikely to consider teaching as their lifelong career. Even if they do, they will likely leave teaching early because of the lack of a respectful professional working environment. The experience of Finland and other successful education systems speaks clearly to this fact.

Finally, we should *properly understand what is driving changes in countries' educational performance rather than making hasty haphazard decisions to try to turn situations for the better.* Changes in a complex system's behavior are always difficult to explain. The Finnish response to worsening education outcomes has had two main interventions: empower teachers and engage students in school. The National Core Curricula are the main vehicles to do that. Equally importantly, the Finnish authorities and education leaders understand that the best way to get educational performance back on an improving course is to address current inequalities in the society and strengthen equity of education. It is too early to judge yet how these ongoing measures will work.

STRESS TEST FOR FINNISH SCHOOLS

The year 2020 started with worrying news about the new coronavirus that was spreading in Wuhan, China, causing the disease that we now know as COVID-19. This new virus came to Europe, then to North America, Asia, and Latin America, and was announced as a global pandemic in March. Governments in many countries had to react quickly to stop the spread of this virus that appeared to be deadly and infectious. Citizens' freedom to move outside was soon restricted, services were closed, public transportation stopped, and eventually school buildings were shut from most children and teachers. In April 2020, UNESCO estimated that over 1.5 billion children were affected by these school closures, and most of them learned at home with digital devices connecting to their teachers by the Internet.

A stress test is a simulation or analysis to determine institutions' ability to deal with external shocks or catastrophe. After the global banking crisis in 2008 banks around the world were stress tested to see how they might survive possible troubled times ahead. Good tests can reveal important insights of these institutions' leadership, risk management, flexibility, and resiliency. Ideally, a stress test can distinguish strong and healthy institutions from weaker ones.

It was Monday evening, March 16, when the Finnish government made a decision to shut down the country in order to stop the COVID-19 pandemic from getting worse. School buildings were ordered to be closed 2 days later, except for the youngest primary school children. This left municipalities that own most schools in Finland to figure out how to arrange teaching and learning during the 4-week period of disruption that was later extended until May 14. Although schools had emergency plans for much smaller incidences, nobody was prepared for anything like this. COVID-19 had become a stress test for Finnish schools.

Because the Finnish education system is decentralized, local governments in 310 municipalities are in charge of schools and how they are organized. The Finnish Agency for Education that provides these local governments with the National Core Curricula set the general guidelines and principles on how remote learning during school closures should be arranged. But most of the details were figured out locally and eventually by teachers and principals in schools. As in most other countries in the world, Finnish schools' readiness to arrange teaching and learning using digital learning platforms was variable. Some schools had much more advanced facilities and personnel to handle teaching and learning digitally. It was clear from the beginning that there would be notable variation from school to school in how this unusual arrangement of teaching over the period of 8 weeks would work.

The COVID-19 pandemic caused an unprecedented social experiment with schools. This experiment tested schools' flexibility, creativity, professionalism, and resiliency. Although there is no systematic research or other evidence available yet about how Finnish schools managed the transition to remote learning and teaching, some survey data collected by the Finnish authorities at the end of the school year suggest that the main challenges were students' lack of access to technology and difficulties in providing online support to students who needed it. The immediate conclusion by state authorities was that schools succeeded very well despite the above-mentioned challenges. "We succeeded in difficult circumstance excellently. The key reason for that is our teachers' and leaders' strong educational background and commitment to their work," said the president of the Trade Union of Education. Next is a summary of the key success factors in coping with the disrupted schooling that are based on my interviews with some leading education experts in Finland in August 2020.

Flexibility. Professional autonomy provides Finnish schools with freedom to find out the best ways to organize teaching and learning within common regulations and guidelines. Absence of national census-based student assessments or external inspections give schools plenty of flexibility in curriculum and how it is implemented. Flexibility was the main reason why the response to the school closures succeeded with only minor complications.

Creativity. National Core Curricula in Finland is built around the idea of creativity and the need to find new ways of teaching and learning. Where schools in many other countries are mostly dealing with compliance with external rules and expectations, Finnish schools can creatively find their own best ways to solve problems and arrange their work. Many authorities and school leaders said that creativity in Finnish schools was a critically important factor in reacting quickly and successfully in the situation where schools were closed.

Resiliency. Collaboration and helping one another are the key values in Finnish education culture. Whereas schools in many other countries cooperate less and compete more with each other, in Finland schools are collectively working for the benefit of their children and families. Resiliency is enhanced by mutual trust between schools and their willingness to support each other. Teachers commented that they were energized and empowered to do their best during remote learning because of the sense of togetherness with other teachers. A sign of *sisu* in all Finnish schools!

What were the first lessons from the lockdown of schools? The Finnish Education Evaluation Centre (2020b) conducted a survey during the first 2 weeks of school closures in April that included 5,000 teachers to find out the impact of remote learning on teachers and students. I also interviewed some education authorities in Finland about this issue in August. Here is my conclusion.

First, everybody emphasized that schools are an integral player in keeping the nation healthy and safe during the health crisis. Educators worked hand in hand with their health care colleagues and medical experts to make sure that while the children were learning from home and especially when they returned back to school in the middle of May, everybody was safe from possible infections. Children's and teachers' health were the most important issue in coping with the crisis, not whether all the learning targets were achieved during school closure. Second, a common view among teachers and the authorities I spoke with was that schools succeeded well in this difficult new situation and that the main reasons were the education system's flexibility and strong trust in schools' capability to find the best ways to respond to common requirements and restrictions. Finally, the biggest concern during the remote learning period among teachers and authorities was to make sure that all children were kept onboard, and that on-time help is available for those children who need it to stay onboard. Approximately one quarter of basic school students in Finland receive special education support in school, and those students were particularly vulnerable when in-person schooling was interrupted.

THE FUTURE OF FINNISH EDUCATION

In the first decade of this millennium, Finland established a global reputation as a model educational nation. International media played a key role in promoting Finland's new position in the global limelight. *Newsweek* titled its May 24, 1999, article about Finland "The Future Is Finnish." The article praised the smart way Finland has been able to create a national vision for an innovation-based society that combines mobile communications and information technologies unlike any other (*Newsweek*, 1999). This book has described how Finland's education system has progressed steadily since the early 1970s until the mid-2000s. Mobile phone makers, symphony orchestra conductors, game designers, and Formula 1 drivers are symbols of what a Finnish culture and society that values ingenuity, creativity, and risk taking is able to nurture. But will the Finnish education system continue to be a model in the future?

On the one hand, Finland's systemic educational leadership since the 1970s, its stable political structure, and its established complementarity among public policy sectors suggest that its educational performance will remain good. On the other hand, PISA survey results, in particular, have created a feeling of complacency among education policymakers, politicians, and the public at large regarding the status of Finnish education. This led to a condition that favored the status quo, where education policies and the leaders of a high-performing system were motivated more by a desire to maintain the current situation than to see what possible reforms the future might require of the Finnish education system.

Finnish education authorities in Helsinki did little to keep the 1990s school improvement movement alive after the first PISA survey ranked the country number one in the world. By the end of the 2000s, the dominant education policy question was how Finland's superior international success and growing fame could be turned into economic profit through education export. At the same time, many other countries increased investments to improve their school systems—often inspired by the ideas from the Finnish Model—but Finland did not follow suit. At the same time, when the financial situation in many municipalities significantly worsened in early 2010s, authorities and many educators spent time and intellectual effort to figure out how Finland's international reputation as an education leader could be converted into commercial products and economic profit.

Not so long ago, Finland had two crown jewels—Nokia and education. In 2013, Nokia was forced to sell its mobile phone business to Microsoft. It is telling that when Apple came out with the iPhone in 2007, Nokia held the dominant position in the cellphone industry and, blinded by its success, didn't recognize the challenge. Nokia had actually invented the touchscreen technology, but failed to take the next step, counting on its global market leadership position. Apple did take that step, and, as a result, leapfrogged over Nokia.

What happened there has some similarities to the situation in Finnish education in 2013. The huge flow of foreigners from all over the world who came to visit the remarkably successful Finnish schools made the authorities and politicians afraid to change anything. The drive for change led by education activists—often maverick school leaders and teachers—in the 1990s was extinguished. Although the Finnish education system still performs well internationally, parts of the strong and equitable education system have broken down, as was explained in Chapter 2. A large majority of school expenditures are covered by local taxes. Catastrophic economic situations in many municipalities, as an experienced educator and leader Peter Johnson describes in Box 5.1, have lowered teacher morale and jeopardized many support functions for students at a time when the need for help and counseling is even greater than before. The future that has been rewritten by the COVID-19 pandemic looks even less optimistic now than before. History may one day show that Finland failed to learn from its own lessons to invest in equity and systemic renewal on time and thus became lost in the journey toward educational change.

Educational change in Finland was driven for decades by culture and emotion in the context of social, political, and economic survival. Finland has shown that there is an alternative way of change to the process many

BOX 5.1: Leading a Local School District

The development of the education system is based on systematic and sustainable fiscal policies. Finnish education depends heavily on public funding. As a result of the global financial crisis in 2008, the Finnish public sector has been hit hard. Municipalities are experiencing rapidly tightening budgets. During the last decade, the debt burden of Finnish municipalities has more than tripled, and the Finnish national debt is bigger than ever before. The COVID-19 pandemic causes even bigger problems for public sector funding, and at the moment we just don't know what will happen in next coming years.

Increasing productivity and cutting public spending are now common public policies in Finland. Merging or closing down small schools is one result of these policies. From an international perspective, Finland is still a country of small schools. The average size of a comprehensive school in Finland is 240 students. In 2020, there are 2,300 comprehensive schools. Since 2000, that number has decreased by 42%.

This has radically changed the density and nature of the comprehensive school network in Finland. More students now travel longer distances to school. According to the latest forecast, for the next 20 years 60% to 70% of schools would be closed in rural areas, where also the number of students is declining. Many small villages are affected when their school closes down. Much of this structural change has been steered by economic rather than educational considerations.

New Finnish schools are much bigger than old ones. In 2000, there were only 13 comprehensive schools that had more than 700 students. Now there are more than 100. Bigger school units are economically more efficient, but require well-designed pedagogy and effective teamwork of teachers to succeed.

The worsening situation of the Finnish public sector has also caused many municipalities to use temporary layoffs of teachers as a cure for their chronic financial crisis. Teachers have been sent home without pay for a few days or, in some cases, weeks. While teachers are on this forced unpaid leave, other teachers have to take care of their classes and students. Savings have often been minor, but the negative implications of this practice for the schools have been severe.

I am concerned about the longer-term effects of these public sector policies. Economic forecasts in Finland do not promise better times ahead. The COVID-19 pandemic causes huge debts in the national economies for a long time—in Finland and globally. On the one hand, we know from experience that simply increasing financial resources does not solve the daily problems of schools. But sustained shrinking of education budgets creates a situation in which some essential structures will be jeopardized. Will schools and municipalities be able to achieve more with less in the future? I think it is possible, but it will require a careful analysis of current structures and practices. We need to be clear about where the savings can be made and where resources can be transferred toward development and renewal. However, without a sufficient slice from the overall public budget to education, this renewal will be very difficult. Cutting budgets and making high-quality education less likely is not a smart way to reward people for their good work.

—Peter Johnson, Senior Advisor of Education, City of Kokkola

other countries have employed. Finns themselves have learned that technical knowledge and political interests are not enough to renew society without emotional engagement. Indeed, global educational reforms show that too rational an approach to change does not work. Renewal requires energy, and energy is driven by emotion. In an era of big changes, emotional passion often emerges from crisis—or a sense of survival—as it did in Finland. But it can also come from recognizing new economical, technological, or cultural opportunities and innovation. In the era of great disruption it may well be that survival is insufficient.

Some Finns are concerned about how the country is seen by other nations in this competitive, globalized world. Several international comparisons indicate that Finland has become one of the most functional and attractive countries in many ways—including well-being, governance, economic performance, sustainable development, education, and happiness. For a rather small and young nation, that seems to be good enough. In 2008, the Ministry of Foreign Affairs invited an influential delegation of thought leaders to think about how to ensure this positive situation—or even strengthen it—in the future. The group's final report suggested that functionality, nature, and education are seen as the key themes on which the future of Finland should be built. It also insisted that—despite or perhaps because of the current positive situation—Finland must continue to ask itself "what shall we do next" in all fields of operations (Ministry of Foreign Affairs, 2010).

The spirit of these general recommendations should also be considered when it comes to education. They place a strong emphasis on the *complementarity* principle by developing the education system as a whole rather than just change some of its parts. All this assumes that the Finnish education system will continue to perform well in the coming years. However, there are some trends within the governance of the education system and within Finnish society in general that seem to be cause for concern.

Some indicators suggest that inequalities in Finnish society and in its education system are increasing. Figure 4.1 suggested that when income equality in a country diminishes, there is bad news on the horizon. In terms of income equality, Finland has been among the top countries in the world, together with other Nordic countries. Figure 5.3 shows how income inequality has changed in Finland since 1987. Increasing inequality is often related to growing social problems, such as increasing violence, diminishing social trust, worsening child well-being, increased poverty, and declining educational attainment, as Wilkinson and Pickett (2009, 2018) have shown. Therefore, the challenge for Finland—where income inequality has increased faster than in other OECD countries—is not just to try to maintain high student performance but to strive to keep the country an equal society and to hold on to its leading position as the most equitable education system in the world.

Figure 5.3. Income Inequality in Finland Using Gini Coefficient for 1987-2017

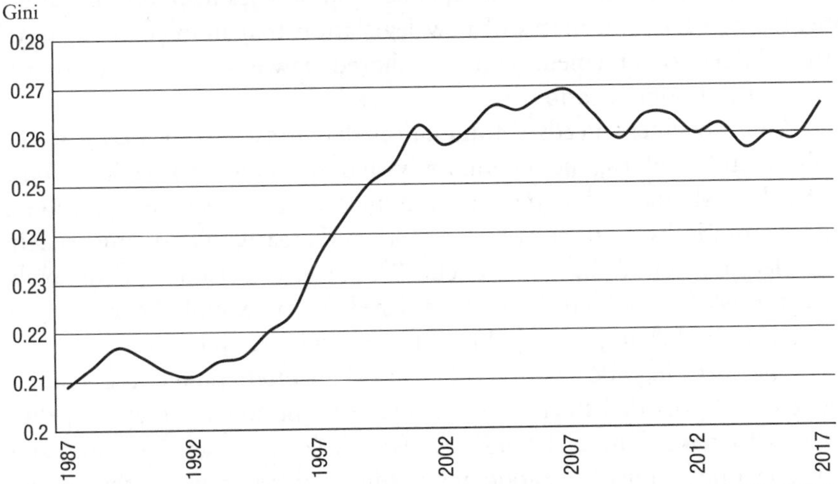

Source: Statistics Finland (n.d.c).

In reforming its education system Finland has actively listened to other countries' advice about what is necessary for raising the quality of student learning and meeting new challenges in education. Finnish education authorities have been particularly attentive to what supranational organizations—the OECD, the European Commission, and United Nations agencies—have considered the necessary steps for Finland's educational policies. The educational research community in Finland has adopted models and ideas from their foreign colleagues. In Finland's current situation, a new orientation is needed. It is still important to maintain ongoing, active communication and collaboration with international partners. Today, however, Finland has become more of a giving partner than a receiving one. As a result, Finland needs to be prepared to collaborate and exchange experiences with other education systems that are trusted sources of inspiration, ideas, and innovation. I have suggested that *new global partnerships* for the leadership of educational change are now needed. These partnerships should be based on systems excellence and good practices, and a willingness to move fearlessly to implement innovative ideas and solutions for the future of education. There are good initiatives in Finland and elsewhere that do that already. The most advanced and best known is the HundrEd.org network, a not-for-profit organization based in Helsinki that seeks and shares inspiring innovations in K–12 education around the world.[3]

But Finland can't be among global leaders without an inspiring and bold new vision for education. After PISA 2000 made Finnish education an international poster child, education policies have brought fragmented projects and pieces of new legislation that municipalities have been obliged to implement without a shared view of the overall direction for the future of education.

Any movement needs a foundation that draws from a core set of values, philosophies, and a commonly shared vision. As I see it, *Finnish School 3.0* should be based on a community of learners where new ideas spark from individual interests, passion, and creativity and aims to help each learner to find their own talent. Whatever the vision is, completely new forms of school have to be considered. The new global partnerships in educational change should kick off from this starting point.

The inspiring idea—or Big Dream—has often united the Finnish people and provided them with a source of emotional energy that they can use to make changes. After World War II, the idea was to give all Finns an equal opportunity for a good public education regardless of their domicile, socioeconomic status, or other life conditions. This became the main principle behind building *peruskoulu* in the early 1970s. The first PISA survey in 2000 proved that the Finnish Dream was fulfilled. The seventh PISA study in 2018 repeats the urgency for that new Finnish Dream.

Some possible reasons for slipping performance of Finnish schools were suggested in Chapter 2. I asked several education experts in Finland their explanations of the downward trends in international tests and national student assessments. Most responses point to two broader issues that together have negatively affected teaching and learning in schools. First, continued budget savings since 2010 have increased school and class sizes, left more children with special needs without adequate support in school, and brought efficiency before pedagogy in educational planning. Second, changing behaviors of young people as a consequence of excessive time spent on digital media and technologies have increased the number of students with psychological, emotional, social, and cognitive challenges in schools. There were some who also thought that bureaucracy in schools has increased and teachers and principals spend much more time in administration and less time with their students. The most worrisome aspect of the Finnish education system that is linked to both two issues above, according to policymakers and many teachers, is rapidly eroding educational equity that once was a bedrock of Finland's equitable school system. In Finland's 2015 national PISA report Ahonen (2018, p. 340) concludes that the development between 2006 and 2015 has gotten to the point where Finnish schools are not anymore able to equalize the differences in student learning that are related to their home background.

Some Finns have called this a crisis. Some others suggest that Finland's education system is simply becoming more like the others with similar challenges and problems. Then there are those who believe that test scores have been declining not because students today are less smart, but because they just lack motivation to take these tests seriously. This book has made it clear that a big part of the initial Finnish success story was based on smart system-wide reforms and inspiring policies that empowered teachers, principals, and other educators to work for the common cause. What is ahead for Finland now? Perhaps Finland needs "to learn to rely less on policy-driven reforms and more on successful ideas that have worked in various cultural settings and powerful networks that are spreading them without the mandate of the authorities" (Sahlberg, 2020a). Or, does the solution lie in the past?

In the midst of one of the worst post–World War II economic crises in the early 1990s, Finland turned again to education and insisted that nothing less than becoming the leading and most competitive knowledge economy of the world was enough to bring Finland back to the trajectory of other advanced economies. The dream then was to make the education system bring about the social cohesion, economic transformation, and innovation that would help Finland become a full member of the European Union and remain a fully autonomous nation. The education system was, as has been discussed in previous chapters, the key driver that raised the nation out of the economic crisis. The past visions of education have been accomplished, and now it is time to form a new vision that is capable of steering educational change in Finland over the next few decades. In conclusion, I offer some seeds for creating this new vision for the future of education in Finland.

The Finnish Dream for the future of Finnish education, inspired by Sir Ken Robinson, should be something like this: *Help all students find their passion in school.* That might be academic, artistic, creative, kinesthetic, or something else. Passion sparks when curiosity drives the discovery of each person's unique talent. Every school needs to be a safe learning community for all students to engage, explore, and interact with other people. School should teach knowledge and skills as they've always done, but they must prepare young people to use their talents, create new ideas, and to learn from failures, too. If people are not prepared to be wrong, as Sir Ken Robinson (2009) says, they will not come up with any valuable new ideas. Being willing to take risks and to tolerate being wrong are the only ways the Finns can make the best use of our scarce human resources.

The existing format of schooling requires radical changes. Massive disruption of schooling that is caused by the coronavirus pandemic is an opportunity to reconsider some of the past practices and structures and challenge the old grammar of schooling (Sahlberg, 2020a, 2020c; Zhao, 2020). First and foremost, Finnish schools must restore the student engagement that was once a hallmark so that more self-directed learning occurs in school. The new Finnish school must be a socially inspiring and safe environment where all pupils can learn the social skills that they will need in their lives. Individualized learning pathways with cooperative learning lead to more specialization but build on the stronger common ground of knowledge and skills. In this new vision for schools, the following new mindsets could be considered.

1. From one-size-fits-all whole-class teaching to flexible self-directed learning. Developing more individualized and activity-based learning eventually leads to a situation where people can learn most of what is now taught in schools through digital devices, anytime and anyplace. Handheld digital devices will provide online access to knowledge and other learners. Shared knowledge and competencies that are becoming an integral part of modern expertise and professional work will also become part of schools and traditional classrooms. Finland and some other countries have shown that it is not the length of the school year or school day that matters most (Figure 2.12). Less teaching can actually lead to more student learning if the circumstances are right and the solutions are smart. Those correct circumstances include trust in schools, adequate support and guidance for all students, and curriculum that can be locally adjusted to meet the interests and requirements of local communities.

Instead of continuing to think of future schooling in terms of allocating time to subjects, right now we should make a bold move and rethink the way time is organized in schools. This would mean devoting less time to conventional subjects, such as mother tongue, mathematics, and science, and more time to integrated themes, projects, and activities. The National Core Curriculum for Preschool Education, Basic Education, and General Upper Secondary Education provide good opportunities for schools to do that by using the common transversal competences as a reference point in designing curricula for schools and learning plans for students. Naturally, organized lessons should be more available in the lower grades of primary school and then should gradually decrease as pupils' ability to manage their own behavior and learning develops. This would also mean making a collective shift in schools from educating toward fixed, predictable outcomes to new, surprising ideas, knowledge, and skills as a result of creative and divergent learning (Sahlberg, 2020a). Doing so would give all students extended time to spend engaged in personally meaningful workshops, projects, and the arts.

2. From impersonal teaching to individualized learning. It is important in the future for each young person to acquire certain basic knowledge and skills, such as reading, writing, and using mathematics. But students should be offered alternative ways to learn these basic things. Children will learn more and more of what we used to learn in school out of school, through media, digital devices, and different social networks to which they belong. As a result, an increasing number of students will find teaching in school less interesting because they have already learned what is meaningful for them elsewhere.

A common trend in most OECD countries is a steadily weakening engagement and declining interest among young people in school learning.

Finland is no exception. Some suggest that the older our children get, the less motivated they are when it comes to what goes on in their schools. My own observation after visiting schools and classrooms around the world is that what is most often missing is a real spirit of curiosity— among both children and adults. If curiosity is related to exploration, experimentation, investigation, and discovery, then it should be a central element of school learning for children of all ages. Curiosity represents a thirst for knowledge and is therefore a major force behind learning and achievement. More play at all levels of schooling is a good and cheap answer, as we explain in our book *Let the Children Play* (Sahlberg & Doyle, 2019).

We need to rethink schools so that learning relies more on personalized individual learning plans and less on teaching drawn from a standardized curriculum. Again, Finland has taken good steps to make this reality in every school. New National Core Curricula will encourage schools to engage students more in codesigning teaching and learning and engage them better in reflecting the success of themselves and their schools. The art of education in the future will be to find a balance between these two. Because of the expanding educational possibilities in our digital world, young children enter schools with huge differences between them in what they already know and are able to do. This also means that young people are interested in a great variety of issues that may be completely foreign to teachers in their schools.

3. From knowledge capital to social capital. In the future, people will spend more time on and give more personal attention to digital media and technologies than they do today. From an educational point of view, this means two things. First, people will generally spend less time together in a concrete social setting. Social interaction will be based on using social networking and other future tools that rely on digital technological solutions. Second, people will learn more about the world and other people through digital gadgets. Expanding engagement in social media and networks will create a whole new source of learning from other people who have similar interests. By default, these new social tools will increase opportunities for creative action, as people can become part of open source projects designing games or digital solutions in collaboration with others in these networks.

Schools need to rethink what their core purpose should be when it comes to educating people. The point of school cannot remain what it is today: to provide the minimum basic knowledge and skills that young people will need in the future. The future for children is now; many young people are already using those skills in their lives today. Schools need to make sure that all students become fluent in reading, mathematics, and science concepts, which is essential for them later in life. Equally important, however, is for all students to develop the attitudes and skills they need to learn more and use the available knowledge and opportunities for achieving their own goals. They will also need to develop better skills for social interaction—both virtual and real—learn to cooperate with people who are very different from themselves, and learn to cope in complex social and information networks, in short, build social capital. What most people in the future will need that they are not likely to learn anywhere other than school is real problem solving in cooperation with other people. This will become one of the basic functions of future schools: to learn empathy, cooperation, leadership, and critical thinking in small groups of diverse individuals.

4. From making a grade to finding passion. Current education systems judge individual talent primarily through standardized knowledge tests and their grades in school. At worst, these tests and exams include only multiple-choice tasks and the negative effects they can have on children are well known (Koretz, 2017). At best, they expand beyond routine knowledge and require analysis, critical thinking, and problem-solving skills. However, they rarely cover nonacademic domains that include creativity, artistic skills, complex handling of information, or communicating new ideas to others. It is not only important to assess how students learn the basic knowledge and skills in school, but also to know how they develop their communication, problem-solving skills, and creativity.

Conventional knowledge tests as we know them now will gradually give way to new forms of assessment in schools. As schools move to emphasize more skills that everybody needs in a complex and unpredictable world, the criteria of being a successful school will also have to change. People will learn more of what they need through digital tools and media, and therefore it will become increasingly difficult to know exactly what role schools have played in students' learning (or *not* learning, if you wish). Two themes will be important in improving Finnish schools in the 2020s.

First, curiosity in school will be more important than ever, serving as an engine of learning and thereby engaging all students in intellectual, social, cultural, and physical activities. A lack of engagement and intrinsic motivation to learn in school are the main reasons for the educational challenges that teachers face in schools and classrooms today. By the end of *peruskoulu*, a growing number of young people find school learning irrelevant and are seeking alternative pathways outside school to fulfill their interests. Therefore, levels of curiosity and engagement in productive learning in school should become an important criterion for judging the success or failure of schools in the future.

Second, students' ability to create something valuable and new in school will be more important than ever—not just for some students, but for all of them. If creativity is defined according to Sir Ken Robinson (2011) as coming up with original ideas that have value, then creativity should be just as important as literacy and should be treated with the same status. Finnish schools have traditionally encouraged risk taking, creativity, and innovation. These traditions need to be strengthened. When the performance of students or the success of schools is measured, the creative aspect of both individual learning and collective behavior should be valued highly. In other words, we should also assess the value of new ideas created by students and teachers in school, not just how much is mastered of what already exists. A successful school is one that is able to take every individual—both students and teachers—further in their ability to create new than they could have gone by themselves.

The COVID-19 pandemic was a real test of professionalism and flexibility for Finnish schools. In March 2020, just in a couple of days teachers and school leaders had to figure out how to keep students learning while they couldn't come to school. This social experiment revealed the strength of an education system that is flexible in reacting to external changes, and that is built on professionalism and trust in teachers' abilities to do what is best for their students. It is fair to say that Finnish schools passed the stress test and showed that also in the future they can be trusted in deciding how to cope with complex crises.

Another positive sign of Finnish schools today is how to teach all children to correctly identify fake news in media. In the 2019 *Media Literacy Index* that is produced by the European Policies Initiative, Finland ranked highest among 35 European countries for the potential of people to resist fake news in media, followed by Denmark, Netherlands, and Sweden (European Policy Initiative, 2019). The ability to resist fake news is associated, according to this survey, with the quality of education, the freedom of media and press, and a high level of trust in these countries. In Finland, children will learn to read and use media critically already in primary school where the National Core Curriculum requires schools to teach digital and media literacy and critical thinking. In mathematics and science lessons children learn to avoid misuse of statistics to convert facts into fiction.

Twenty-three hundred years ago, Aristotle said that happiness is the ultimate purpose of human existence. Happiness has indeed become one of the indices used to measure the success of nations. Some education systems, like Finland's, view children's well-being and happiness as integral goals of schools. I believe that happiness occurs when people can do the things they like, which they find meaningful and rewarding. Happiness flourishes when we get closer to our element, which Sir Ken Robinson (2009) says is "about discovering yourself, and you can't do this if you're trapped in a compulsion to conform. You can't be yourself in a swarm" (p. 148).

What we need to turn my suggested four new mindsets into reality in Finland is not just another educational reform but a renewal, a continuous and systemic transformation of teaching and learning, moving step by step toward the new Big Dream. Finland has what it takes to make that happen. It requires new global partnerships and leadership in educational change. An important lesson from Finland is that there are different pathways to system excellence. These paths differ from the Global Educational Reform Movement discussed in the previous chapter. One way of increasing productivity and improved efficiency may lead to financial savings and perhaps temporarily better services, but shrinking budgets will never create sustainable improvements unless there are simultaneous investments in something new. Forecasts for the Finnish economy and society in general suggest that more investments are needed to bring about new ideas and innovations in both education and economic development, and to maintain the high level of social capital that has traditionally been the driver of strong educational performance.

At the end of the 1990s, Finland was able to benefit from one of the most competitive national economies. Experimentation, creativity, and networking were seen as the heart of school improvement, and trust in teachers and schools was endorsed as a key principle of education management. Educational change should provide encouragement and support for risk taking so that creativity will flourish in classrooms and schools, leading to new ideas and innovation. This is possible only with continuous renewal of Finnish education, guided by wise educational leadership in close relation with other public sector policies.

What many countries are looking for now is a socially just education system with schools that inspire teachers and students alike to do their best. Seymour Sarason (1996) reminded educational reformers that "teachers cannot create and sustain contexts for *productive learning* unless those conditions exist for them" (p. 367). Finnish educational policy fits precisely with this conviction. The Finnish government understands the importance of teachers and accordingly invests heavily not only in teacher education and professional development but also in work-conducive environments so that the teaching profession attracts and retains talent.

Well before the surge in attention to Finnish education following the publication of the PISA 2000 results, I had the privilege to host Seymour Sarason in Helsinki for a week in 1995. He was finalizing the revision of his book *The Culture of the School and the Problem of Change*, from which the observation above is drawn. I took Seymour to visit schools, talk to professors, and tell senior education authorities about the laws of school change as he saw them. He also read the Finnish 1994 National Curriculum Frameworks for basic and upper-secondary schools and the education development plans we had prepared for the future of schooling. In our final meeting, I asked Seymour to summarize his findings. He said: "Why did you bring me here? Your school system to me looks very close to what John Dewey had in mind and what I have been writing about teaching and schools for the last three decades."

Indeed, John Dewey dreamed of the teacher serving as a guide to help children formulate questions and devise solutions. Dewey saw the pupil's own experience, not information imparted by the teacher, as the critical path to understanding. Dewey also contended that democracy must be the main value in each school, just as it is in any free society. The education system in Finland is, as Sarason pointed out, shaped by these ideas of Dewey's and flavored with Finnish principles of practicality, creativity, and common sense. What the world can learn from educational change in Finland is that creating a good and equitable education system for all children is possible, but it takes the right mix of ingenuity, time, patience, and determination.

The Finnish Way of educational change should be encouraging to those who have found the path of competition, choice, test-based accountability, and performance-based pay to be a dead end. Moreover, the future of Finnish education described above can offer an alternative means to customized learning. For the Finns, personalization is not about having students work independently at computer terminals. The Finnish Way is to address the needs of each child with flexible arrangements and different learning paths. The wisdom of Finnish education is simple: The teacher's task is to help students to do their best.

As a countervailing force against the Global Educational Reform Movement that is driving school systems around the world, the Finnish Way continues to reveal that creative curricula, professionalism of teachers, courageous leadership, and high education systems performance go together. It is built on a pedagogical imperative that teaching and learning in school are systematically tailored to the needs of each and every student, taking into account their individual differences. It is guided by a clear purpose to educate the whole child, to learn what to do with what you know, and to grow into humanity. The Finnish Way makes plain that collaboration with teachers, not confrontation, is the path to better results. The evidence is clear—and the road ahead should be, too.

Afterword

The Evolving Story

I am often asked if there are any countries that are providing nationally for the sorts of education that I advocate. Finland, I say, and over the past 252 pages, Pasi Sahlberg has clearly explained why that might be. He has described how and why the Finnish system has evolved as it has, how it works now, the principles on which it is based, and the challenges it faces in the future. Is education in Finland perfect? Of course not. Will it stay as it is forever? How could it?

Like all human systems, Finnish education is in a constant process of becoming. It is embedded in the numerous economic, social, and cultural changes that are affecting Finland's overall way of life. And they, in turn, are part of larger global trends that are affecting all of us, wherever we are. National systems of education have to evolve for precisely that reason. How they should evolve is exactly what this book is about.

The main theme of *Finnish Lessons* is that transforming education is about creating the best conditions for young people to become engaged learners, fulfilled individuals, and compassionate, productive citizens. The Global Educational Reform Movement (or GERM, as Pasi so deftly puts it) may declare this intention, but the practices it has promoted in schools have largely had the opposite effects. In country after country, the standards movement has narrowed curricula, dampened morale, lowered aspirations, heightened anxiety, and hampered achievement among students and teachers alike. The countries that have done well on the standards agenda are often paying a heavy price in a loss of creativity, innovation, and engagement in students, the very qualities on which personal, cultural, and economic vitality now depend.

In recent years, my own work has focused on the importance of creativity in schools and on enabling students to develop their personal talents and passions. In his final chapter, Pasi argues that these must be priorities in the next phase of evolution in Finnish education. What does that involve?

I define creativity as the process of having original ideas that have value. There are various misconceptions about creativity. One is that it is a special power that only a few people have. It is not. It is a process that draws on a wide range of capacities that we all have. Another is that creativity is limited to certain sorts of activities, especially the arts. It is not. As essential as they are in education, creativity is not just about the arts. We can be creative in any activity that involves our intelligence, including mathematics, sciences, technology, and whatever else you might do.

I make a distinction between *general* and *personal* creativity (Robinson, 2011). One of the obstacles to original thinking is conventional patterns of thought that we take for granted: We can all be too easily entrapped in common sense. There are techniques of general creative thinking that anyone can learn and practice for challenging accepted habits of thought and for generating new ideas and perspectives. These techniques should be taught routinely in schools like other core skills. They should also be part of the professional development of teachers so that they can use them for themselves and help their students to do the same.

In *The Element: How Finding Your Passion Changes Everything*, I look more closely at *personal* creativity (Robinson, 2009). We all have unique patterns of aptitudes and interests. Being in your element is partly about finding what those are. It's not enough to know what you're good at. Many people are good at things they don't care for. You may have an aptitude for music or math or design or cooking, but not enjoy it. To be in your element, you have to love it. If you do love something that you're good at, it never feels like work. On the contrary, you get energy from doing it and often a new sense of purpose, too.

There are some things that we want all students to know, understand, and be able to do. But they also need to discover and develop their unique interests and abilities. When they do, they are much more likely to face their lives with confidence and enthusiasm and to meet the challenges they face with resilience and resourcefulness.

Helping all students to find their element has implications for the structure of the school curriculum, for methods of teaching and learning, and for assessment and accreditation. It is also at the heart of what it means to personalize education. As Pasi argues, doing that in a full-blooded and determined way is now the leading challenge for education systems that are serious about helping young people succeed in a world that is changing more rapidly than ever before.

For the past 15 years, Finland has been well ahead of the curve in education. The rest of the world has much to learn from these Finnish lessons. One of the most important lessons is that this story is still evolving and is far from over.

—Sir Ken Robinson

Notes

Introduction

1. The World Bank and OECD have used Finland as an example in Aho, Pitkänen, and Sahlberg (2006) and OECD (2011a). The McKinsey Company refers to Finland as a global benchmark of good practice in Barber and Mourshed (2007) and in Auguste, Kihn, and Miller (2010). Schleicher (2018) refers to Finland as the most successful country in PISA. The World Economic Forum has also regularly reported about Finland's extraordinary education performance.

2. There was a public debate in the Finnish media soon after the first OECD PISA results were published. Several members of the Finnish academic community rejected the results by arguing that the tests didn't measure "pure" mathematics or physics, but rather some forms of common everyday knowledge that are irrelevant for further studies in these subjects. More detailed description of these debates is in Sahlberg (2018).

3. Howard Gardner visited Finland in May 2010, and his interview was published in *Helsingin Sanomat* on May 28, 2010 (p. B9).

Chapter 1

1. *Peruskoulu* is the Finnish term that refers to 9-year basic school, which consists of six grades of lower comprehensive school (primary school) and three grades of upper comprehensive school (lower-secondary school). Today, the structure of Finnish basic schools has become unified, and the administrative line between the earlier two phases are disappearing.

2. The Second Republic refers to the period of 1946 to 1994 in Finnish history in Alasuutari (1996).

3. Tenth grade is a voluntary additional year following the completion of compulsory basic education. Students have individualized learning plans that are typically blended with academic and practical subjects or themes. One of the key purposes of the 10th grade is to provide young people with a second chance to improve their knowledge and skills so that they will be successful in upper-secondary school. Tenth grade is arranged as part of normal *peruskoulu* and is taught by their teachers.

4. www.washingtonpost.com/blogs/answer-sheet/wp/2014/03/20/weird-list -of-topics-avoided-on-california-high-school-exit-exam.

5. The Aquarium Project was a government-funded school improvement initiative to support the shift from a centrally steered system of management to local leadership and continuous improvement. A good description can be found (in Finnish) in the doctoral thesis of Hellström (2004).

6. The National Institute for Health and Welfare (THL; www.thl.fi/en/web /thlfi-en) is a research and development institute under the Finnish Ministry of Social Affairs and Health. THL seeks to serve the broader society in addition to the scientific community, actors in the field, and decisionmakers in central government and municipalities. The aim is to promote health and welfare in Finland.

7. The Finnish National Agency for Education is the state-level education authority that is assigned to develop education and training, early childhood education, and lifelong learning, and to promote internationalization in Finland (https://www.oph.fi/en/education-and-qualifications/national-core-curriculum -ecec-nutshell).

Chapter 2

1. KiVa is an antibullying program that has been developed in the University of Turku, Finland, with funding from the Ministry of Education and Culture. The program is evidence-based, which means that the effectiveness of KiVa has been proven scientifically. KiVa offers a wide range of concrete tools and materials for schools to tackle bullying. More information can be found at https://www.kivaprogram.net.

2. The International Association for the Evaluation of Educational Achievement conducts PIRLS and TIMSS studies in 4-year or 5-year cycles. TIMSS (Trends in International Mathematics and Science Study) measures trends in mathematics and science achievement at the 4th and 8th grades. It has been conducted on a regular 4-year cycle since 1995, making TIMSS 2011 the fifth assessment of mathematics and science achievement trends. PIRLS (Progress in International Reading Literacy Study) measures trends in reading comprehension at the 4th grade. First assessed in 2001, PIRLS has been on a regular 5-year cycle since then. Both TIMSS and PIRLS were assessed in 2011, when the cycles of both studies came into alignment. More information and results are available at timssandpirls.bc.edu.

3. Data for all countries but the United States come from OECD, *Education at a Glance 2019* (Paris: OECD, 2019), Table D4.2, p. 429, https://www .oecd.org/education/education-at-a-glance. The data for the United States come from S. E. Abrams, The Mismeasure of Teaching Time, Working Paper, Center for Benefit-Cost Studies of Education, Teachers College, Columbia University, January 2015, https://www.cbcse.org/publications/the-mismeasure-of-teaching -time. Abrams's documents that the OECD data for the United States derive from a faulty teacher survey the country uses to collect its data and bases his numbers instead on teacher contracts and school schedules. The other countries use statutory data based on teacher agreements. For additional information re-

garding the methodology employed by countries for gathering data on teaching time, see OECD, *Education at a Glance 2019: Annex 3, Sources, Methods, and Technical Notes*, Table X3.D4.1, pp. 289–292, https://www.oecd-ilibrary.org /education/education-at-a-glance-2019_d138983d-en.

4. The city of Helsinki provides detailed information about population with foreign background in Helsinki. Statistics on population with foreign background, with a foreign mother tongue or with a foreign nationality, namely their demographic structure, migration, housing, education, and employment can be found here: https://ulkomaalaistaustaisethelsingissa.fi/en/content/education.

Chapter 3

1. Vipunen is the education administration's reporting portal. The Ministry of Education and Culture and the Finnish National Agency for Education are jointly responsible for its content. Vipunen's statistics are based on data and registers collected by the Statistics Finland, the Ministry of Culture and Education, and the Finnish National Agency for Education. You can use this service to access statistics and indicators for education in a number of educational sectors, placement of students after completion, research conducted in higher education institutions, the population's educational structure, and the socioeconomic background of students. Link: https://vipunen.fi/en-gb.

2. The Bologna Process is an intergovernmental initiative that currently has 46 signatories. It aims at creating a European Higher Education Area with harmonized degree systems and the European Credit Transfer System (ECTS). Teacher education is described in Pechar (2007) and Jakku-Sihvonen and Niemi (2006).

3. Pan-European collaboration in teacher education has increased due to the Bologna Process and specific exchange programs in Europe, but strong and active research links have remained between Finnish universities and their North American, British, and Australian counterparts.

4. There has been continuous debate over whether the matriculation examination negatively affects the way that teachers teach in upper-secondary schools. Some of the empirical research findings are reported in Häivälä (2009).

5. Finland was part of the International Teacher Policy Study that was funded by the National Center on Education and the Economy (NCEE) and the Ford Foundation in 2014–2017. The country case study is available in Hammerness et al. (2017), and a short video illustrating Finland's teacher training schools is available here: https://edpolicy.stanford.edu/node/1520. The video shows students working with supervising teachers. The student–supervisor relationship helps the students to build trust between students and their clinical mentors. An additional aspect of this clinical teacher education model is the teachers' collaborative relationship with education faculty at the university that is essential in connecting the theory of teaching to classroom practice.

Chapter 4

1. These are the two main academic journals dedicated to school improvement and educational change.

2. The initial idea of "a new educational orthodoxy" comes from Andy Hargreaves. See Sahlberg (2011).

3. I was coleading a national project called Creative Problem-Solving in Schools that had close links to Finnish innovation enterprises such as Nokia, Kone, and Vaisala. It was administrated and funded by the National Board of General Education. Part of the inspiration for this project was the Creative Problem-Solving initiative based in Buffalo, New York.

4. The World Economic Forum (WEF) is a Switzerland-based international organization that coordinates research on economics. Similar comparisons of national economic competitiveness are done by the International Institute for Management Development (IMD). In the European Union's internal ranking of its member states' economic competitiveness, Finland ranked at the top with Sweden in 2010.

Chapter 5

1. A salient example of this accountability culture is the well-known and controversial "deliverology" approach, which relies on targets, measuring, and accountability to manage and monitor the implementation of education reform policies and strategies. For a prodeliverology perspective, see Barber, Moffit, and Kihn's (2011) "field guide." For a critical perspective, see Seddon's (2008) critique.

2. For example, Hargreaves (2003), Schleicher (2007), and Grubb (2007) have underscored the importance of alternative education policies in transcending the conventional educational reforms.

3. HundrED.org is a not-for-profit organization, which seeks and shares inspiring innovations in K–12 education around the world. It is based in Helsinki, Finland, and led by Saku Tuominen, an experienced Finnish entrepreneur, innovator, and activist. HundrEd.org describes its vision like this: The world is changing faster than schools, but beautiful things are still happening in education all over the world. We call them education innovations: practices, programs, or organizations that are scalable and impactful in K–12 education. The world is full of them and they are helping children flourish, but it can be difficult for them to spread. We envision a future where every child has access to the best possible educational innovations that provide quality education for all. More about this initiative can be found at https://hundred.org/en#header.

4. Cultural factors have been discussed by external observers of Finnish education. See Hargreaves et al. (2008), Schleicher (2006), Grubb (2007), Abrams (2016).

References

Abrams, S. E. (2015). *The mismeasure of teaching time.* Working Paper, Center for Benefit-Cost Studies of Education. Teachers College, Columbia University. www.cbcse.org/publications/the-mismeasure-of-teaching-time

Abrams, S. E. (2016). *Education and the commercial mindset.* Harvard University Press.

Adams, R. J. (2003). Response to "Cautions on OECD's recent educational survey (PISA)." *Oxford Review of Education, 29*(3), 377–389.

Adamson, F., Åstrand, B., & Darling-Hammond, L. (Eds.). (2016). *Global education reform: How privatization and public investment influence education outcomes.* Routledge.

Aho, E. (1996). *Myrskyn silmässä* [In the eye of the storm]: *Kouluhallituksen pääjohtaja muistelee.* Edita.

Aho, E., Pitkänen, K., & Sahlberg, P. (2006). *Policy development and reform principles of basic and secondary education in Finland since 1968.* World Bank.

Ahonen, A. (2018). Muuttuvatko koulut? In J. Rautopuro & K. Juuti (Eds.), *PISA pintaa syvemmältä. PISA 2015 Suomen pääraportti* (pp. 311–342). Suomen kasvatustiteteellinen seura.

Ahtiainen, R. (2017). *Shades of change in Fullan's and Hargreaves's models: Theoretical change perspectives regarding Finnish special education reform.* PhD thesis, University of Helsinki.

Alasuutari, P. (1996). *Toinen tasavalta: Suomi 1946–1994.* Vastapaino.

Allerup, P., & Mejding, J. (2003). Reading achievement in 1991 and 2000. In S. Lie, P. Linnakylä, & A. Roe (Eds.), *Northern lights on PISA: Unity and diversity in Nordic countries in PISA 2000* (pp. 133–146). University of Oslo, Department of Teacher Education and School Development.

Alquézar Sabadie, J., & Johansen, J. (2010). How do national economic competitiveness indices view human capital? *European Journal of Education, 45*(2), 236–258.

American Statistical Association. (2014). *ASA statement on using value-added models for educational assessment.* www.amstat.org/asa/files/pdfs/POL-ASAVAM-Statement.pdf

Amrein, A. L., & Berliner, D. C. (2002). High-stakes testing, uncertainty, and student learning. *Education Policy Analysis Archives, 10*(18).

Asplund, R., & Maliranta, M. (2006). Productivity growth: The role of human capital and technology in the road to prosperity. In A. Ojala, J. Eloranta, & J. Jalava (Eds.), *The road to prosperity: An economic history of Finland* (pp. 263–283). SKS.

Atjonen, P., Halinen, I., Hämäläinen, S., Korkeakoski, E., Knubb-Manninen, G., Kupari, P., . . . Wikman, T. (2008). Tavoitteista vuorovaikutukseen. Perusopetuksen pedagogiikan arviointi [From objectives to interaction: Evaluation of the pedagogy of basic education]. *Koulutuksen arviointineuvoston julkaisuja, 30*, 197. Koulutuksen Arviointineuvosto.

Au, W. (2009). *Unequal by design: High-stakes testing and the standardization of inequality.* Routledge.

Auguste, B., Kihn, P., & Miller, M. (2010). *Closing the talent gap: Attracting and retaining top third graduates to a career in teaching.* McKinsey & Company.

Baker, E., Barton, P., Darling-Hammond, L., Haertel, E., Ladd, H., Linn, R., . . . Shepard, L. (2010). *Problems with the use of student test scores to evaluate teachers: Briefing paper 278.* Education Policy Institute.

Barber, M., Moffit, A., & Kihn, P. (2011). *Deliverology 101: A field guide for educational leaders.* Corwin.

Barber, M., & Mourshed, M. (2007). *The McKinsey report: How the world's best performing school systems come out on top.* McKinsey & Company.

Bautier, E., & Rayon, P. (2007). What PISA really evaluates: Literacy or students' universes of reference? *Journal of Educational Change, 8*(4), 359–364.

Berliner, D., & Sahlberg, P. (2017). Foreword: PISA: A good servant but a bad master. In S. Sellar, G. Thompson, & D. Rutkowski (Eds.), *The global education race: Taking the measure of PISA and international testing* (pp. vii–xii). Brush Education.

Berry, J., & Sahlberg, P. (2006). Accountability affects the use of small group learning in school mathematics. *Nordic Studies in Mathematics Education, 11*(1), 5–31.

Bracey, G. (2005). Research: Put out over PISA. *Phi Delta Kappan, 86*(10), 797.

Breakspear, S. (2012). *The policy impact of PISA: An exploration of the normative effects of international benchmarking in school system performance.* OECD Education Working Papers, No. 71. OECD Publishing.

Brophy, J. (2006). *Grade repetition: Education Policy Series 6.* International Institute for Educational Planning.

Campbell, D. T. (1976). *Assessing the impact of planned social change.* Paper #8. Dartmouth College, Public Affairs Center.

Carnoy, M. (with A. Gove & J. Marshall). (2007). *Cuba's academic advantage: Why students in Cuba do better in school.* Stanford University Press.

Castells, M., & Himanen, P. (2002). *The information society and the welfare state: The Finnish model.* Oxford University Press.

Center for American Progress & The Education Trust. (2011). *Essential elements of teacher policy in ESEA: Effectiveness, fairness, and evaluation.* www

.americanprogress.org/issues/education/report/2011/02/23/9167/essential
-elements-of-teacher-policy-in-esea-effectiveness-fairness-and-evaluation

Chaker, A. N. (2014). *The Finnish miracle*. Talentum.

Coleman, J., Campbell, E., Hobson, C., McPartland, J., Mood, A., Weinfeld, F.,
& York, R. (1966). *Equality of educational opportunity*. U.S. Government
Printing Office.

Cunha, F., & Heckman, J. (2010). *Investing in our young people* (NBER Working Paper 16201). National Bureau of Economic Research. www.nber.org
/papers/W16201.pdf

Dahlman, C., Routti, J., & Ylä-Anttila, P. (2006). *Finland as a knowledge economy: Elements of success and lessons learned*. World Bank.

Darling-Hammond, L. (2006). *Powerful teacher education: Lessons from exem-
plary programs*. Jossey-Bass.

Darling-Hammond, L. (2010). *The flat world and education: How America's
commitment to equity will determine our future*. Teachers College Press.

Darling-Hammond, L., Burns, D., Campbell, C., Goodwin, A. L., Hammerness,
K., Low, E. L., McIntyre, A., Sato, M., & Zeichner, K. (2017). *Empowered
educators: How high-performing systems shape teaching quality around
the world*. Jossey-Bass.

Darling-Hammond, L., & Lieberman, A. (Eds.). (2012). *Teacher education
around the world: Changing policies and practices*. Routledge.

Department for Education. (2010). *The importance of teaching: The schools
white paper*. Department for Education.

Dohn, N. B. (2007). Knowledge and skills for PISA. Assessing the assessment.
Journal of Philosophy of Education, 41(1), 1–16.

Economist. (2020, October 3). *A rising tide*. www.economist.com/graphic
-detail/2020/10/03/its-better-to-be-a-poor-pupil-in-a-rich-country-than-the
-reverse

Elley, W. B. (Ed.). (1992). *How in the world do students read?* Grindeldruck.

Engel, L., & Rutkowski, D. (2019, March 28). *Is PISA worth its cost? Some
challenges facing cost-benefit analysis of ILSAs*. Laboratory of International Assessment Studies blog series. https://bit.ly/2Wp3c9S

Engel, L., & Rutkowski, D. (2020). Pay to play: What does PISA participation
cost in the US? *Discourse: Studies in the Cultural Politics of Education,
41*(3), 484–496.

European Policy Initiative. (2019). *Just think about it. Findings of the Media
Literacy Index 2019*. Open Society Institute.

Finnish Education Evaluation Centre. (2016). National Plan for Education
Evaluation 2016–2019. FINEEC.

Finnish Education Evaluation Centre. (2020a). *National Plan for Education
Evaluation 2020–2023*. FINEEC.

Finnish Education Evaluation Centre. (2020b). *Poikkeuksellisten opetusjärjest-
elyjen vaikutukset tasa-arvon ja yhdenvertaisuuden toteutumiseen*. Karvi.

https://karvi.fi/app/uploads/2020/05/Poikkeuksellisten-opetusjärjestelyjen
-vaikutukset-osa-I-Karvi-7.5.2020-1.pdf

Finnish Institute for Health and Welfare. (2019). *Kouluterveyskyselyn tulokset.*
https://thl.fi/fi/tutkimus-ja-kehittaminen/tutkimukset-ja-hankkeet/kouluter
veyskysely/kouluterveyskyselyn-tulokset

Finnish National Agency for Education. (2014). *National Core Curriculum for
Preprimary Education.* Finnish National Agency for Education.

Finnish National Agency for Education. (2016). *National Core Curriculum for
Basic Education.* Finnish National Agency for Education.

Finnish National Agency for Education. (2018). *National Core Curriculum for
ECEC in a nutshell.* Finnish National Agency for Education. www.oph.fi/en
/education-and-qualifications/national-core-curriculum-ecec-nutshell

Finnish National Agency for Education. (2020). *Core Curriculum for General
Upper Secondary Schools in a nutshell.* Finnish National Agency for Education. www.oph.fi/en/statistics-and-publications/publications/core-curricu
lum-general-upper-secondary-schools-nutshell

Fischman, G., Sahlberg, P., Silova, I., & Marcetti Topper, A. (2019). International large-scale student assessments and their impact on national school
reforms. In Larry E. Suter, E. Smith, & B. Denman (Eds.), *The handbook of
comparative studies in education.* SAGE Publishing.

Fullan, M. (2010). *All systems go: The change imperative for whole system
reform.* Corwin.

Fullan, M. (2011). *Choosing wrong drivers for whole system reform* (Seminar
Series 204). Centre for Strategic Education.

Fullan, M. (2016). *The new meaning of educational change.* Teachers College
Press.

Fuller, K., & Stevenson, H. (2019). Global education reform: Understanding the
movement. *Educational Review, 71*(1), 1–4.

Gameran, E. (2008, February 29). What makes Finnish kids so smart? *Wall
Street Journal.* wsj.com/article/SB120425355065601997.html

Gardner, H. (1983). *Frames of minds: The theory of multiple intelligences.* Basic
Books.

Gardner, H. (2010, January 10). *The ministers' misconception.* www
.thegoodproject.org/the-ministers-misconceptions

Gardner, H. (2020). *A synthesizing mind: A memoir from the creator of multiple intelligences theory.* MIT Press.

Goldstein, H. (2004). International comparisons of student attainment: Some
issues arising from the PISA study. *Assessment in Education: Principles,
Policy & Practice, 11*(3), 319–330.

Grek, S. (2009). Governing by numbers: The PISA "effect" in Europe. *Journal
of Education Policy, 24*(1), 23–37.

Grubb, N. (2007). Dynamic inequality and intervention: Lessons for a small
country. *Phi Delta Kappan, 89*(2), 105–114.

Haertel, E. H. (2013). *Reliability and validity of inferences about teachers based on student test scores.* Educational Testing Service.

Häivälä, K. (2009). *Voice of upper-secondary school teachers: Subject teachers´ perceptions of changes and visions in upper-secondary schools.* Annales Universitatis Turkuensis, C 283 (in Finnish). University of Turku.

Halme, K., Lindy, I., Piirainen, K., Salminen, V., & White, J. (2014). *Finland as a knowledge economy 2.0: Lessons on policies and governance.* World Bank.

Hammerness, K., Ahtiainen, R., & Sahlberg, P. (2017). *Empowered educators in Finland: How high-performing systems shape teaching quality.* Jossey-Bass.

Hanushek, E., & Woessmann, L. (2019). *The economic benefits of improving educational achievement in the European Union: An update and extension.* EENEE Analytical Report No. 39. The European Commission.

Hargreaves, A. (2003). *Teaching in the knowledge society: Education in the age of insecurity.* Teachers College Press.

Hargreaves, A., Crocker, R., Davis, B., McEwen, L., Sahlberg, P., Shirley, D., & Sumara, D. (2009). *The learning mosaic: A multiple perspectives review of the Alberta initiative for school improvement.* Alberta Education.

Hargreaves, A., Earl, L., Moore, S., & Manning, M. (2001). *Learning to change: Teaching beyond subjects and standards.* Jossey-Bass.

Hargreaves, A., & Fink, D. (2006). *Sustainable leadership.* Jossey-Bass.

Hargreaves, A., & Fullan, M. (2012). *Professional capital: Transforming teaching in every school.* Teachers College Press.

Hargreaves, A., Halasz, G., & Pont, B. (2008). The Finnish approach to system leadership. In B. Pont, D. Nusche, & D. Hopkins (Eds.), *Improving school leadership, Volume 2: Case studies on system leadership* (pp. 69–109). OECD.

Hargreaves, A., Lieberman, A., Fullan, M., & Hopkins, D. (Eds.). (2010). *Second international handbook of educational change.* Springer.

Hargreaves, A., & Shirley, D. (2009). *The Fourth Way: The inspiring future of educational change.* Corwin.

Hargreaves, A., & Shirley, D. (2012). *The Global Fourth Way: The quest for educational excellence.* Corwin.

Hausstätter, R., & Takala, M. (2010). Can special education make a difference? Exploring the differences of special educational systems between Finland and Norway in relation to the PISA results. *Scandinavian Journal of Disability Research*, 1–11.

Hautamäki, J., Harjunen, E., Hautamäki, A., Karjalainen, T., Kupiainen, S., Laaksonen, S., . . . Jakku-Sihvonen, R. (2008). *PISA06 Finland: Analyses, reflections and explanations.* Ministry of Education.

Hautamäki, J., Kupiainen, S., Marjanen, J., Vainikainen, M.-P., & Hotulainen, R. (2013). *Oppimaan oppiminen peruskoulun päättövaiheessa. Tilanne vuonna 2012 ja muutos vuodesta 2001.* [Learning to learn at the end of basic education. Results in 2012 and changes from 2001.] Faculty of Behavioral

Sciences, Department of Teacher of Education Research Report No. 347. University of Helsinki.

Hellström, M. (2004). *Muutosote. Akvaarioprojektin pedagogisten kehittämishankkeiden toteutustapa ja onnistuminen* [The way of change—The implementation and success of pedagogical development projects at the experimental schools of the Aquarium Project]. University of Helsinki.

Itkonen, T., & Jahnukainen, M. (2007). An analysis of accountability policies in Finland and the United States. *International Journal of Disability, Development and Education, 54*(1), 5–23.

Jakku-Sihvonen, R., & Niemi, H. (Eds.). (2006). *Research-based teacher education in Finland: Reflections by Finnish teacher educators.* Finnish Educational Research Association.

Jennings, J., & Stark Rentner, D. (2006). *Ten big effects of the No Child Left Behind Act on public schools.* Center on Education Policy.

Jensen, B., Weidmann, B., & Farmer, J. (2013). *The myth of markets in school education.* Grattan Institute.

Jimerson, S. (2001). Meta-analysis of grade retention research: Implications for practice in the 21st century. *School Psychology Review, 30,* 420–437.

Jokinen, H., & Välijärvi, J. (2006). Making mentoring a tool for supporting teachers' professional development. In R. Jakku-Sihvonen & H. Niemi (Eds.), *Research-based teacher education in Finland: Reflections by Finnish teacher educators* (pp. 89–101). Finnish Educational Research Association.

Joyce, B., & Showers, B. (1995). *Student achievement through staff development: Fundamentals of school renewal* (2nd ed.). Longman.

Joyce, B., & Weil, M. (1986). *Models of teaching* (3rd ed.). Prentice Hall.

Jussila, J., & Saari, S. (Eds.). (2000). *Teacher education as a future-moulding factor: International evaluation of teacher education in Finnish universities.* Higher Education Evaluation Council.

Kangasniemi, S. (2008, February 27). Millä ammatilla pääsee naimisiin? [With which profession to get married?] *Helsingin Sanomat Koulutusliite,* pp. 4–6.

Kärnä, A., Voeten, M., Little, T., Alanen, E., Poskiparta, E., & Salmivalli, C. (2011). Going to scale: A nonrandomized nationwide trial of the KiVa antibullying program for comprehensive schools. *Journal of Consulting and Clinical Psychology, 79,* 796–805.

Kasvio, M. (Ed.). (2011). *The best school in the world: Seven Finnish examples from the 21st century.* Museum of Finnish Architecture.

Kauffman, S. (1995). *At home in the universe: The search for the laws of self-organization and complexity.* Oxford University Press.

Kirjavainen, T., & Pulkkinen, J. (2017). Pisa-tulokset heikentyneet huippuvuosista—kuinka paljon ja mistä se voisi johtua? [PISA results have declined—How much and why?] *Talous ja yhteiskunta, 45*(3), 8–12. www.labour.fi/ty/tylehti/ty/ty32017/unnamed-file.pdf/ty32017Kir

Kiuasmaa, K. (1982). *Oppikoulu 1880–1980: Oppikoulu ja sen opettajat koulujärjestyksestä peruskouluun* [Grammar school 1880–1980: Grammar school and its teachers from school order to comprehensive school]. Kustannusosakeyhtiö Pohjoinen.

Kivi, A. (2005). *Seven brothers* [*Seitsemän veljestä*, R. Impola, Trans.]. Aspasia Books. (Original work published 1870)

Komatsu, H., & Rappleye, J. (2017). A new global policy regime founded on invalid statistics? Hanushek, Woessmann, PISA, and economic growth. *Comparative Education, 53*(2), 166–191.

Komatsu, H., & Rappleye, J. (2020, July 22). TINA comes to European education? The European Commission, PISA, PIAAC, and American-Style Knowledge Capital Theory. *NORRAG blog.*

Koretz, D. (2017). *The testing charade: Pretending to make schools better.* University of Chicago Press.

Koskenniemi, M. (1944). *Kansakoulun opetusoppi* [Didactics of primary school]. Otava.

Kreiner, S., & Christensen, K. B. (2013, June). Analyses of model fit and robustness: A new look at the PISA scaling model underlying ranking of countries according to reading literacy. *Psychometrika,* 1–22.

Kupari, P., & Välijärvi, J. (Eds.). (2005). *Osaaminen kestävällä pohjalla. PISA 2003 Suomessa* [Competences on the solid ground. PISA 2003 in Finland]. Institute for Educational Research, University of Jyväskylä.

Kuusi, P. (1961). *60-luvun sosiaalipolitiikka* [Social politics of the 1960s]. WSOY.

Laukkanen, R. (2008). Finnish strategy for high-level education for all. In N. C. Sognel & P. Jaccard (Eds.), *Governance and performance of education systems* (pp. 305–324). Springer.

Lavonen, J., Krzywacki-Vainio, H., Aksela, M., Krokfors, L., Oikkonen, J., & Saarikko, H. (2007). Pre-service teacher education in chemistry, mathematics and physics. In E. Pehkonen, M. Ahtee, & J. Lavonen (Eds.), *How Finns learn mathematics and science* (pp. 49–68). Sense Publishers.

Lawrence, M. (2020). *Testing 3, 2, 1: What Australian education can learn from Finland.* Melbourne Press.

Lehtinen, E. (2004). *Koulutusjärjestelmä suomalaisen yhteiskunnan muutoksessa* [Education system in the changing Finnish society]. Sitra.

Lehtinen, E., Kinnunen, R., Vauras, M., Salonen, P., Olkinuora, E., & Poskiparta, E. (1989). *Oppimiskäsitys* [Conception of knowledge]. Valtion painatuskeskus.

Lewis, R. (2005). *Finland, cultural lone wolf.* Intercultural Press.

Liiten, M. (2004, February 11). Ykkössuosikki: Opettajan ammatti [Top favorite: Teaching profession]. *Helsingin Sanomat.* www.hs.fi/artikkeli/Ykk%C3%B6ssuosikki+opettajan+ammatti/1076151893860

Linnakylä, P. (2004). Finland. In H. Döbert, E. Klieme, & W. Stroka (Eds.), *Conditions of school performance in seven countries: A quest for understanding the international variation of PISA results* (pp. 150–218). Waxmann.

Linnakylä, P., & Saari, H. (1993). *Oppiiko op-pilas pe-ruskoulussa? Pe-ruskoulu arviointi 90 tutkimuksen tuloksia* [Does the pupil learn in peruskoulu? Findings of the Peruskoulu 90 research]. Jyväskylän-yliopiston kasvatustieteiden tutkimuslaitos.

MacKinnon, N. (2011). The urgent need for new approaches in school evaluation to enable Scotland's Curriculum for Excellence. *Educational Assessment, Evaluation and Accountability, 23*(1), 89–106.

Martin, M. O., Mullis, I. V. S., Gonzales, E. J., Gregory, K. D., Smith, T. A., Chrostowski, S. J., . . . O'Connor, K. M. (2000). *TIMSS 1999 international science report: Findings from IEA's repeat of the third international mathematics and science study at the eighth grade.* Boston College.

Matriculation Examination Board. (2020). *Digital matriculation examination.* www.ylioppilastutkinto.fi/en/matriculation-examination/digital-matriculation-examination

Matti, T. (Ed.). (2009). *Northern lights on PISA 2006. Differences and similarities in the Nordic countries.* Nordic Council of Ministers.

Meyer, H.-D., & Benavot, A. (2013). PISA and the globalization of education governance: Some puzzles and problems. In H.-D. Meyer & A. Benavot (Eds.), *PISA, power, and policy: The emergence of global educational governance* (pp. 9–26). Symposium Books.

Miettinen, R. (1990). *Koulun muuttamisen mahdollisuudesta* [About the possibilities of school change]. Gaudeamus.

Ministry of Education. (2009). *Ensuring professional competence and improving opportunities for continuing education in education* (Committee Report 16).

Ministry of Education. (2019). *PISA18 ensituloksia. Suomi parhaiden joukossa.* OKM julkaisuja #40. Ministry of Education.

Ministry of Foreign Affairs. (2010). *How Finland will demonstrate its strengths by solving the world's most intractable problems: Final report of the country brand delegation.*

Mortimore, P. (2009). *Alternative models for analysing and representing countries' performance in PISA.* Paper commissioned by Education International Research Institute. Education International.

Mortimore, P. (2013). *Education under siege: Why there is a better alternative.* Policy Press.

Mourshed, M., Chijioke, C., & Barber, M. (2010). *How the world's most improved school systems keep getting better.* McKinsey.

Murgatroyd, S. (2007). *Accountability project framework—Developing school-based accountability.* Unpublished report. Innovation Expedition.

National Board of Education. (1999). *A framework for evaluating educational outcomes in Finland.*

National Institute for Health and Welfare (2020). *Varhaiskasvatus 2019*. Tilas-
    toraportti 33/2020. www.julkari.fi/bitstream/handle/10024/140541/Tr33
    _20.pdf?sequence=1&isAllowed=y

National Youth Survey. (2010). *KNT 2010*. 15/30 Research.

Newsweek. (1999, May 24). *The future is Finnish*. www.newsweek.com/1999
    /05/23/the-future-is-finnish.html

Ng, P. T. (2018). *Learning from Singapore: The power of paradoxes*. Routledge.

Nichols, S. L., & Berliner, D. C. (2007). *Collateral damage: How high-stakes
    testing corrupts America's schools*. Harvard Education Press.

Niemi, H. (2008). Research-based teacher education for teachers' lifelong learn-
    ing. *Lifelong Learning in Europe, 13*(1), 61–69.

Nuikkinen, K. (2011). Learning spaces: How they meet evolving educational
    needs. In M. Kasvio (Ed.), *The best school in the world: Seven Finnish ex-
    amples from the 21st century* (pp. 10–19). Museum of Finnish Architecture.

OECD. (2001). *Knowledge and skills for life: First results from PISA 2000*.

OECD. (2004). *Learning for tomorrow's world: First results from PISA 2003*.

OECD. (2005). *Equity in education: Thematic review of Finland*.

OECD. (2007). *PISA 2006: Science competencies for tomorrow's world* (Vol. 1).

OECD. (2008). *Trends shaping education*.

OECD. (2010). *PISA 2009 results: What students know and can do. Student
    performance in reading, mathematics and science* (Vol. 1).

OECD. (2011). *Strong performers and successful reformers in education: Les-
    sons from PISA for the United States*.

OECD. (2012). *Equity and quality in education*.

OECD. (2013a). *PISA 2012 results: What students know and can do. Re-
    sources, policies and practices* (Vol. 1).

OECD. (2013b). *PISA 2012 results: What makes schools successful: Resources,
    policies and practices* (Vol. 4).

OECD. (2013c). *OECD skills outlook: First results from the survey of adult
    skills*.

OECD. (2014a). *TALIS 2013 results: An international perspective on teaching
    and learning*.

OECD. (2014b). *Measuring innovation in education: A new perspective*.

OECD. (2016). *PISA 2015 results. Excellence and equity in education*.

OECD. (2018). *Equity in education: Breaking down barriers to social mobility*.

OECD. (2019a). *PISA 2018 results: What students know and can do*.

OECD. (2019b). *PISA 2018 results: Where all students can succeed*.

OECD. (2019c). *PISA 2018 results: What school life means for students' lives*.

OECD. (2019d). *Education at a glance: Education indicators*.

OECD. (2019e). *PISA 2018: Insights and interpretations*.

OECD. (2019f). *TALIS 2018 results. Teachers and school leaders as lifelong
    learners*.

OECD. (2020a). *Education at a glance. Education indicators*.

OECD (2020b). *PISA 2018 results. Effective policies, successful schools.*

Ofsted (Office for Standards in Education, Children's Services and Skills). (2010). *Finnish pupils' success in mathematics: Factors that contribute to Finnish pupils' success in mathematics.*

O'Neill, O. (2002). *A question of trust.* Cambridge University Press.

Opetushallitus. (2017). *Opettajat ja rehtorit Suomessa 2016. Raportit ja selvitykset 2.* Opetushallitus.

Panzar, K. (2018). *Finding Sisu: In search of courage, strength, and happiness the Finnish Way.* Hodder & Stoughton.

Patel, D., & Sandevur, J. (2019). *A Rosetta stone for human capital.* Published on Harvard University's website. https://scholar.harvard.edu/files/devpatel /files/rosetta_stone.pdf

Pechar, H. (2007). "The Bologna Process": A European response to global competition in higher education. *Canadian Journal of Higher Education, 37*(3), 109–125.

Popham, J. (2007). The no-win accountability game. In C. Glickman (Ed.), *Letters to the next president: What we can do about the real crisis in public education* (pp. 166–173). Teachers College Press.

Prais, S. J. (2003). Cautions on OECD's recent educational survey (PISA). *Oxford Review of Education, 29*(2), 139–163.

Prais, S. J. (2004). Cautions on OECD's recent educational survey (PISA): Rejoinder to OECD's response. *Oxford Review of Education, 30*(4), 569–573.

Pulkkinen, J., Räikkönen, E., Jahnukainen, M., & Pirttimaa, R. (2020). How do educational reforms change the share of students in special education? Trends in special education in Finland. *European Educational Research Journal, 19*(4), 364–384.

Quintero, E. (Ed.). (2017). *Teaching in context: The social side of education reform.* Harvard Education Press.

Ramirez, F., Luo, X. W., Schofer, E., & Meyer, J. (2006). Student achievement and national economic growth. *American Journal of Education, 113*(1), 1–29.

Rautopuro, J., & Juuti, K. (Eds.). (2018). *PISA pintaa syvemmältä.* PISA 2015 Suomen pääraportti. Suomen kasvatustieteellinen seura.

Ravitch, D. (2010). *The death and life of the great American school system: How testing and choice are undermining education.* Basic Books.

Ravitch, D. (2013). *Reign of error: The hoax of the privatization movement and the danger to America's public schools.* Alfred A. Knopf.

Ravitch, D. (2020). *Slaying Goliath: The passionate resistance to privatization and the fight to save America's public schools.* Alfred A. Knopf.

Riley, K., & Torrance, H. (2003). Big change question: As national policymakers seek to find solutions to national education issues, do international comparisons such as TIMSS and PISA create a wider understanding, or do they serve to promote the orthodoxies of international agencies? *Journal of Educational Change, 4*(4), 419–425.

Rinne, R., Kivirauma, J., & Simola, H. (2002). Shoots of revisionist education policy or just slow readjustment? *Journal of Education Policy, 17*(6), 643–659.

Robert Wood Johnson Foundation. (2010). *The state of play: Gallup survey of principals on school recess.*

Robinson, K. (with L. Aronica). (2009). *The element: How finding your passion changes everything.* Viking Books.

Robinson, K. (2011). *Out of our minds: Learning to be creative.* Capstone Publishing.

Robitaille, D. F., & Garden, R. A. (Eds.). (1989). *The IEA study of mathematics II: Context and outcomes of school mathematics.* Pergamon Press.

Saari, S., & Frimodig, M. (Eds.). (2009). Leadership and management of education: Evaluation of education at the University of Helsinki 2007–2008. *Administrative Publications, 58.* University of Helsinki.

Sahlberg, P. (2006). Education reform for raising economic competitiveness. *Journal of Educational Change, 7*(4), 259–287.

Sahlberg, P. (2007). Education policies for raising student learning: The Finnish approach. *Journal of Education Policy, 22*(2), 173–197.

Sahlberg, P. (2009). Ideat, innovaatiot ja investoinnit koulun kehittämisessä [Ideas, innovation and investment in school improvement]. In M. Suortamo, H., Laaksola, & J. Välijärvi (Eds.), *Opettajan vuosi 2009–2010* [Teacher's year 2009–2010] (pp. 13–56). PS-kustannus.

Sahlberg, P. (2010a). Rethinking accountability for a knowledge society. *Journal of Educational Change, 11*(1), 45–61.

Sahlberg, P. (2010b). Educational change in Finland. In A. Hargreaves, A. Lieberman, M. Fullan, & D. Hopkins (Eds.), *Second international handbook of educational change* (pp. 323–348). Springer.

Sahlberg, P. (2011). The fourth way of Finland. *Journal of Educational Change, 12*(2), 173–185.

Sahlberg, P. (2012). The most wanted: Teachers and teacher education in Finland. In L. Darling-Hammond & A. Lieberman (Eds.), *Teacher education around the world: Changing policies and practices* (pp. 1–21). Routledge.

Sahlberg, P. (2013a). Teachers as leaders in Finland. *Educational Leadership, 71*(2), 36–40.

Sahlberg, P. (2013b, May 15). What if Finland's great teachers taught in U.S. schools? *Washington Post.* www.washingtonpost.com/blogs/answer-sheet /wp/2013/05/15/what-if-finlands-great-teachers-taught-in-u-s-schools-not -what-you-think

Sahlberg, P. (2015a). Developing effective teachers and school leaders. In L. Darling-Hammond (Ed.), *Teaching in a flat world* (pp. 30–44). Teachers College Press.

Sahlberg, P. (2015b). Finnish schools and the Global Educational Reform Movement. In J. Evers & R. Kneyber (Eds.), *Flip the system: Changing education from the ground up* (pp. 162–174). Routledge.

Sahlberg, P. (2016a). Global Educational Reform Movement and its impact on teaching. In K. Mundy, A. Green, R. Lingard, & A. Verger (Eds.), *The handbook of global policy and policymaking in education* (pp. 128–144). Wiley-Blackwell.

Sahlberg, P. (2016b). The Finnish Paradox: Equitable public education within a competitive market economy. In F. Adamson, B. Åstrand, & L. Darling-Hammond (Eds.), *Global education reform: How privatization and public investment influence education outcomes* (pp. 130–150). Routledge.

Sahlberg, P. (2018). *FinnishEd Leadership: Four big, inexpensive ideas to transform education.* Corwin Press.

Sahlberg, P. (2019). *Facts and myths about Finnish Schools.* Seminar Series 290. Centre for Strategic Education.

Sahlberg, P. (2020a). Will the pandemic change schools? *Journal of Professional Capital and Community, 5*(3/4), 359-365. DOI 10.1108/JPCC-05-2020-0026.

Sahlberg, P. (2020b). Lessons for the United States from International Education Systems. In M. Soskil (Ed.), *Flip the system US: How teachers can transform education and save democracy* (pp. 139–146). Routledge.

Sahlberg, P. (2020c). Does the pandemic help us make education more equitable? *Educational Research for Policy and Practice,* pages not available.

Sahlberg, P., & Doyle, W. (2019). *Let the children play: How more play saves our schools and helps children thrive.* Oxford University Press.

Sahlberg, P., & Johnson, P. (2019, August 30). What Finland is really doing to improve its acclaimed schools? *Washington Post.* www.washingtonpost .com/education/2019/08/30/what-finland-is-really-doing-improve-its -acclaimed-schools

Sahlberg, P., & Walker, T. (2021). *In teachers we trust: The Finnish way to world-class schools.* Norton.

Sarason, S. B. (1996). *Revisiting "the culture of the school and the problem of change."* Teachers College Press.

Schleicher, A. (2006). *The economics of knowledge: Why education is key for Europe's success.* Lisbon Council.

Schleicher, A. (2007). Can competencies assessed by PISA be considered the fundamental school knowledge 15-year-olds should possess? *Journal of Educational Change, 8*(4), 349–357.

Schleicher, A. (2018). *World class. How to build a 21st-century school system.* OECD Publishing.

Schleicher, A. (2019). The state of the teaching profession. *ACER Teacher Magazine.* www.teachermagazine.com.au/columnists/andreas-schleicher/the-state -of-the-teaching-profession

Schulz, W., Ainley, J., Fraillon, J., Losito, B., Agrusti, G., & Friedman, T. (2018). *Becoming citizens in a changing world.* IEA International Civic and Citizenship Education Study 2016 International Report. Springer Open.

Seddon, J. (2008). *Systems thinking in the public sector: The failure of the reform regime . . . and a manifesto for a better way.* Triarchy Press.

Sellar, S., & Lingard, B. (2013). The OECD and the expansion of PISA: New global modes of governance in education. *British Educational Research Journal, 40*(6), 917–936.

Sellar, S., Thompson, G., & Rutkowski, D. (2017). *The global education race: Taking the measure of PISA and international testing.* Brush Education.

Silliman, M. (2017). *Targeted funding, immigrant background, and educational outcomes: Evidence from Helsinki's "positive discrimination" policy.* Working Papers 134. VATT Institute for Economic Research.

Simola, H. (2005). The Finnish miracle of PISA: Historical and sociological remarks on teaching and teacher education. *Comparative Education, 41*(4), 455–470.

Simola, H. (2015). *The Finnish education mystery: Historical and sociological essays on schooling in Finland.* Routledge.

Spieghalter, D. (2013, December 3). *East Asian countries top global league tables for educational performance. Guardian.* www.theguardian.com/world/2013/dec/03/east-asian-top-oecd-education-rankings

Statistics Finland. (n.d.a). *Education.* www.stat.fi/til/kou_en.html

Statistics Finland. (n.d.b). *Research and development.* www.stat.fi/til/tkke/index_en.html

Statistics Finland. (n.d.c). *Income and consumption.* www.stat.fi/til/tul_en.html

Statistics Finland. (n.b.d). *Isät tilastoissa 2019.* www.stat.fi/tup/tilastokirjasto/isat_tilastoissa_2019.html

Teddlie, C. (2010). The legacy of the school effectiveness research tradition. In A. Hargreaves, A. Lieberman, M. Fullan, & D. Hopkins (Eds.), *The second international handbook of educational change* (pp. 523–554). Springer.

Toom, A., Kynäslahti, H., Krokfors, L., Jyrhämä, R., Byman, R., Stenberg, K., . . . Kansanen, P. (2010). Experiences of a research-based approach to teacher education: Suggestion for the future policies. *European Journal of Education, 45*(2), 331–344.

Tucker, M. (2011). *Surpassing Shanghai: An agenda for American education built on the world's leading systems.* Harvard Education Press.

Tyack, D., & Tobin, W. (1994). The "grammar" of schooling: Why has it been so hard to change? *American Educational Research Journal, 31*(3), 453–479.

UNICEF. (2020). *Worlds of influence: Understanding what shapes child well-being in the rich countries.* Innocenti Report Card #16.

Välijärvi, J. (2004). Implications of the modular curriculum in the secondary school in Finland. In J. van den Akker, W. Kuiper, & U. Hameyer (Eds.), *Curriculum landscapes and trends* (pp. 101–116). Kluwer.

Välijärvi, J. (2008). Miten hyvinvointi taataan tulevaisuudessakin? [How to guarantee welfare also in future?]. In M. Suortamo, H. Laaksola, &

J. Välijärvi (Eds.), *Opettajan vuosi 2008–2009* [Teacher's year 2008–2009] (pp. 55–64). PS-kustannus.

Välijärvi, J., Kupari, P., Linnakylä, P., Reinikainen, P., Sulkunen, S., Törnroos, J., & Arffman, I. (2007). *Finnish success in PISA and some reasons behind it.* University of Jyväskylä.

Välijärvi, J., Linnakylä, P., Kupari, P., Reinikainen, P., & Arffman, I. (2002). *Finnish success in PISA and some reasons behind it.* Institute for Educational Research, University of Jyväskylä.

Välijärvi, J., & Sahlberg, P. (2008). Should "failing" students repeat a grade? A retrospective response from Finland. *Journal of Educational Change, 9*(4), 385–389.

Vanhempainliitto. (2017). *Reforming early childhood education and care.* Vanhempainliitto. https://vanhempainliitto.fi/wp-content/uploads/2018/12/early-childhood-education-and-care.pdf

Voutilainen, T., Mehtäläinen, J., & Niiniluoto, I. (1989). *Tiedonkäsitys* [Conception of knowledge]. Kouluhallitus.

Weiss, E. (2013, September 12). *Mismatches in Race to the Top limit educational improvement: Lack of time, resources, and tools to address opportunity gaps puts lofty state goals out of reach.* Education Policy Institute.

Westbury, I., Hansen, S.-E., Kansanen, P., & Björkvist, O. (2005). Teacher education for research-based practice in expanded roles: Finland's experience. *Scandinavian Journal of Educational Research, 49*(5), 475–485.

Wiborg, S. (2010). *Swedish free schools: Do they work?* Centre for Learning and Life Chances in Knowledge Economies and Societies. www.llakes.org

Wilkinson, R., & Pickett, K. (2009). *The spirit level: Why more equal societies almost always do better.* Allen Lane.

Wilkinson, R., & Pickett, K. (2018). *The inner level: How more equal societies reduce stress, restore sanity and improve everyone's well-being.* Allen Lane.

Schulz, W., Ainley, J., Fraillon, J., Losito, B., Agrusti, G., & Friedman, T. (2018). *Becoming citizens in a changing world.* IEA International Civic and Citizenship Education Study 2016 International Report. Springer Open.

World Bank. (2011). *Learning for all: Investing in people's knowledge and skills to promote development.* World Bank.

Yliopisto. (2018). Heikkenevä PISA-menestys ei tarkoita, että nuoret olisivat tyhmempiä—vaan tuhmempia. www.helsinki.fi/fi/uutiset/opetus-ja-opiskelu-yliopistossa/heikkeneva-pisa-menestys-ei-tarkoita-etta-nuoret-olisivat-entista-tyhmempia-vaan-tuhmempia

Zhao, Y. (2014). *Who's afraid of the big bad dragon: Why China has the best (and worst) education system in the world.* Jossey-Bass.

Zhao, Y. (2020). Speak a different language: Reimagine the grammar of schooling. *International Studies in Educational Administration, 48*(1), 4–10.

Index

Note: Page numbers followed by "*b*", "*f*", and "*t*" indicate boxes, figures, and tables respectively; and those followed by "n" indicate notes.

About the Author

Pasi Sahlberg, PhD, is a professor of education policy at the University of New South Wales in Sydney. He has worked as a schoolteacher, teacher educator, and education policy advisor in Finland and as an education expert for several international organizations and consulting firms. During the last 3 decades he has analyzed education reforms around the world and has worked with education leaders and policymakers of more than 60 countries, including the United States, Canada, Australia, New Zealand, Ireland, and the United Kingdom. Dr. Sahlberg was a former staff member of the World Bank in Washington, DC, and the European Training Foundation in Turin, Italy. He won the 2012 Education Award in Finland, the 2013 Grawemeyer Award in the United States, the 2014 Robert Owen Award in Scotland, and the 2016 Lego Prize for his work on improving education around the world. He is an adjunct professor at the University of Helsinki and at the University of Oulu and was visiting professor at Harvard Graduate School of Education (2014–2016). He lives with his family in Sydney, Australia. Follow his writings and work on Twitter @pasi_sahlberg or visit www.pasisahlberg.com.